Marriage: It's in Your Hands

How to Cultivate Your Marriage so it Grows and Flourishes

Bobby L. Sneed, Jr.

All That I Am Publishing

Austin, Texas

Marriage: It's in Your Hands

ISBN- 9780615586885

ISBN- 9780615399577

Copyright © 2015 by Bobby L. Sneed Jr.

This edition is published by All That I Am Publishing Group

All rights reserved. No part of this publication may be reproduced or transmitted in any form or by any means, electronic or mechanical, including photocopy, recording, or any information storage and retrieval system, without the prior written permission of the publisher.

Printed in the United States of America

This book is fondly dedicated to my close family and friends for the encouragement and support I have received from them and to my parents for the love and guidance they have given me throughout my life. They are my role models.

God may your plan and purpose be fulfilled through this book. I can do all things through you as you give me strength.

CONTENTS

Be-Do-Have --1

Spiritual Warfare --6

The Origin of Men and Women ---9

There is No Place Like Home ---12

Submission to God ---18

The First Marriage ---25

The Honeymoon is Over ---33

No Where to Run or Hide --47

Lazy Leadership and Mismanagement -------------------------------55

What Kind of Man Are You? ---63

What is a Husband? ---75

Part I: Developing The Marriage Relationship

Development ---88

The Four Kinds of Love --95

Agape Love ---99

Self-Control ---132

Having a Vision ---135

Personal Management--139

Marital Interdependence--143

Marital Interdependent Leadership--------------------------------172

Marriage Systems---178

Marital Interdependent Management--------------------------------191

Marital Interdependent Communication-----------------------------200

Marital Interdependent Cooperation-------------------------------206

Self-Renewal---211

Part II: Protecting The Marriage Relationship

Protection---218

The Weeds of Sexual Immorality-----------------------------------221

The Emotional Weeds of Immorality--------------------------------253

What is a Wife?--269

Unconditional Respect--285

Building The Marriage Foundation---------------------------------294

Acknowledgements

No work of this magnitude can be achieved by one person alone. I want to acknowledge God for guiding me and speaking His words to me as I wrote this book. He has been with me every step of the way, and without Him, this book would not have been possible.

There are many people who I wish to thank. My wonderful parents who introduced me to Christ as a young man and have supported, loved, and encouraged me to become all that I can become: I love you, Dad and Mom. Thank you!

To my sisters, you are the best sisters in the world. You are always there to encourage and support me in whatever I choose to do. Just so you know, the only reason I decided to attend Texas A&M University was because I wanted to be just like the two of you.

To my nieces, I love you so much. I pray that this book gives each of you a clear picture of what type of man you should allow into your life to be your husband and what type of woman you must become to be his wife.

To my close friends Tim Scott, Zairreus Patterson and Kenneth Cotton, Jr., God has definitely blessed me because of our friendships. Thank you for encouraging me to write this book.

Many thanks to all my family and friends for being supportive in all that I do. This book would not have been possible without your support.

Finally, to the people who have purchased this book, I pray that you experience and enjoy marriage the way God envisioned it at creation. It is my earnest desire that you experience a transformation from the inside out, realizing that the success of your marriage is truly in your hands. Forgiveness is my inspiration.

Prologue: It's in Your Hands

David was a young man who lived in Austin, Texas who had recently graduated from college. Every day after work David would travel to a nursing home to play cards with an elderly man named Bill. Bill, in his late 80s, was very smart and witty. Every time they played cards, Bill would win, because he was so wise and always seemed to have an answer for everything. David would often ask him random riddles and Bill always answered them correctly. One day David decided that he had enough and was finally going to outsmart Bill, so he went home that day and began to brainstorm. He thought long and hard and finally came up with a full proof plan to outsmart Bill. His plan was to catch a grasshopper, go up to Bill with it in his hands and ask him a question. The question would be whether the grasshopper in his hands was alive. If Bill said no, David was going to open his hands and let the grasshopper go free, proving Bill wrong. If Bill said yes, David was going to crush the grasshopper with his hands, also proving Bill wrong. The next day he went to visit Bill at the nursing home with the grasshopper in his hands and asked him the question. "Bill, what do I have in my hands?" Bill replied, " A grasshopper is in your hands." David laughed to himself. He then asked Bill, "Is the grasshopper alive, or is it dead?" Bill paused for a minute. He then said to David, "*That* is in your hands."

It is the same concept with marriage. If you desire a successful marriage, it is in your hands. Whether your marriage will last is up to you! Marriage can be a beautiful relationship when you are the right person and you are married to the right person. However, it can be a nightmare if you are not the right person or you marry the wrong person. As the saying goes, "The right person at the wrong time is the wrong person."

I was married for two and a half years, only to have it end in a distasteful divorce. To be honest, one of the main reasons our marriage did not work was because of a lack of integrity and maturity on my part. Looking back, I was often inconsistent, impatient, immature and selfish. That is a hard mirror to look into. And so, I have learned that in order for a marriage to be harmonious there must be a giving of yourself to the other person and a willingness to serve them in love and with respect. I was not willing to do this consistently at that point in my life. I got married when I was twenty-three years old. My desire was to be a good husband but not a great one. Honestly, I didn't know what a being a husband was. Furthermore, I had limited knowledge and skills and lacked the proper tools necessary to perform the roles and responsibilities of a husband successfully. Now, I was familiar with the everyday things like pursuing a career, paying the bills on time, and the like, but as far as maintaining a marriage was concerned, I was far off the mark. When we got married, God placed me in the position to lead and manage the marriage in collaboration with my wife. I was not successful and I experienced setback after setback. From my perspective, I felt that it was my wife who needed to change and I would often petition God to change her. She was not perfect and neither was I, but I expected her to be perfect and expressed that by often placing unrealistic expectations on her. I judged myself by my intentions and my wife by her actions. Our shared challenges were dealt with in frustration by me instead of attacking and analyzing our challenges with love. As I reflect, I can finally admit to myself that I brought a lot of deep-seated addictions and strongholds into the marriage, which placed a lot of strain and stress on my wife and our relationship. So, as the man, the appointed leader and manager of the marriage, I take full responsibility for the failure of my marriage.

So why did I write this book and for whom did I write it?

The answer may shock you. Three years after I was divorced and still healing, I was sitting at my kitchen table eating dinner when out of nowhere I asked myself the following question. "Why didn't our marriage last?" As I sat there alone at the table I heard a voice that seemed to resonate from within me. The voice answered and said, " Do you really want to know why your marriage ended in divorce?" I replied, "Yes I do." The voice then said, "I know you think it was all on her but let's start with you. The main reason why your marriage ended in divorce was because you never became a husband you were just a married man." As I thought about what I heard, I put my fork down and tears began to roll down my face. My next question was, "God, what is a husband and will you show me how to become one?" I asked God to reveal what biblical marriage was through His lens. From that day forward, God began to reveal to me principles of marriage from the Bible and other resources that I had never noticed before. My desire for knowledge increased, and I started waking up in the middle of the night just writing what I heard from the deepest part of my soul. I began reading books on marriage and other relationship-related topics. I listened to sermons and presentations on marriage for hours upon hours. I attended seminars on relational care. For three years I wrote down in a notebook what I was hearing and learning from this inner voice. There was no doubt in my mind that the words that I heard and wrote down, which would eventually become a marriage book were not my own. I believe that a divine authority gave them to me for the sole purpose of helping to save and strengthen marriages and prevent divorce.

Who Should Read This Book?

In America, there is approximately one divorce every 36 seconds. That's nearly 2,400 divorces per day, 16,800 divorces per week and 876,000 divorces a year. On average, nearly 20 people per minute are physically abused by an intimate partner in the United States. During one year, this equates to more than 10 million women and men. Every 9 seconds in the US, a woman is assaulted or beaten and 1 in 3 women and 1 in 4 men have been victims of some form of physical violence by an intimate partner within their lifetime. On a typical day, there are more than 20,000 phone calls placed to domestic violence hotlines nationwide.

This book is written for ambitious, resilient men and women who desire to achieve marital success. It will serve as your step-by-step guide to achieving a successful marriage and preventing divorce and domestic violence from happening to you. I wrote *Marriage: It's In Your Hands* for men and women, who are either single, married, divorced or widowed. I want to help men become authentic husbands and empower them to love their wives unconditionally. I also want to help women become authentic wives and empower them to respect their husbands unconditionally. Additionally, it is important that a man pursues the right woman to be his future wife and it is equally important that a woman selects the right man as her future husband. I aspire to help as many married couples as I can to have a great marriage and family. I desire to help single men and women become the right people so they can attract the right person.

My objective for writing this book is to help save and strengthen biblical marriages, develop strong families, prevent divorce and domestic violence- Bobby L Sneed Jr.

Chapter 1

Be-Do-Have

Today married couples appear to be failing in developing and protecting their marital relationships. In reality, there is a more than 50% chance that your marriage will end in divorce. Married couples now divorce two-and-a-half times more than couples did 50 years ago. Between 40% and 60% of new marriages will eventually end in divorce. People between the ages of 25- 39 make up 60 percent of all divorces, and over one million children are affected by divorce each year. *Divorce Magazine* reported in 2002 that only 52 percent of married people reach their fifteenth anniversary.

But why is this happening? Why are so many marriages ending in the courts?

Perhaps some were like me not understanding the institution of marriage, its purpose and how I was supposed to operate in it.

Many people stand on the side-lines and admire couples who have successful marriages and desire that same success. With this hope, they too get married. It appears that each person is meeting the other's needs and sometimes, wants. It's as if the relationship is a match made in heaven. However, soon after when reality steps in, things fall apart.

It is is very important therefore that couples both young and old understand that when they stand at the altar and say "I do," that they are making a sacred agreement stating that they have become the type of people who are willing and capable to do all of the things they are supposed to do in a marriage. Therefore, if you go to the altar unequipped, incapable and unwilling to do everything necessary to have a great marriage, you are not being honest with yourself or the other person (your marriage partner).

The key here is to become that person first. Saying what you will do in the future is not enough. You must have success evidenced with self first before you can have success evidenced with another person in a committed, lifelong relationship. Desire alone will not guarantee you a great marriage although it is the first step. There are some people with a desire to have a successful marriage, but they do not have the discipline, character, or integrity to practice a lifestyle that will prepare them for such.

If you say you are an effective marriage partner, there are things that effective marriage partners do. Your desire to become an effective husband or wife must be greater than the resistance to doing those things necessary to become that person.

Many ask the question, "What must I do to have a successful marriage?" However, this is the incorrect question to ask. What you should ask is, "Who do I need to become to have a successful marriage?" What we do does not make us who we are; it merely reflects who we already were. If I want things to change for me, I must change. If I do not change, my situation or circumstances will not change for me. We cannot make anyone change unless they want to. Why? Because the person will never be able to do what you are suggesting until they change their mindset to do those things as a result of—not despite—the new thinking and person they have become. Life is designed so that we must grow in our conscience before we can experience a better life and better relationships.

The order is Be-Do-Have. I must become the person willing and capable to do and learn the things necessary to have an effective marriage. It is critical to understand that you have to choose to develop into who you will be as a husband or wife instead of wishing and dreaming about who you want to become.

So who do you need to be? What do you need to do? What do you need to learn to be ready to enter into or continue a healthy marital relationship? These questions will be answered as you keep reading. There are many self help books on marriage that have great information, but if you have not deliberately made the choice to become an effective marriage partner in your mind and heart then those books are useless to you. You might do them for a little while, but it won't last because you do not see yourself as a person who does the things that effective married people do. How do you become that person?

"As a man thinks in his heart, so is he." Proverbs 23:7

We become what we think about. What influences your thoughts? Most of the time, we allow others to control our thinking, or we have developed warped views about the biblical roles of a husband or wife.

When you believe something and you choose an attitude, opinion, or a point of view associated with it, you become what that something is. I am who I believe I am and who I choose to be. You have the power to change your mind and thoughts about who you are and who you desire to become. It is your choice. If you want to be an effective husband or wife and that is your core desire, then the next step is to find out what type of specific knowledge, skills/tools and definite plan you will need to reach that goal. This book will give you guidance, instruction, encouragement, and correction to help you accomplish this. This book will not help unless you have made a deliberate choice to become someone different. This book is about assisting you in the development of your private, personal life to have a successful marriage.

The next step is the doing part so that you can have success in marriage. If you have not become that person who will take responsibility for your actions and address destructive and unhealthy habits, you will find excuses for not doing the things in this book that will allow you to have a successful marriage.

Why? It will not be a natural response or action cycle that you will take and apply, and it most certainly won't fit the image of who you are.

"If you really want to be someone or do something, you'll find a way. If you don't, you'll find an excuse." -Jim Rohn

As a believer, you must make a commitment to God and to

yourself first and honor that commitment before you can make a legitimate commitment to someone else.

This is my commitment statement. "As a husband, I will love my wife unconditionally. I will be faithful to her and live with integrity and honor. I will submit to God in every area of my life. I will acquire the specific knowledge, skills/tools, definite plans, strong desire and persistence to become that which I choose to be. I will be a life long learner and a student husband."

I would encourage you to develop your own commitment statement. When you replace your current way of thinking with this way of thinking, a renewing of your mind will begin to take place, and you will consciously begin to become the husband or wife that you desire to be.

I believe that the Bible is one of the most practical books from which you can gain specific knowledge, correction, encouragement and instruction pertaining to marriage. I believe in God, Jesus, and the Holy Spirit; these co-equal persons are the foundation of my faith and this book. I believe this book will be an eye-opener to men and women who are dating, engaged, married or divorced. It is my earnest desire that as I share with you my mistakes and many shortcomings that you will capitalize on them and learn from them. My prayer is that you will avoid and prevent divorce from happening to you and instead grasp the concept that the success or failure of your marriage is truly in your hands.

Chapter 2

Spiritual Warfare

Let us take a trip back in time to the very beginning of human existence. This will allow you to understand in great detail why we as men and women have difficulty in the areas of marriage and relationships and how we can have success in them. It will also make you aware of an enemy whose primary goal is to bring confusion, chaos, and destruction to the marriage relationship or any godly relationship for that matter. Our trip will begin in Genesis. It is the first book of the Bible and tells the story of the first male-female relationship.

"In the beginning God created the heaven and the earth." Genesis 1:1

According to the storyteller, before the earth was fully developed, it was just like any other planet without life. God decided that he wanted to take some of His divine glory and create a race of angels to worship Him. God and His angels lived in heaven. One of the angels God created was an anointed cherub, which meant that he was a supreme angel above all other angels. His name was Lucifer, meaning, "shining one." When God created Lucifer, He wanted to create a masterpiece. Lucifer was God's right-hand angel, so to speak. God had given him a certain amount of power and authority and created a home for him on a mountain in heaven called the Mountain of Eden. Although he was a perfect being created by God, he was given volition. He was given the choice to worship and serve God or not.

God wanted Lucifer and the created race of angels to relate to Him in worship by their own free will. Lucifer, who presided over the music department in heaven became jealous of the power of God. Pride, because of his immaculate beauty was found in his heart. In the Bible, Ezekiel describes how Lucifer got beside himself as pride began to take over his heart.

What does this have to do with marriages? Before the first man and woman were created, there was a spiritual conflict going on between good and evil in heaven. This conflict was transferred to earth when Lucifer was expelled there. Ezekiel was given special insight as to what happened between God and Lucifer in heaven. Why was he given special insight? To answer that question you need to know who Ezekiel was and what he encountered that led God to speak a prophetic word to him. According to the storyteller, Ezekiel was a man who loved and honored God. He was a servant of God in Babylon for 22 years telling everyone about God, salvation, and judgment. He obeyed God, faithfully proclaimed His word, and foretold the future blessings for God's people.

Ezekiel lived in a city called Tyre, just north of Israel, close to Jerusalem. Tyre dominated the sea trading routes while Judah dominated the land trading routes. Tyre and Judah competed for the lucrative trade traffic that came through their lands from Egypt and other nations. The King of Tyre was a greedy king and a man full or pride and arrogance. He was also very intelligent and witty. He used his knowledge and talents to amass a huge fortune in the trading industry. Because of all the notoriety he received, he became proud and boastful. He believed that he was God. He believed that he was wiser than God and that he deserved to sit on the throne of God. God was not pleased with the king's attitude and sent Ezekiel to him to warn him. Ezekiel scheduled an appointment, and then he met with the king. During their conversation God gave spiritual insight to Ezekiel and described to him how Lucifer paralleled to the King of Tyre in his ambitions of being God. This conversation can be found and read in Ezekiel chapter 28 verses 13 through 17.

Lucifer like the King of Tyre desired to have dominion over God and refused to continue to serve Him. He believed that he did not need God and that he could operate independently from Him. In the book of Isaiah he describes how Lucifer rebelled against God. Reading Isaiah chapter 14 verses 11 through 14 will give you a detailed description of Lucifer's rebellion against God.

God was not pleased with Lucifer's rebellion.

"So I banished you from the mountain of God. I expelled you…So I threw you to the earth…" Ezekiel 28:16

Lucifer, or "shining one," was expelled from the mountain of Eden in heaven and cast down to Earth to await judgment from God. His name was changed to Satan. With him, he took one-third of the angels who also decided to rebel against God and not serve Him. It is important to know that Satan was here on earth before the first man and woman were created. The nature of Satan is to bring chaos and confusion to any environment he is in. The earth is now in a chaotic state of darkness because Satan and his rebellious angels now occupy it.

Chapter 3

The Origin of Men and Women

In the beginning, before the first man or woman was ever created, God renovated the earth. Earth's change from a chaotic state to a stable state had to be done before human creation could take place. Genesis chapter one records how this was done.

The first man and woman were created in God's image and put here on the earth to rule under God and over Satan and the fallen angels.

"The earth was without form, and void; and darkness was upon the face of the deep [another **word for chaos**]. ***And the Spirit of God moved upon the face of the waters. And God said, "Let there be light: and there was light." Genesis 1: 2-3***

God renovated the earth and created the Garden of Eden.

"And the Lord God formed man of the dust of the ground, and breathed into his nostril the breath of life; and man became a living soul." Genesis 2:7

Why were man and woman created in the first place? Was God in a man-making mood? God could have destroyed Satan and the fallen angels, but instead, He decided to take another route. He wanted to show Satan that He could do more with less, when less obeyed Him than He could do with more when more disobeyed Him. So God created a garden on earth like the mountain of God in heaven and decided to create man lesser than the angels. Man would rule over Satan and the fallen angels here on earth, and the war of man versus Satan would begin. In Psalms 8:3-8, David describes man's dominion over the earth.

"For you have made man a little lower than the angels, and you have crowned him with glory and honor..." Psalms 8:3-8

Then God said, *"Let us make people in our own image to be like ourselves. They will be masters over all life, the fish in the sea, the birds in the sky and all the livestock, wild animals and small animals. So God created people in His own image; God patterned them after himself as male and female. God blessed them and told them, 'Multiply and fill the earth and subdue it.'" Genesis 1:26-28*

Marriage was God's idea. God is the originator of marriage, so He is the only one who has legitimate authority to define what marriage is and what it is not. This is a key principle that someone wanting to marry or someone already married must understand. God intended for a man and woman to have dominion and rule over Satan in marriage. Satan hates biblical marriage. Satan seeks to disrupt this union between a husband and wife and bring about chaos and disorder, shifting the dominion to him. Your primary enemy will not be your husband or wife; your primary enemy will be Satan and people under his influence. Satan is going to attack every biblically based marriage. The greatest lie that was ever told was that Satan does not exist.

"This is not a wrestling match against a human opponent. We are wrestling with rulers, authorities, the powers who govern this world of darkness, and evil spiritual forces that control evil in the heavenly places." Ephesians 6:12

If you choose to get married, you will be choosing the plan God has for a man and woman to live together as one flesh.

God created the first man in His image, to have dominion over the earth. His name was Adam, and he was made very differently to the animals God later created. Adam consisted of three parts: body, soul, and spirit. The body is the human container that houses the soul and the spirit of men and women. The soul of man, which is the personality, consists of four parts: self-awareness, imagination, conscience, and will. Self-awareness and imagination give us our ability to think, reason, and dream. The conscience is our ability to understand right from wrong and express our emotions. Our will is our ability to choose or make decisions. Whereas, the four parts of our soul make our personality, we wouldn't be complete without our spirit. Men and women were created in the image of God for dominion.

Chapter 4

There is No Place Like Home

After God created Adam, He did something interesting. He placed Adam where he wanted him to be in the Garden of Eden.

"The Lord God planted a garden eastward in Eden; and there he put the man whom he had formed. Out of the ground made the Lord God to grow every tree that is pleasant to the sight, and good for food; the tree of life also in the midst of the garden, and the tree of knowledge of good and evil."

Genesis 2:8,9

At this time, God made Adam the leader of the garden, so to speak. Although he did not own it, he was responsible for managing it. Adam communicated with God daily. Adam was so interested in pleasing God that he and God were in constant communication. They often took walks together, and Adam's spirit communicated with the Holy Spirit of God. I imagine Adam asking God, " God how do you want me to take care of what you have created and placed me in charge of managing?" This is the first example of submission. The man as the husband is to first and foremost submit to God before he can expect his wife to submit to him.

"The Lord God placed the man in the Garden of Eden to tend and care for it. But the Lord God gave him this warning: "You may freely eat any fruit in the garden except fruit from the tree of the knowledge of good and evil. If you eat of its fruit, you will surely die." Genesis 2:15-17

Adam was created a perfect being just like Lucifer and the angels to duplicate the same scenario that had existed in heaven now on earth. God gave Adam volition, the choice to submit to Him as his Lord or to follow his own will and make choices without input from Him. Adam, made in the image of God, possessed some, but not all, of the divinity that makes God who He is, so Adam had limitations. He was a perfect, limited human being. He was perfect in the sense that no sin was within him, but as a created being, he had limits. God is a perfect, sinless, limitless being. God has no limits, no boundaries.

Bobby L. Sneed Jr.

Playing House Versus Taking Care of a Home

There are several procedures a person must go through before becoming a homeowner. With no upfront capital but a desire to purchase a house or condo, there are a few options. One of these options is to get a loan from a bank to purchase a home. Few mortgage companies will allow you to select a house, live in it for a couple of years, and then let you decide whether you want to purchase it at the end of the term. Before you can move in and call a house your home, a financial commitment to a financial institution must be made. You must have insurance for protection of the property and you must be willing to maintain the house through proper maintenance. These are just a few things that are required. The point is that you do not get to enjoy any of the benefits until you make the commitment. Why? Because the financial institutions understand that there could be severe consequences if they did otherwise. So, how does this all fit into your relationships and marriage? What does commitment have to do with it anyway?

Truth is, that very often we can allow people to have access to our bodies, souls, and spirits without requiring marriage or the commitment that comes with it. As a result, many women and men are left scared, scarred and broken, not knowing what to do with their lives.

Let's look at a scenario involving two young people. Stacie is a 24-year-old college student and has a boyfriend named Nick. Nick, 26 is a teacher and provides educational services to children with disabilities. They met at church and were physically attracted to each other so they began to date and spend a lot of enjoyable time together. Six months passed, and it seemed that they were really in love. Either he was at her apartment or she was always at his apartment.

On the surface, Nick seemed like a great guy but he was addicted to pornography and would often masturbate. Lust not love drove many of his decisions and sometimes those decisions were impulsive and erratic. It was hard to focus on Stacie and the relationship because pornography had rewired Nick's mind about what true intimacy was. He was also a very insecure man and many times was inconsistent with his words and actions. Stacie was molested when she was nine years old and was a habitual liar. Fear not faith drove many of her decisions. She was embarrassed by what happened to her and refused to talk about it to anyone. She was hurt, angry and afraid and she wanted to develop closeness with Nick but many times avoided it and pushed him away unconsciously.

Another six months went by, and then the question came up. "Since we are always at each other's apartments, should we just move in together?" Stacie asked one night as they were cuddling after having sex. They decided to live together. They were engaging in sex and had been since two months into the relationship. Then Stacie started to feel ill every morning for about two weeks. Thinking that it was just the flu, she ignored it, but the feeling would not go away. She called her mother, who by the way was against her moving in with Nick but realized that she was an adult and must make her own decisions. Her mother suggested that she make an appointment to see the family doctor. She did and found out that she was pregnant. Stacie got really emotional and scared because she did not know what to do. Later that night she told Nick, who responded with a blank stare on his face and asked. "Are you going to keep it?" "Yes, I do not believe in abortion, Nick," Stacie said. "Well, I am not ready to take care of a baby I thought you were on birth control," Nick replied.

Six months later Stacie began to put on a lot of weight and physically was not the same person she was when she met Nick. She began to notice that Nick was spending a lot more time on the computer and would quickly log off when she came home. Nick's physical attraction to her appeared to have waned. Meanwhile, he felt that his responsibilities had dramatically increased. There was always something to do for Stacie and the unborn baby. "Stacie, I'm going to go hang out with my friends. I will be back later," became a pattern. He was always staying away from the apartment and Stacie became insecure and concerned. "Nick is never here," she frequently complained to her girlfriends.

Three months later, Nick and Stacie had a baby boy named Jeremy. Nick loved his son but was not ready to be a father. He had no personal time for himself anymore. Most of his money went to the baby, and Nick still had a lot of selfish desires. He decided that he needed space and moved out, leaving Stacie with a newborn son. Stacie did not finish college because after she got pregnant, she decided to drop out. What should she do now? How should she deal with the father of her child who no longer wants either of them?

There is an old saying: "Why buy the cow when you can get the milk for free?" Stacie wanted Nick to act like her husband when he was only her boyfriend. There is a difference between being a husband and being a boyfriend. A husband is a spiritual leader, protector, and provider. A wife is a helper, assisting and giving to her husband. There are some things a woman should help and assist only her husband with. There are some things a woman should only give to her husband. Stacie gave Nick things that should be reserved for her husband. Stacie felt that because she was having sex with Nick that he felt the same way she did. She wanted him to financially support her as if he was her husband prior to her getting pregnant. They played house but never made their apartment a home through marriage. Nick as a boyfriend received the benefits of a husband without actually having to make the commitment and sacrifice of actually being a husband. Stacie as a girlfriend received some of the benefits of a wife without actually having to make a commitment and sacrifice of being a wife. In short, there were too many unwritten agreements and expectations and as the results have shown that is never good.

A successful marriage is built on love and respect. To give love and respect, you must love and respect yourself. Allowing people relational access to the invaluable resources that make you who you are without the commitment of marriage will be detrimental to your life. There is a difference between playing house and building a home. If you want the benefits of a wife or husband, then make a marriage commitment and honor it.

Commitment is not based on how you feel or what you feel like doing. Rather, it is saying that you are willing to do whatever is necessary for the relationship, even at the expense of your own feelings. Women should recognize and select a man who understands the difference between being a married man and being a husband who is married. A man should pursue a woman who understands that her main role in the relationship is to help not hurt, to complement and not complicate, whether verbally, emotionally, or physically.

Chapter 5

Submission to God

"But I want you to understand that the head of every man is Christ, the head of a wife is her husband, and the head of Christ is God." 1 Corinthians 11:3 (ESV)

Barack Obama was elected as the 44th President of the U.S.A. Joe Biden was elected as his Vice President, not Michelle Obama. When Barack the husband of Michelle became President, Michelle his wife became the First Lady, not the Vice President. Many people voted for Barack Obama, and many other people did not. The majority of the votes were for him. Whether you agree or disagree with, like or dislike Barack Obama, you must respect his position as the 44th President of the U.S. You have to submit to his leadership and management during his tenure in office even if you do not agree with him. Democracy is a political form of government in which governing power is derived from the people. This is how our government functions. God, on the other hand, operates and functions from a theocratic position. God operates and instructs us to operate as a theocracy not a democracy in marriage. A **theocracy** is a form of government in which God is recognized as the supreme ruler of the heavens and earth. For believers, a theocracy is a form of government in which divine power governs an earthly human state, either in a personal incarnation or more often, via religious institutional representatives (i.e., a church), **replacing or dominating the civil government**. Theocratic governments enact theocratic laws (rules). Men and women can become frustrated because God's laws on marriage do not always coincide with human opinions on marriage.

"My dear brothers and sisters, be quick to listen, slow to speak, and slow to get angry. Your anger can never make things right in God's sight." James 1: 19-20 (NIV)

God wants us to be quick to hear what He thinks, feels, or would decide on a matter. Then He instructs us to be slow to speak what we think, feel, or would decide on a matter. Our ways are not God's ways of doing things, and obeying God will often time make us angry because we will have to go against what we want or desire. According to God's theocratic laws (rules) for marriage, a husband is called to become the Commander in Chief or President of the home, and his wife is to become the First Lady and his personal advisor and encourager of the home. **No other woman should have a greater impact, influence or voice than a man's wife.** Together, they operate in one life, one vision and one direction. The President is the Chief Executive Officer, and the First Lady submits to the President. This is how God has called us to operate in marriage under His theocratic rule.

Does God know more about marriage and life than you? Do you believe that God can show and teach you what you need to know about marriage? Do you believe that God's approach to marriage is a better approach than yours and that following His guidelines will give you better results? If you answered yes to the previous questions, then you believe God has more knowledge and experience in the area of marriage than you. If we believe that God's way is a better way, why then do many choose not to submit to His ways?

Contrary to what you may have heard, according to God's theocratic laws, there is a hierarchy in marriage: God-Jesus-Husband-Wife-Children. In the Garden it was God-Adam-Eve-Cain-Abel-Seth...God has called and elected men to be the leaders and managers of the home in marriage. This means that everyone has someone to answer to. Therefore, God primarily holds the husband responsible for the success, vitality or failure of the marriage. If a marriage is not operating the way it is supposed to, the first person God is going to have a conversation with is the man! There is no such thing as two husbands or co-husband in a marriage. There is only one husband and one wife and a woman cannot be a husband. This position is reserved for men only. A man cannot be a wife, this position is reserved for women only.

Beware of false teaching that says men and women are the "husbands" of the relationship. Or women are the "vice-husbands" in a marriage. A woman is not to lead or manage a man in marriage, this is God's job, not hers! She is to complement her man and help him lead and manage - a big difference. It is time for men to be held accountable and to take their position in the home seriously. It is not your wife's job to lead or manage the marriage relationship. God has commanded the husband to do this.

To submit means to give over or yield to the power or authority of another.

The word "give" means to present voluntarily or to place in someone's care.

The word "authority" means the right to control, command, or determine.

How do we submit to God? As Christian husbands and wives, we are to submit to God in six areas of our lives.

1. Our Heart- By loving Him more than any relationship, activity, achievement, or possession.

2. Our Will- By committing ourselves completely to Him through our choices and decisions.

3. Our Mind- By seeking to know Him and His Word, so His principles and values form the foundation of all we think, believe, and feel.

4. Our Body- By recognizing that our strengths, talents, and sexuality are given to us by God to be used for pleasure and fulfillment according to His rules and not ours.

5. Our Finances- By deciding that all of the resources we have ultimately come from God and that we are managers of these resources. We do not own them.

6. Our Future- By deciding to make service to God and man the main purpose of our life's work. When someone submits to another, he or she voluntarily places himself or herself in that person's care, giving that person the right to control, command, or determine where his or her life will go. A Christian husband has to first submit to Christ, voluntarily placing himself in the care of Christ, giving up his right as a man to allow Christ to now control, command, and determine how he will interact with his wife and family and the direction of the marriage. A wife is then to submit to him as he submits to Christ. Most men do not want to submit to Christ and follow His agenda but still expect the wife to submit to them and follow their agenda.

The last instruction that was given to Adam in the garden was not to eat from the tree of knowledge of good and evil. It is important to know that there were many trees in the garden he could freely eat from. Among the other trees, God placed two very important trees at the center of the garden. They were called the tree of life and the tree of knowledge of good and evil. One may think that God was tempting Adam to eat from the tree of knowledge of good and evil. Why else would he place it in the middle of the garden for Adam to see day in and day out? Well, the tree of knowledge of good and evil gets a lot of attention; however, there was another tree next to it. It was called the tree of life. Adam was given instructions about the two trees. If he would have eaten from the tree of life, he would have lived forever in the garden in a god-like state on Earth. Here is the point I want to make: God has infinite knowledge and wisdom, which means He is an all-knowing, all-powerful God. He knows everything about everything. He has always been and will always be. God knows a lot more than you and me about the things of this world and what is best for us. Remember that when God created man, He created him in His own image. He gave man a human earth suit called the body. Inside the body, He gave man a soul. The soul consists of the mind, emotions, and will. Then He gave man His spirit. This is the way we are able to communicate with the Holy Spirit of God. What is God's Holy Spirit?

I believe that God's Holy Spirit is God's personality. It is what God thinks about a matter, what He feels about a matter, and the choice He would make about a matter. Back in the garden, Adam had a choice between two trees. Adam knew what God had told him. However, his mind, emotions, and will were also having a conversation within him. If we choose to listen to our soul instead of the spirit that God has placed inside of us when we become Christians, we are literally saying, "God, my way is better than your way, and I choose not to follow you." When God wanted to communicate with Adam, He would communicate with him through the spirit He placed in him. The Holy Spirit of God fed and communicated with the spirit of man. The spirit of man would dominate the soul, and the soul would then instruct the body what to do. At this point, Adam is dependent on God for the leadership and management of the garden God had created and placed him in. God allowed Adam to use his soul to make decisions as long as it did not conflict with God's spirit that was placed in him.

"And the Lord God commanded the man, saying, 'Of every tree of the garden you may freely eat but of the tree of the knowledge of good and evil you shall not eat, for in the day that you eat of it you

shall surely die.'" Genesis 2:16, 17 (NKJV)

So you see Adam has the freedom to eat from many trees. If on Monday he wanted a pear, he had the freedom to freely eat a pear. If on Thursday he wanted a plum, he had the freedom to freely eat as many as he wanted. He was given the freedom to use his soul for decision-making as long as it did not interfere with what God was saying through His Holy Spirit. You see this again in Genesis 2:19 (NLT) below.

"So the Lord God formed from the soil every kind of animal and bird. He brought them to Adam to see what he would call them, and Adam chose a name for each one."

Once again, God gave Adam the freedom to use his soul (his mind, emotions, and will) to determine what the animals' names would be, as long as he was operating within the boundaries set by God.

I played basketball as a kid. One of the first things I had to learn was the rules of the game. There are more than 100 rules in basketball. One day, I got so frustrated with all the rules that I asked my coach, "Why are there so many rules in basketball?" He told me my safety was the reason the game has so many rules. By not having rules, it would become chaotic and disorderly, and I would not be able to enjoy it the way it was meant to be enjoyed.

God places limitations on how far we can operate from within our soul. He does this because although we believe we know what is best for our situations and decisions we are faced with, God ultimately knows what is best for us. He has seen the beginning to the end. God gave us the Ten Commandments as a minimum standard. He did not give the Ten Commandments so that we could earn His love. He gave them to us so that our lives would have order. Disobeying what God has said about marriage in His Word allows chaos to reign in the marriage relationship. God is so great that He protects us from seen and unseen danger and at times, from ourselves. God had only one objective for commanding Adam to not eat from this tree. God wanted to see whether Adam would submit to Him. Would Adam trust God with His infinite knowledge of the world He created? Or would Adam use his own human determination or his soul to determine what was best for him and his family?

Chapter 6

The First Marriage

When God created Adam, he gave him a job or purpose and instructed him to do three things before he got married: cultivate (i.e., develop), keep (i.e., protect), and submit (i.e., not eat from the tree of knowledge of good and evil). God said that it was not good for Adam to be alone. Why did God say this? When you look at the word "alone" it can be broken up into two words, "all" and "one." So when God created man, He created him like Himself—all one person. In this state Adam is 100% whole; he is all-one, or **alone**. God said it wasn't good for Adam to be all-one like Him. I believe God was saying, "I have made Adam separate, apart, or isolated. I have made him to live solitarily the way I live. I have made him without aid or help, and this is not good." Why is this not good? Let me pause here to share something with you that was shared with me. I asked God, "Why did you create a woman for the man?" This is the answer I received from the Lord God. He led me to Genesis 1:27 and 28 (KJV). It says:

"So God created man in his own image, in the image of God created he him; male and female created he them. And God blessed them, and God said unto them, Be fruitful, and multiply, and replenish the earth, and subdue it: and have dominion over the fish of the sea, and over the fowl of the air, and over every living thing that moveth upon the earth."

As I was lying in my bed one night, God spoke these words to me. Moved by His spirit, I began to write down the words I heard Him speak to my spirit. God said to me:

*"After I renovated the earth, I assigned Adam to develop the land and protect it. I knew Satan wanted to undo the renovations I had made and Adam's job was to prevent this from happening. I gave him dominion over Satan and the garden. Satan was furious, and he hated Adam and his position over him. This would be a large task for one man to accomplish by himself. The plan was to allow Adam to create a race of humans to rule along side of him. Adam was just like me, but with limits. I did not want him to have the power to create life the same way I am able to create life. Because he was all-one or alone, I had to make a way for him to have the ability to create other human beings. So what I did was take part of him and made a woman. The power would now lie in the hands of them both to create a race of humans to rule along side of them. From Adam came the woman. Now as a married couple, his seed and her egg came together and formed a fertilized egg inside of her. This fertilized egg grew inside of the woman and would bear my image. Inside of her, it **developed** into a fetus, and she **protected** the fetus until it was time to be born. They must work together as one (**submit**) to create life. I do not need anyone else to create life. I wanted the man and woman to experience what I experienced when I created the heavens and the earth and called it good. I am the only one true God who has been able to create something from nothing. I wanted Adam to be able to create life just like me. He needed help in doing that. I did not want him to think he was me, so he would not be able to create another life as I have created him without the woman's egg. I am God; there is none other like me. So from one I made two, so that when the two **become** one again, they will have the power of creation."*

After I received this revelation from God, it was confirmed in the book of Malachi.

"Hasn't he made the two of you one? Both of you belong to him in body and spirit. And why has he made you one? Because he was looking for Godly children." Malachi 2:15 (NIRV)

Creation means to bring into existence that which has not existed before. When a man and woman get married, they create a marriage between the two that has not existed before. Love and respect are used as tools to keep the marriage united. Creation is synergistic because through cooperation, you have created something together that you otherwise would not be able to create separately. Because Adam is a created being, not God but like Him in a much lesser form, Adam does not have the human ability to operate as God operates. God is His own source of power. He needs no one and nothing to aid Him in accomplishing anything that He desires to accomplish. So God takes Adam, who is all-one person and makes another person from him. He is going to use material from Adam, so he is no longer a whole one person anymore.

God chose not to make a woman from the dust of the ground the same way he made man because then she too would be all-one or alone. He takes a part of Adam and decides He is going to make a woman from it. God chose to take and use a rib. When God took the material from Adam to make woman, He wanted two people from the same origin to function in synergy. Adam was not made like any man who has ever lived. Adam was made like God, all-one or alone. God lives alone. Then God says, "This is not good. I have made Adam just like me in a lower form, nevertheless, he is like me and that is not good." When God removed the rib from Adam, He removed part of Himself from Adam as well. At this junction, Adam is less than one, or not whole, because he is now missing a body part. He is missing a rib. So what you have now is a man and a rib. What is important now is what God does with this rib with part of His image attached to it.

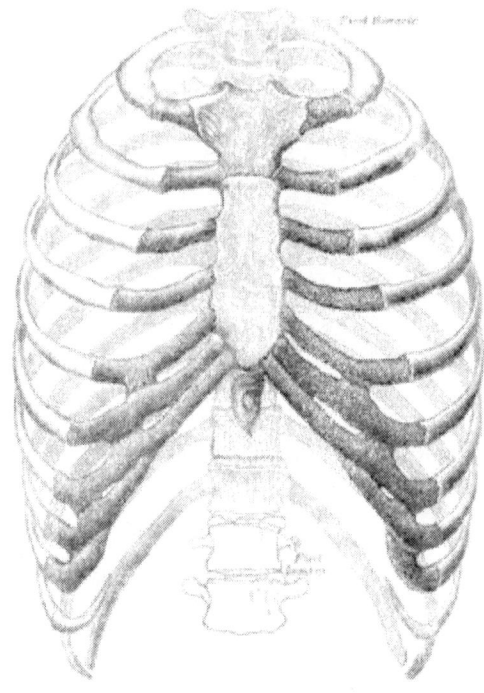

Only the ribs have the role of **protecting** the internal organs from damage. They also give structure to the body, as all bones do. The main purpose of the rib cage is protection. The rib cage forms a barrier that encloses the heart and lungs. The rib cage also offers a chamber in which the lungs can expand for breathing. Muscles between the ribs lift the rib cage upon inhalation and move down to squeeze air out during exhalation.

The function of a rib is to protect the vital organs. So God *made* a woman from material that is used primarily for protection of vital organs. She was not made from material from the cranium to rule over him or the hind foot to be walked over by him. She was made from a rib to help protect him. The word "made" means to bring into existence by shaping or changing material. God changed and shaped the rib into a woman and placed some of His divinity in her.

Adam was not complaining that he was by himself. Adam needed help; this is why in Genesis 2:18 God said, "I will make a helper suitable for him." So what does Adam need help with? It has been determined that Adam needed help creating the human race. He also needed help in the garden. Later on in marriage, he would need help and collaboration in efficiently operating the marriage systems. Woman was not created from the dust of the ground as Adam was. She was created from material taken from Adam.

From the beginning, men and women were designed to be interdependent on each other. If you observe our sexual organs, they are designed to complement and be interdependent with each other. When the woman was created, she was created to complement Adam—not compete with him; her agenda would be to help, not hurt him. When the woman was brought to Adam, he was to be responsible for informing her of the instructions God had commanded him to do. Adam was to be responsible for her. He would still be responsible for managing the garden God placed him in. God now extends Adam's responsibilities and places His daughter in Adam's care.

Now Adam is in a marital relationship with a woman and is to continue to develop, protect, and submit to God. God's instructions to Adam did not change after the woman was created. He was to continue doing what God had instructed him to do as the leader and manager of the garden. He also was to follow those same directions in the garden of marriage. Now Adam had a First Lady literally because she was the first woman created and the Cabinet Advisor. The woman was not given to Adam to do Adam's job. The woman was given to Adam to help Adam do his job more effectively and efficiently. I believe that when God created man, He created him for a purpose and placed him in his calling. He purposely took out some things that reflected His image and put them into the woman to help Adam do what He told him to do in the first place. (It says in the Bible that man and woman were created in God's image.) Adam was not going to be able to do what God was asking him to do by himself; he needed help. Companionship, although important was not God's first intention for creating the woman. Men, our calling or purpose in life precedes our sexuality; that is, having someone by you who can help you achieve what God has called you to do is more important than companionship. So I believe as husbands, we are called to lead and manage (very broad), for example, the home. As husbands, we are called to be both the positional and functional head of our homes. God expects it and God demands it. But there is no authority without limitations. As President, we have the authority to do what we are supposed to do—not necessarily the authority to do what we want to do. As husbands, we must submit to God because submission runs all the way down the hierarchal chain; Christ is the head of every man. To receive and obey God's orders or instructions, we must have a relationship with him—not an attachment. The only way you can have a relationship with God and receive salvation is through His Son Jesus Christ. Jesus is the only way to establish a relationship with God.

In 1 Timothy 2, Paul told us to pray for everyone. Then he said,

"This is good and acceptable in the sight of God our Savior, who desires all men to be saved and to come to the knowledge of the truth. For there is one God, and one mediator also between God and men, the man Christ Jesus, who gave Himself as a ransom for all" (vv.3-6).

A mediator is a go-between, someone who can stand between two parties that are at odds with each other and bring them together. On the cross, Jesus literally hung between two estranged parties: His Father and the human race, to bring us to God. Husbands have to function under divine authority in order to have legitimate marital authority. This means as husbands, we look to the Bible and Christ for direction, correction, and instructions on how to effectively love our wives the way Christ loved the church.

Genesis 2:23 and 24 (NIV) describes the first wedding between a man and woman. Adam says,

"'This is now bone of my bones and flesh of my flesh she shall be called woman because she was taken out of man.' For this reason a man will leave his father and mother and be united to his wife, and they will become one flesh."

So as they came together sexually as one, the output from this oneness would equal five, one hundred, one thousand and more. What two people can do together is greater than what they each can do alone when it is done right. When Adam and his wife came together as one, they had three sons named Cain, Abel, and Seth. Their oneness produced five, because they now had a family of five instead of a family of two. This statement paints a picture of synergy.

At this point everything seems to be going well for the newly married couple. Adam is excited that he now has someone to help him do the tasks that God has called him to do. The woman is excited about her husband and the new marriage. Genesis 2 comes to an end with Adam and the woman as a married couple, with neither one of them feeling ashamed.

Chapter 7

The Honeymoon is Over

Knock, Knock. Who's there? Satan. Satan who? Satan who has come to kill you. Adam said, "Come on in."

It is worth noting that Chapter 1 of Genesis explains what God did in creating the earth. Chapter 2 of Genesis explains how He did it. Adam never had a girlfriend or wife, so there was no relational baggage that he brought into the marital relationship. Adam didn't even come from a dysfunctional family. The same can be said about the woman God created. Here you have two created human beings in their purest form, yet in Chapter 3 there is chaos. Here is my point: no matter who you marry, that person will not be as pure as Adam and Eve were. He or she will not be perfect. You must be willing to work through your differences. It did not take long for Adam and Eve to have their first disagreement. Chapter 3 of Genesis starts out with the woman and Satan having a conversation.

Before we dissect the conversation between the serpent and the woman, we need to look at the conversation between God and Adam that took place beforehand. It is found in Genesis 2:16 and 17 (NIV):

"And the Lord God commanded the man, saying, 'of every tree of the garden thou may freely eat from them. But of the tree of the knowledge of good and evil, you shall not eat of it. For in the day that you eat from it you shall surely die.'"

God is very detailed in what he told Adam. Let's recap:

1. There are many trees in the garden in which Adam (not the woman because she had not been created yet) can *freely* eat from except one tree that is off limits.

2. God tells Adam which tree he cannot *eat* from and that it's off limits to him so that Adam does not get confused and eat from the wrong tree by mistake. The tree is called "the tree of the knowledge of good and evil."

3. God tells Adam the day *he* eats from tree of the knowledge of good and evil *he* will surely, without a doubt, die.

Next to the tree of the knowledge of good and evil is another tree. It is the *tree of life*.

"And out of the ground made the Lord God to grow every tree that is pleasant to the sight, and good for food; the tree of life also in the middle of the garden, and the tree of knowledge of good and evil." Genesis 2:9 (NIV)

The tree of life was a beautiful tree, pleasant to the sight, and provided good food. In fact, all of the trees in the garden were beautiful and provided good food except one. The tree of the knowledge of good and evil was an attractive tree, but it was not good for food. Many people think that there was only one tree in the middle of the garden, but there were two trees and they were the two most powerful trees. They were planted side by side. Some may ask, "Why did God tempt Adam by putting the two trees there in the middle of the garden?" But God did not tempt Adam; God gave Adam a choice. When God made man, he put an expiration date on him. He was not made eternal, but he was designed to live eternally if he ate from the tree of life. On one tree you have the fruit of eternal life; on the other tree you have the fruit of knowledge and death. He told Adam to choose.

Now let's look at the conversation that the woman had with the serpent being controlled by Satan.

Before we begin, it must be pointed out that there are two words that are very important. The two words are "ye" and "thou." The King James Version of the Bible uses these words in the account of the conversation between the woman and serpent. Many other translations mix up these words, causing even more confusion to understand what was being said and to **whom it was being said.**

The word "ye" is the plural of the word "thou," or meaning more than one (we). The word "thou" is singular and used to denote a person or thing addressed (I or you).

Gen 3:1-7(KJV)

"Now the serpent was more subtle [sneakier] *than any beast of the field which the Lord God had made. And he said unto the woman, Did God say, 'Ye* [Adam and you] *shall not eat of every tree of the garden?'*

2 And the woman said unto the serpent, 'We may eat of the fruit of the trees of the garden.'

3 But of the fruit of the tree which is in the middle of the garden, God hath said, ye [Adam and I] *shall not eat of it, neither shall ye* [Adam and I] *touch it, lest ye* [Adam and I] *die.*

4 And the serpent said unto the woman, Ye [Adam and you] *shall not surely die:*

5 For God doth know that in the day ye [Adam and you] *eat thereof, then your eyes shall be opened, and ye* [Adam and you] *shall be as gods knowing good and evil.*

*6 And when the woman saw that the tree was good for food, and that it was pleasant to the eyes, and a tree to be desired to make one wise, she took of the fruit from it, and did eat, and gave also unto her husband **with her**; and he did eat.*
*7 And the eyes of them **both** were opened, and they knew that they were naked; and they sewed fig leaves together, and made themselves aprons.*

Now let's dissect the conversation between the woman and the serpent.

1.The serpent starts out asking the woman a question to find out exactly what she knows, or what information has been passed on to her pertaining to what God said to Adam when He gave him the instructions about the trees in the garden. He already knows the answer to the question before he even asked, but he wanted to see what she knew. He does not ask Adam because Adam received firsthand instructions about the garden and him. The serpent knew that because the woman had secondhand information, he had a better opportunity to deceive her and bring deception and confusion into the marital relationship. Notice what he first asks her before she says anything. The serpent asked, "Woman, did God say that ***Adam and you*** must not eat of every tree of the garden?" This question is very important because the serpent needed to know if the woman knew and believed that the command applied only to Adam. So does the woman believe that God said that ***Adam*** must not eat or ***Adam and she*** must not eat? Well, the woman believes that God told Adam that ***they*** both could eat from every tree of the garden except one particular tree. God clearly said ***Adam*** must not eat from one particular tree, with no mention of the woman because she had not been created yet.

So how did the serpent know what God said to Adam in order to ask the woman if she knew about the conversation God had with Adam? Remember God had the conversation with Adam, but the serpent was listening to the conversation, taking detailed notes of what was being said so that he could twist the truth in order to deceive and conquer. He was also watching as God created the woman and brought her to Adam. The serpent was listening to the conversation that Adam and the woman had about the trees in the garden. He wanted to see whether Adam was going to leave out something or forget to mention something to the woman that he could use to deceive her. He also wanted to see whether the woman was paying attention and fully understood everything Adam was telling her. This is why effective communication is so important in a marriage.

2. The woman responds to the question by saying, "We may eat of the fruit of the trees of the garden." This is not what God told Adam. Here you see the woman misquoting God for the first time. He told Adam that *he* could *freely* eat. Adam then tells his wife that because God has allowed him to freely eat she may freely eat from certain trees as well. The word *freely* means not affected or restricted by a given condition or circumstance. So there were no restrictions on the thousands of trees that *he* could *freely* eat from. When she left out the word *freely*, she made God more restrictive than He was and the serpent capitalized on this later in the conversation. So does this mean that the woman could not freely eat from the trees in the garden since God did not say whether she could? What this means is that Adam was responsible for informing the woman about the access and restrictions he himself was informed about by God. Adam was to submit to God. The

woman was to submit to Adam. When God instructed Adam about the garden, He told him what he had access to, what he was restricted from and gave him a consequence if he decided to disobey Him and access the tree that was restricted.

God has authority over Adam. God then extends His authority to Adam to lead and manage the relationship with the woman. When Adam instructs his wife about the trees she can freely eat from and the one tree she can't eat from, he does so because he wants to protect his wife from danger. The command Adam gives to his wife is from him and not from God. However, Adam does not assign a consequence to her if she chooses to go against his instructions. If she chooses to eat from a tree that her husband has told her not to eat from, then she is disobeying her husband, not God.

It is also worth noting that the serpent did not ask about what Adam as the leader or manager could or could not do. He asked about what *they* could and could not do. He was planting a seed of role reversal, rebellion, and independence in the mind of the woman, and she had no clue. Independence is not a bad thing; it is necessary to experience a level of personal success. It is when you choose to operate solely from an independent mindset as you seek to share your life with someone that is harmful and counterproductive.

As a married couple interacts interdependently, they are able to accomplish more working together than as separate married independent individuals. When the serpent said *they*, what he meant and implied was that Adam and the woman were the same in their position and function as it applied to their roles in the garden and their marriage. Sameness and oneness have different meanings. An orchestra is not made up of all of the same instruments. There are different instruments that make different sounds and have different functions that make up an orchestra. When these different instruments play together in a harmonic melody, you have oneness among the different instruments operating in their purpose. Satan was not promoting **oneness,** he was promoting **sameness** through competition! Whenever I believe we share the same leadership and management position and have the same authority from God to operate from this position, there is a great possibility and temptation to overrule you, because I believe I am a more qualified leader and manager than you. Remember, Adam was the President of the garden before the woman was created and received his instructions and consequences from God. Adam operated and submitted to God. When God created the woman, she was to operate and submit to Adam as he operated and submitted to God. The woman was not to operate as a co-husband, but as a wife. God was Adam's Lord, and Adam was to be the woman's lord in the garden.

The serpent's intent was to imply that God created man and woman functionally and hierarchically the same. God created man and woman ontologically the same. A man is not valued more than a woman in the eyes of God. God is our Father, and we are His sons and daughters. But as men and women, we have different functions and roles. This is why men can't have babies. We were not designed to give birth to children; this is not our function. The serpent used the term *we* to make the woman feel that there were two Presidents in the garden and that she was not the First Lady or Adam's Cabinet Advisor; she was President just like him. He implied that she did not need to submit to Adam or God. She was her own woman and should think independently of Adam, not function interdependently with him. The serpent placed in the woman's mind that in a marriage body there should be two heads—not one. He implied that she should be leading and managing this garden. So Satan placed seeds of doubt and mistrust in the woman's mind. God said the two shall become **one** not the **same**, and His plan was that married couples would function interdependently. Satan's plan was to divide the **oneness** so that there were two people who each would operate independent of the other person, creating two Presidents with equal authority.

3. Hear what the woman said next as she continues her response to Satan's first question. The woman says, "But of the fruit of the tree which is in the midst of the garden, God has said, ye (***Adam and I***) shall not eat of it, neither shall ye (***Adam and I***) touch it, *lest* ye (***Adam and I***) die." This is not what God told Adam. Here you see the woman misquoting God a second and third time by stating that they could not touch the tree, lest they would die. Remember there are two trees in the middle of the garden. They are the tree of life and the tree of the knowledge of good and evil. The woman speaks as if there is only one tree when there are two. She then goes on to tell the serpent that ***they*** cannot eat of it or ***touch it lest they*** **would die**.

It is important to know that God gave Adam a command and a consequence attached to that command. If he was to disobey the command he would receive the consequence. Adam gave the same command to the woman but without a consequence attached to it because God did not issue the command or the consequence to the woman; he issued it only to Adam. As she is talking with the serpent, the woman took the lead role of the relationship by speaking for Adam about the restrictions of the garden. The coward in Adam prevents him from doing what he was supposed to do, which was to protect (or keep the serpent out of) the garden.

The woman begins speaking on behalf of Adam and herself. She told the serpent that God said she could not eat. God did not say the woman could not eat—Adam told the woman she could not eat. The woman, through having a conversation with the serpent, has now confused herself and has mixed up the instructions and consequences that God told Adam. At this point she has taken over the leadership and management role of the relationship and in her mind has become the husband or house-binder. Adam has taken the role of helper or wife.

What you now have is role reversal. The serpent was listening when God told Adam he could not eat the forbidden fruit and what would happen if he did, and he knew that God said nothing about the woman because she had not been created yet. This is what the serpent used to deceive the woman. God never said anything about *touching the fruit*. He did not tell Adam if he touched it he might die. He said to Adam if he ate it he would surely die. When the woman misquoted God for the second time and said that God commanded that they could not even touch it, she made God more restrictive.

4. The woman told the serpent *lest* we die. The problem here is the word *lest*. The word "lest" means out of fear one should not do something because some consequence might happen. Did God tell Adam he **should not** eat or he **must not** eat? He told Adam and not the woman not to eat from the tree of the knowledge of good and evil, and if he did he would surely die. Once again the woman misquotes God for the third time saying lest (we might) die if we eat. God never said this.

5. The serpent has a rebuttal. He says, "And the serpent said unto the woman, Ye (*Adam and you*) shall not surely die." This is

partly true. The woman was not going to die if she ate solely, as we will see later on. Now Satan is calling God a liar, so the woman has to make a decision about who is telling the truth. Does she obey Adam and submit to him, believing what he has instructed her is in her best interest? Or does she lean to her own understanding and lead with emotion, believing what Adam has said is not accurate information from God? Remember, Adam told her not to eat without telling her the consequence of doing so. Even if Adam told the woman she would surely die like him, it would not have happened, because God did not say that when He gave the instructions to Adam about the two trees. Satan knew this as well.

Genesis 3:5 says *"For God knows that in the day you eat from it, then your eyes shall be opened, and ye (**Adam and you**) shall be as gods, knowing good and evil."*

The serpent told the woman that her eyes would be opened and she and Adam would become like gods. Satan goes on to say, "Adam and you will not die if you eat from the tree of the knowledge of good and evil." Once again this is partially true, but it is not the whole truth. Again, let me reiterate that the woman has taken the lead role in the relationship and Adam has taken a passive, cowardly role. The serpent was only telling the partial truth. The serpent knew that if the woman ate she would not die, unless Adam ate too, because the command to not eat was not given to her by God but was given to her by her husband without a consequence attached to it. Adam had a consequence attached to his disobedience from God.

6. *"And when the woman saw that the tree was good for food, and that it was pleasant to the eyes, and a tree to be desired to make one wise, she took of the fruit thereof, and did eat, and gave also*

unto her husband with her; and he did eat."

When the woman touched the fruit nothing happened. She did not fall out, nor were her eyes opened. Then she ate the fruit and still nothing happened. So she was convinced that what Adam said about this particular tree was not accurate. Remember, the woman believed that she was President just like Adam and that she was equal in function and position, that whatever God told Adam also applied to her, including his consequences. So the serpent convinced the woman to go against her husband. Notice that I said against her husband and not directly against God. Adam was in a sense the god-head of the relationship in the garden. He was the little god of the garden. When the woman ate the fruit she rebelled against Adam because he gave her the command not to eat. So the woman disobeyed Adam, who was her lord and Adam disobeys God, who was his Lord. Let's see what happens next.

7. *"And the eyes of them both were opened, and they knew that they were naked; and they sewed fig leaves together, and made themselves aprons."*

Notice that their eyes were not opened until Adam ate. The woman touched the fruit and nothing happened. Then the woman ate first and nothing happened. Why? Once again the command was not given to her by God; it was given to Adam. If Adam would not have eaten, their eyes would have remained closed to their nakedness and shame. Adam and the woman *dying* depended on whether Adam ate from the tree of the knowledge of good and evil—not her. Adam was to operate under God's authority, and the woman was to operate under the man's authority given to him by God. In relation to the man, his death was based on what God said. For the woman, her death was based on the actions of Adam since he was her god-head. Why were the woman's eyes opened when Adam ate the fruit? Remember, Adam was formed first by God. Then God took material from Adam and made the woman. Whatever spiritual blessings Adam received from God the woman benefited from. Consequently, whatever punishment Adam received through God the woman was also the beneficiary.

What would have happened if the woman chose not to eat the forbidden fruit but Adam chose to eat the forbidden fruit? They both would have surely died. Some may ask, "If God did not give the command to the woman not to eat, why then would she die if Adam ate and she didn't?" When a woman is pregnant with a child, the child is in her womb for the duration of the pregnancy. The woman is to care and protect that child. If she drinks alcohol or uses drugs, the baby is exposed to the alcohol or drugs, because the baby is in submission to the mother. If the mother dies because she makes a poor decision, then the baby inside of her also dies. So what kind of death happened? During pregnancy, a mother and her baby are connected by an umbilical cord. An umbilical cord, or funicle connects the embryo, or fetus, with the placenta of the mother, transporting nourishment from the mother and wastes from the fetus. When God created man, He established a spiritual umbilical cord with Adam. When He created the woman from Adam, He extended the spiritual umbilical cord to the woman through the man. God said to Adam that the day that he ate from the tree of the knowledge of good and evil, He would sever the spiritual umbilical cord between Him and Adam and Adam would die spiritually [denied access to the Holy Spirit of God]. He would sever the spiritual connection. Adam's spirit would no longer be fed by the Holy Spirit of God. Adam's spirit would die and he would have to rely on his soul for direction. There were two spiritual umbilical cords: one connecting God to Adam and the other connecting Adam to the woman. The woman received spiritual nutrients from God because she was connected to Adam and Adam was connected to God. When Adam disobeyed God and ate from the tree God commanded him not to eat from, the spiritual umbilical cord between Adam and God was severed. Both Adam and the woman's eyes were then opened because they were both cut off from God because of the severed connection between God and Adam. I can hear some women saying, "I do not need a man to be connected to God." You are absolutely right. You need Jesus to be connected to God. Remember Jesus was not in the garden; it was only God, Adam, and the woman.

After sin entered into the world through disobedience, God made a way for us to be reconnected to Him and have access to His Holy Spirit through His Son Jesus. Jesus became the spiritual umbilical cord that connects each of us to God when we receive His salvation. This way, the Holy Spirit of God can feed the spirit that has been **born again** [our spirits must be born again] in a man or woman. Because of Jesus and the cross, we can be united to God forever. In a marriage as a woman, you elect your husband as President. He becomes the head leader and manager of the marital relationship. He is not to become or replace God because he does not own the relationship, God does. You still have a spiritual connection to God through the spiritual umbilical cord of Jesus Christ. As a wife, you are now called to submit to and respect your husband in the same way you submit to and respect Jesus for connecting you back to God. Thus, as a Christian man, before you have a second marriage with one woman, you are in a marriage with Jesus. The man and God are married and have a primary marriage. The man is the bride of Christ. God is his husband. The woman, as a believer, is married to Jesus in a primary marriage and married to her husband in a secondary marriage. The husband is to submit to Jesus primarily and follow Jesus Christ's example, using love to relate to his wife. The wife is then to submit to Jesus in her marriage to Him and then to her husband in her secondary marriage, using respect as she relates to her husband.

Chapter 8

No Where to Run or Hide

"Toward evening they heard the Lord God walking about in the garden, so they hid themselves among the trees. The Lord God called to Adam, 'Where are you?'

He replied, 'I heard you, so I hid. I was afraid because I was naked.'

'Who told you that you were naked?' the Lord God asked. 'Have you eaten the fruit I commanded you not to eat?'" Genesis 3:8-11 (NLT)

After Adam and the woman ate the fruit, God goes looking for Adam—not the woman. Here in these verses, you see that God asks Adam a very important question. He asked him who told him he was naked. God also asked Adam if he had eaten the fruit that He commanded him not to eat. Notice that God did not ask if Adam and the woman had eaten the fruit. He only asked whether Adam ate because God never told the woman not to eat from the forbidden tree. He only told Adam not to eat the fruit.

Genesis 3:12 (NLT) "'Yes,' Adam admitted, 'but it was the woman you gave me who brought me the fruit, and I ate it.'"

Adam admits to disobeying God, but he blames God and the woman for what he did. It is amazing that today we are still blaming God and others for our own disobedience.

Genesis 3:13 (NLT) "Then the Lord God asked the woman, 'How could you do such a thing?' 'The serpent tricked me,' she replied. 'That's why I ate it.'"

When God asked the woman how she could do such a thing, He was not referring to her disobeying Him. God was disappointed with the woman for disobeying her husband Adam, who He placed over her as her lord. You will see later that God gives the woman her consequence for disobeying her husband—not for disobeying Him. The woman witnessed how Adam reacted so she figured that she would react in the same way and blame the serpent for what she did. Everybody is blaming somebody and nobody is taking responsibility for their actions.

Genesis 3:14 and 15 (NLT): "So the Lord God said to the serpent, 'Because you have done this, you will be punished. You are singled out from all the domestic and wild animals of the whole earth to be cursed. You will grovel in the dust as long as you live, crawling along on your belly. From now on, you and the woman will be enemies, and your offspring and her offspring will be enemies. He will crush your head, and you will strike his heel.'"

In the later part of Genesis 3:15, God gave a preview of the coming of Jesus and how He was going to redeem the sins of man. God is stating that Satan is going to strike the heel of Jesus on Calvary, but on the third day Jesus is going to crush the head or headship of Satan when He raises Himself from the dead. Then all power in heaven and earth will be in the hands of Jesus Christ. God had already set in motion the plan of redemption for the sins of man as He gives a preview to the coming of Jesus Christ. God said, "He will crush your head." The "He" God is referring to is Jesus Christ. Jesus would be born of a virgin woman and as the reincarnate of God in the form of man. As a man, He is going to crush the headship of Satan. But there is more. God is speaking about future marriages as well and how the husband and wife will have the power to prevent divorce. Look closer at what God says. "He will crush your head, and you will strike his heel." Remember in a marriage relationship, not attachment, the man represents Christ and the woman represents the church.

Ephesians 5:33 says "Husbands love your wives as Christ loved the Church and gave himself for it..." God is speaking on an even deeper level saying that every husband with the power of the Holy Spirit, the Word of God and effective prayer, functioning under divine authority along with the help of his wife, will have the power to crush the headship of Satan as he attacks the marital relationship. How will Satan attack your marital relationship? He will deal massive blows to the heels of the marital relationship.

So how does this verse in Genesis 3:15 relate to marriage? Christ is a representative of the husband, and the wife is a representative of the church. Christ and the church must be in agreement. A husband and wife must be in agreement about how they will interdepend on and interact with each other. In the marital agreement, a man decides who he will be to his wife and his wife decides who she will be to him. Life and marriage are about agreements, even the unwritten ones. When a marriage relationship starts to shift to a marital attachment, i.e., just existing not relating, the marital relationship has stopped working and becomes a marital attachment, because the agreement to make it a relationship has been broken. Either one or both parties have made a choice to no longer be who they said they would be in how they would relate and interact with each other. When this happens, you stop doing the things you agreed to do or begin doing things you did not agree to do. What causes this to happen? When you change your mind about who you are and decide to relate to the person in a different way outside of the original agreement, you break that agreement. Once again, how can two people walk together unless they are agreed or in agreement? This is where Satan comes in. We use our feet to walk and balance the body, and Satan seeks to strike the heels of our feet so we are unable to walk together in agreement and have balance in our marital relationships.

You normally do not see people out in public walking around with no shoes on their feet. People wear shoes to protect their feet and to prevent injury. It is very difficult to walk and balance the body with feet that are bruised or severely damaged. Satan seeks to strike and step on the toes of each person in the marital relationship and make the other person think their spouse was the one who struck his or her heel. The heels represent your ability to agree and maintain agreements with each other. Satan's mission is to strike the heels of every marital relationship, damaging your ability to agree, or to want to agree, by influencing and manipulating your thoughts, emotions, and choices, which affect your behavior. This is done when we allow Satan to install his "demonic program files" onto the hard drive of our hearts. We then allow him to manipulate us through the reprogramming of our hearts and mind. This causes us to break our agreements on who we said we would be and what we said we would do as we interact with each other in marriage. Damaged, bruised feet won't walk far together. If we are limping along, eventually we are destined to stop walking altogether. So when Satan begins striking the heels of your marital relationship, how do you get him to stop?

*"Put on all of God's armor so that you will be able to stand firm against all strategies of the devil. For we are not fighting against flesh-and-blood enemies, but against evil rulers and authorities of the unseen world, against mighty powers in this dark world, and against evil spirits in the heavenly places. Therefore, put on every piece of God's armor so you will be able to resist the enemy in the time of evil. Then after the battle you will still be standing firm. Stand your ground, putting on the belt of truth and the body armor of God's righteousness. For **shoes**, put on the peace that comes from the Good News so that you will be fully prepared."* Ephesians 6:11-15 (NLT)

Are you walking around bare footed? If you are, you must protect your feet by putting on your spiritual combat shoes of peace.

Satan's strategy is to strike the heels of the marital relationship so that there is discord, dissension and division between a husband and wife. When you are wearing the shoes of peace, you are able to protect your feet so that you can continue to walk together in agreement. The shoes of peace represent a state of mutual harmony between a husband and wife. With your spiritual shoes on as a proactive defensive strategy, you are now ready to crush Satan's head with repeated punches. How do you punch Satan in the head? You punch Satan in the head using the Word of God and effective prayer as an offensive weapon. The Word of God and prayer become your spiritual boxing gloves. When we obey God in what He has said about marriage in His Word, we make a choice not to operate and interact with each other based on our feelings or our moods. We choose godly principles to be our guide as we respond and interact with the challenges and concerns of the marital relationship. When we do this, it is like giving Satan an uppercut to the jawbone because the Word of God is a weapon. Each time Satan tempted Jesus in Matthew chapter 4, Jesus punched Satan in the head with the Word of God. It is written…, It is written…, It is written… Ephesians 5:33 explains how you can punch Satan in the head when he begins striking the heels of your marriage.

"Each one of you must love his wife as he loves himself and the wife must respect her husband."

As a husband, you must understand that when or if your wife is disrespectful to you, it becomes a strike to your heel. Her operating in the flesh as she interacts with you is many times, her being influenced by Satan without her even knowing it. He wants you to think she is attacking you when in reality he has been successful in manipulating her personality in how she is interacting with you. As the husband, when you move pride aside, pray willingly and love unconditionally by addressing her disrespect in a loving way, you are using godly principles to relate to her. When she is disrespectful, you put on the **shoes of peace** and use your spiritual boxing gloves of effective prayer and unconditional love to uppercut punch the devil in the head to stop him from using your wife to strike your heel. The same is true for a husband who is being unloving toward his wife. By not reacting with unhealthy emotional warfare, but using effective prayer and being respectful using godly principles to relate to him and address the unloving behavior in a respectful way, you put on the **shoes of peace** and use your spiritual boxing gloves of unconditional respect to deal a massive blow to the head of Satan. Satan will not want to trade blow for blow with you. Receiving a blow to the head causes more damage than a strike to the heel. But if you do not deal massive blows to the head of Satan, he will continue striking the heels of your marriage until one of you or both of you make a decision to no longer walk together in agreement. When this happens, divorce happens.

Genesis 3:16 (NLT): "Then he said to the woman, 'You will bear children with intense pain and suffering. And though your desire will be for your husband, he will be your master.'"

Here, God is saying to the woman that because she took over the leadership and managerial roles of the relationship without His divine authorization, her desire will be for her husband. Desire is a strong feeling, worthy or unworthy, that impels to the attainment or possession of something that is (in reality or imagination) within reach. In other words, God is saying she will have a *strong feeling that impels her to the attainment* to be and function as the husband. This means that at times, she will desire to control, lead, and manage her husband and their marital relationship, but he will rule over her as God rules over him. When God handed out the punishment to the serpent and Adam, he explained first what they did and then enforced the consequences. With the woman, God does not do that because she did not break His commandment. She disobeyed and dishonored Adam by taking over the leadership and management responsibilities of the relationship. On behalf of Adam, God issued her consequence: pain during childbirth. God knew the desire to be the head leader and manager of the marriage had not left the woman's conscience. She had tasted the power of leadership and management and now God had to give her a command so that she would not step out of her place again to be the head leader and manager of the marriage relationship when he designed her to be the helper to her husband. Thus, God is saying, "Woman, I know you want to lead and manage the marital relationship over your husband because you may think he is not competent and capable of leading at times, but your husband will be your master and you must submit to him as he submits to my Son Jesus."

Genesis 3:17-20 (NLT): "And to Adam he said, 'Because you listened to your wife and ate the fruit I told you not to eat, I have placed a curse on the ground. All your life you will struggle to scratch a living from it.
 It will grow thorns and thistles for you, though you will eat of its grains. All your life you will sweat to produce food, until your dying day. Then you will return to the ground from which you came. For you were made from dust, and to the dust you will return.' Then Adam named his wife Eve, because she would be the mother of all people everywhere."

Here you see God reaffirm what I have been saying throughout this chapter. He says that Adam listened to his wife and ate the fruit that He told him not to eat. Remember, the command was given to Adam—not to the woman. So God told Adam what he did wrong and the consequences that were going to be associated with his actions.

Genesis 3:21-23 "And the Lord God made clothing from animal skins for Adam and his wife. Then the LORD God said, 'The people have become as we are, knowing everything, both good and evil. What if they eat the fruit of the tree of life? Then they will live forever!' So the Lord God banished Adam and his wife from the Garden of Eden, and He sent Adam out to cultivate the ground from which He had been made."

To "cultivate" means to develop. As men, we are commanded by God to develop our relationships in marriage until death. A wife is to help her husband with this great task.

Life in the Garden of Eden was a paradise, much like living in heaven. When Adam disobeyed God, God removed him from the garden. He no longer deserved the paradise that was created for him. It is important to know that God evicted Adam from the garden, but because Eve was his wife, she also was evicted. Once again what Adam did affected her. The only way she could have stayed in the Garden of Paradise was if Adam was living there. Since he got evicted, she was evicted as well.

Chapter 9

Lazy Leadership and Mismanagement

After the wedding bells have stopped ringing and the emotional bliss of the wedding has begun to subside, there is a tendency to become lazy in leadership and management. Why? I believe that time can be the killer of enthusiasm. Anything new is exciting, and when the excitement wears off, often times complacency sets in. The word "lazy" means to be averse or disinclined to work in an activity or the lack of exerting effort to a *purpose*. The word "leadership," as you learned before, means the act or instance of leading, guiding, or directing. Management means to bring about or succeed in accomplishing something in the most effective and efficient way. Adam was to follow God's leadership as he led and managed the marital relationship. This means one must start with a clear understanding of the destination. It means to know where you're going so that you better understand where you are now and so you know that the steps you need to take are always in the right direction. Godly leadership is knowing where God is leading you and what God wants you to accomplish for Him. By faith you begin the journey that God has led you to accomplish for Him. Remember, leadership is a process by which a person influences others to accomplish an objective. Leaders carry out this process by applying their leadership attributes, such as beliefs, values, ethics, character, knowledge, and skills. God outlined His leadership plan to Adam and told him what objectives He wanted Adam to accomplish for Him. The goal was dominion or rulership over the Garden of Eden. Adam was to accomplish this goal by cultivating (*developing*), keeping (*protecting*), and submitting (*following the plan of God*). When Adam and the woman were married, Adam's leadership goal for marriage from God did not change. Adam was to continue to cultivate the marriage (***develop it***), keep the marriage (***protect it***), and submit to God in marriage (***obey His instruction on how to be a husband and function as one***). The honeymoon is over; now let's evaluate what kind of leader Adam was and whether he followed the leadership outline God gave him.

Genesis 3:1-3: "Now the serpent was sneakier than any beast of the field which the Lord God had made. And he said unto the woman, Did God say, 'Ye [Adam and you] *shall not eat of every tree of the garden?' And the woman said unto the serpent, 'We may eat of the fruit of the trees of the garden: But of the fruit of the tree which is in the midst of the garden, God hath said, Ye* [Adam and I] *shall not eat of it, neither shall ye* [Adam and I] *touch it, lest ye* [Adam and I] *die.'"*

One of two things has happened. Either Adam told the woman if they touched or ate the fruit from the forbidden tree they might die, or the woman assumed that if they touched it or ate it they might die.

Either way, Adam is responsible for making sure that the correct message was delivered and understood. Why? God appointed him as the President of the garden. Let's look at an example to see what this means. Let's say Adam is the CEO of Best Buy. One day you decide that you want a flat screen TV. You go online and place an order for a 46-inch Sony Bravia Flat Screen TV. A month and a half passes by and the Super Bowl is airing in one week, and your TV has not been delivered. You call the customer service number, and you ask to speak to a Best Buy representative. Eve works for Best Buy and takes your call. She is the one who handles all of the online orders and somehow she has deleted your order. Now you are upset that this has happened and you e-mail the CEO, Adam, explaining why he is responsible for your order being deleted. Adam responds and says, "I apologize but that is not my fault. I did not process your online order and accidentally delete it. My assistant Eve did that." You respond and say, "But you are the CEO. You may not have processed my order, but you are responsible for the company and training of your employees to make sure things like this do not happen. In the case of the garden, Adam was responsible and at fault because the woman was not the appointed CEO or President of the garden. Adam deferred his God-given leadership and managerial duties to his wife and submitted to her leadership and management.

Genesis 3:6: "And when the woman saw that the tree was good for food, and that it was pleasant to the eyes, and a tree to be desired to make one wise, she took of the fruit thereof, and did eat, and gave also unto her husband with her; and he did eat."

There was no struggle to persuade Adam to eat the fruit. Adam didn't even question the woman. Adam was in total submission to her. The Scriptures say that Adam just took the fruit and ate it. He completely disregarded God's command in submitting to Him; instead, he chose to give over or yield his power or authority to the woman and follow her lead.

But wait. Doesn't it say in Ephesians 5:21 that husbands and wives are to submit to one another? Isn't a husband supposed to submit to his wife? This is what the verse says,

"Submitting yourselves one to another in the fear of God."

This simply means if a husband is about to make a decision that is not godly and his wife urges him to follow God, he should submit to his wife because of the godly advice she is giving him.

The woman was out of line for having a spiritual conversation about the leadership and management of the marriage and God's provisions for the marital relationship. The woman was also out of line for suggesting that Adam should disobey God even if she had good intentions. I believe she had good intentions for wanting to be wise to better help her husband. But her method of achieving wisdom was outside of the will of God. You can be sincere, but sincerely wrong. What she was suggesting was not godly advice. The conversation between the woman and the serpent should have never taken place, because Adam's job was to protect the woman from the serpent. Adam became lazy in his leadership and management of the relationship, and the woman took over the relationship. The woman did not leave the garden to have a conversation apart from Adam; it happened right where they lived. The serpent came to them wanting to speak to her, and Adam did nothing to stop it. Adam and the woman were together when the serpent approached the woman. Adam, like many men today, got married and started to relax in his leadership and management duties. He was given the position by God to be the President of the marriage, but he began slacking. If Adam was proactive, when he saw the serpent—who he knew was the enemy God had warned him about—he would have removed the threat or problem immediately. If Adam was reactive, he would have waited to see what the outcome of the conversation would be and what his wife was going to do. Adam became passive. Adam knew what to do because God instructed him—not her. Adam knew what direction the relationship was supposed to go in. God said, "Be fruitful and multiply." Not only did God provide the leadership, but he also provided the management of how Adam was to accomplish this. God instructed Adam to develop, to protect two valuable assets of the garden, about Satan and the fall of him and his angels, and about the two trees. Adam had all the information to lead and manage successfully. Before the woman was created, Adam was given a management class by God as well. How do we know this? Adam says something profound at the end of Genesis 2.

Genesis 2:23 (KJV): "And Adam said, 'This is now bone of my bones, and flesh of my flesh: she shall be called woman, because she was taken out of man.'"

The phrase "This is now" is not referring to the woman; it is referring to the marriage and oneness [not sameness] that he has experienced. Next Adam describes the woman by saying, "She shall be called woman, because she was taken out of man." Adam is now married and is expected to operate as the husband. He is to follow godly leadership as he leads the marital relationship. He is to follow godly management as he manages the marital relationship. In the very next verse, notice that God tells Adam something that is very profound and important to making the marriage successful. This is what God says, *"Therefore shall a man leave his father and his mother, and shall cleave unto his wife: and they shall be **one flesh**."* [Not the same flesh] Before marriage a man is to develop his personal and private life. Before he signs a marital agreement with a woman to be his wife, he must have and keep the agreement he has made with God. The idea is that when he leaves his father and mother, he is a developed man capable of independent living in which he has achieved success with himself. He is to leave his family and create a new life and family with his wife as they operate interdependently. Parents are given a charge by God to develop their children so they will be able to form successful relationships. Since Adam did not have earthly parents, he received his instructions from God Himself.

Proverbs 22:6 (KJV) states, *"Train up a child in the way he should go: and when he is old, he will not depart from it."*

This proverb is saying that the training a child receives from his parents is invaluable. If a young boy is taught how to treat his wife and family when he is young, he is more able to function effectively in a marital relationship when he gets older. This same principle would apply to a woman receiving training from her parents on how to be a godly wife to her husband and a godly mother to her children. The parents are responsible for teaching, instructing, and correcting a child when he or she is young. When the child is older, he or she is more likely not to depart from it. Even if a child is taught the right way, he or she still has to make a decision to live the right way. Many parents today are having children at younger ages, and many of these children are the by-products of single parents. The children of yesterday become the parents of today, and many of them did not receive correct instructions on how to be successful with themselves from their parents, let alone how to be successful in and have meaningful relationships. They were exposed to dysfunctional relationships, and now a dysfunctional relationship seems normal while functional relationships are many times viewed as dysfunctional. The second part of Genesis 2:24 states that he shall cleave or "merge" with his wife and they shall be one flesh. This is the ***public life*** they experience as a couple. In order to come together and operate as one in an interdependent relationship, you must first be effectively self-developed as individuals. Adam and Eve were perfectly created individuals with limitations. Learning never ceases, so developing yourself is a process—not a destination. If Adam is responsible for teaching and informing the woman, he has to continue to be taught and submit to God's instructions. Adam stopped submitting to God and began to do things his way; no wonder there were gaps in what Eve believed she knew about what God had said. If the woman has not developed herself in the areas of maturity, character, and integrity, she will not cooperate, interact respectfully, and communicate effectively with her husband to have a successful interdependent relationship. To operate as one in an interdependent relationship, you must have effective interaction(win-win), effective communication (***understand first and then be understood***), and effective cooperation (***synergy***). How we interact, communicate, and cooperate all determine whether two people can operate in oneness in a marriage or dating relationship.

In Matthew 5:25 Jesus said, *"Every household divided against itself will not stand."* Who is mentoring you as an individual as you prepare for marriage? Who is providing instruction to you as a couple to stand together?

More than fifty percent of couples in their first marriage fail to become ***one***, which ultimately leads to some form of divorce. This is because of one of the following: each person has not taken the time to become the right person in his and her private life, or each person does not know how or chooses not to effectively interact with each other, effectively communicate with each other, and effectively cooperate with each other. Secondly, the husband and wife do not implement love, respect, sexual fulfillment and romance on an ongoing basis thereby losing interest in each other. This book provides the tools that will help you to understand who you first must become so that you can do the things necessary to keep your marriage together. It will also prepare you as an individual before marriage to be the person who is capable of experiencing self-development to achieve success with yourself and then others. If you want a better healthy marriage, become a better healthy person.

If you are looking for a great man, become a great woman. If you are looking for a great woman, become a great man.

In order to become great, you must...

1. Learn - grow and develop yourself mentally, emotionally and spiritually every day. The wisdom of the world is in books.

2. Live - Get... a life - you must take care of your body and not allow others to abuse it mentally, emotionally or spiritually.

3. Love - Relational health - you must be able to love and receive it.

As you practice these 3 principles, you will begin to discover your voice in life. What is your Voice?

Your Voice is your personal unique contribution to mankind and is made up of 4 parts.

1. Talent - what are your natural gifts and strengths (everyone has talent)?

2. Passion - what are those things that naturally inspire, energize, excite, and motivate you?

3. Need - What does the world need that you could provide assistance by using your talents?

4. Conscience- that small voice inside you that compels you to act and make a difference.

When you tap into your talent and passion you discover a need and feel drawn by your conscience to do something about it.

Chapter 10

What Kind of Man are You?

Many men wrestle with the ideal of what kind of man they are or will become. There is this notion that if you are male and over the age of eighteen, you are a man. Well, there is a difference between a masculine man and a grown-up boy. When you look at today's modern men, you see that so many have the wrong mindset about what masculinity is. (I can say this because I too had a distorted mindset.) We can all make a change. The next seven years can be different to the last seven years if we choose to change.

Ladies, it is important that you are able to recognize and select a great man to become your future husband. What separates men from grown-up boys? It's simple, men's principles, beliefs, attitudes, actions, and habits are not the same as grown-up boys. You cannot expect a grown-up boy to act like a grown-up masculine man because they are two different people. I was listening to a sermon on marriage by Pastor Mark Driscoll, the preaching and speaking pastor of Mars Hill Church in Seattle, Washington. In one of his sermons, he describes the difference between the two. Here is a recap of what he said.

What is a grown-up boy? He is a male who reaches the legal adult age but does not have the maturity of an adult. He does not accept responsibility for his words and actions. He is not dependable and is not developed in the areas of maturity, integrity, or character.

Grown-up boys fall into two categories when it comes to how they relate to others. They are the pitfalls of omission and commission.

The pitfall of commission simply means **doing** what you're not supposed to do. This leads to the development of chauvinism in a man. The pitfall of omission means **not doing** what you're supposed to do. These pitfalls can create a situation where men become cowardly. Men, it is vitally important to develop the inner qualities that separate you from the men who are chauvinistic or cowardly. I believe any man can achieve this.

Chauvinistic Man

A chauvinistic man is a grown-up little boy, parading like a confident man whose behavior and attitude toward women indicate a belief that they are innately inferior to men.

Iceberg Ike. Ike is a person who defines himself as being a masculine man when in face he is not. He believes the way to be a man is to do the opposite of what a woman does. For example, if she hugs, he does not hug. If she cries, he does not cry. If she expresses how she feels, he does not. If she is nurturing, he is not nurturing. Why would he be? That stuff is for weak men according to him. He is fearful of showing emotion and love because in his mind real men do not do that. He was always told that real men don't cry or show love, and if you show emotion, you are acting like a weak man. He is a person who commits himself to operate in an unloving way because to him, demonstrating love does not fit the pattern of being a masculine man.

Success-and-Status Sean. Sean is a person who defines masculinity as accumulating material possessions. The more stuff he has, the more of a man he believes he is. Sean will sacrifice anything for the all-mighty dollar. His wife and kids suffer because he is never around to provide love and affection to them. He is completely devoted to his career or business, while his marriage falls apart. Sean believes that as long as he financially provides for his family, that he has done his job. His life revolves around status, so he has to keep up with the latest trends and fashions. He is more concerned about what other people think of him than what he thinks about himself. He is arrogant and ego-driven and believes the world revolves around him. The fear of criticism is the driving force in his life.

Hell-Raising Howard. Howard is a walking time bomb just waiting to explode on someone. Because of his anger, pride, jealousy, insecurity and selfishness, Howard does not have a positive mental attitude about life. He is a person who blames others for his anger, attitude, and abusive behavior. Howard believes that a masculine man must use fear to control his girlfriend, wife or kids. He is abusive with his words and actions in an attempt to intimidate his spouse or children through fear. Howard is a person who is verbally and physically abusive and believes that when a woman does not do what he says, he must verbally, physically or emotionally abuse her. As with other men who have similar mindsets, he saw his dad treat his mother this way, and he adopted this behavior believing that it's evidence of manhood. But he is not a man; he is a little boy. When you are around Hell-Raising Howard, you have to be careful of your actions because any little thing will set him off. Howard may seem to be all right at times, but if you disagree with him or do not do what he tells you to do the way he wants it done, he is going to explode on you with violence and give you hell about it. Howard is a controlling, abusive person who, deep down inside, is angry with himself.

I'm-the-Boss Brian. Brian is a person who is full of pride and ego. Brian believes that because he is a male, women are beneath him.

His only rationale for a woman doing what he asks or demands is not because what he is asking is honorable or right but because he is a man and she is a woman. Brian believes that a woman has to do whatever he says. Whatever a woman says or asks of him will result in him doing the opposite or ignoring her because he thinks he is the boss and she is his employee. He tells her what to do, and she should do what he says without questioning him. Brian takes advantage of his marital authority and has a distorted view of biblical leadership and management in marriage. He is an inconsiderate, self-centered, arrogant, prideful person. Brian believes that ordering around a woman makes him a man and no one can tell him what to do, so he does not submit to a higher authority. He believes that he has the final say in all matters and has to answer to no one. No one can hold him accountable for his destructive behavior because he chooses to shut down and disregard positive intervention or instruction. He either doesn't know or doesn't accept that God, and not him is in charge of everything. He fails to understand that he has a boss—God—and that he must submit to the leadership and management of God to have authentic authority in marriage. If he does understand, it still is not good enough because Brian decided long ago he would lead and manage his own way—not God's. Why? Because in his eyes, he is the boss!

It's-my-Money Mike. Mike is cheap. He is a miser—extremely stingy with his money and possessions and unwilling to share. It is one thing to be a great steward over money, but Mike takes it to another level. Mike is so tight with his money that to save on the monthly water bill, he has a house rule for using the toilet. "If it's yellow, let it mellow. If it is brown, flush it down." Mike seldom gives his wife money or allows her to spend her own money. He takes saving money to an extreme. Mike is so tight with his money that he has developed a love for it, which is greater than his love for his family. Mike does not believe in having a life insurance plan. Why? Because, "It's my money, and I'm not leaving any of it to you when I die."

The Cowardly Man

The second type of undeveloped man is the cowardly man. He is a person who lacks courage in making decisions or facing danger, difficulty, opposition, or pain. He is timid or easily intimidated. He is a person who fails to take responsibility for himself and his family.

Little-Boy Leroy. Leroy is an immature little boy who has not had success in his private life, but he believes he will be successful in a committed relationship. He still lives at home with his mom, and she pays all his bills. Leroy gets stressed out easily, so he only works part-time or complains that he can't find a job that suits him. He prides himself in having other women take care of him. Leroy wants to find someone to take care of him the way his mother does, so he can play video games and watch TV all day. He wants to stay at home while his girlfriend or wife goes to work. He is not interested in working or providing for his family because that would stress him out or give him a headache. Leroy also makes excuses for not working or making himself a better person by reading books, attending the seminars, going to school to get a degree or attending a trade school. He is not dependable and it is always someone else's fault why he cannot get a job or start a business. He expects his woman to pull half of his load and all of hers while she obeys his every command and accepts his excuses. Little-Boy Leroy is a man who will weigh a woman down and suck the life and resources from her and the relationship with his immature behavior.

Bring-Home-the-Bacon Bill. Bill is a guy who works very hard and is very dependable but checks out mentally and emotionally when he gets home. Bill believes that because he has worked all day he does not have any responsibility to the function of the home. Bill believes that it is the woman's job to take care of any and all household responsibilities. All Bill wants to do when he gets home is to channel surf, check his fantasy football, baseball and basketball standings as he watches the latest sports updates on ESPN. If he is not watching TV he is spending countless hours at the gym working out. He is not interested in having quality time with his kids or wife. He hears nothing they say to him because he is in his own world when he gets home. So Bring-Home-the-Bacon Bill is a guy who is present and absent at the same time. He is committed and motivated to solving complex problems and situations as they arise at his job, but when it comes to problems in his relationship with his wife or with his children he does not have the energy to use his creative abilities and logic to solve them.

Super-Spiritual Stanley. Stanley is a guy who knows every verse in the Bible. He can quote scriptures like T.D Jakes and Joel Osteen. Stanley is a person who preaches at people instead of first seeking to understand them. He is a person who judges and is often a hypocrite at the same time. He claims to believe in and follow God, but his actions toward his wife, family and friends say otherwise. He does not always live what he preaches. No one wants to hear what Stanley has to say because his negative actions speak louder than his positive words. Stanley can be one way at home and another way at church or at his job, so he confuses many people including his wife and kids. He is embarrassing at times because he does not apply wisdom to his knowledge, so quite often he turns people away from the gospel.

All I Want is Sex Stuart. Stuart is a person who is motivated solely by having sex with as many women as he can. For the most part, he is only lustfully attracted to a woman's body. He does not care that she has a brain, a wonderful personality or a spiritual connection to God. He is out for one thing and one thing only, finding a woman to experience sexual ecstasy with him. His pursuit of women is tied only to his erection. Once he is satisfied sexually, the women are put back on the "I only call or text her for sex" shelf until it is time to utilize them again. He has no ambition to respect and love any of these women. Why? His motto: "You can't turn a whore into a housewife, and why buy the cow when the milk is free." He has emotionally tricked women into believing that the way to show him love is giving him unauthorized, unconditional sex. He has tricked women into believing that if they have sex with him, he will eventually marry them. Stuart prides himself on this. His mission is to "smash" and "dash" meaning as soon as he has sex with you he leaves you. He will never be able to connect emotionally with a woman in a healthy way, but he makes her think he is so that he can continue to connect with her sexually when he gets horny. The only time Stuart will call is when he wants sex or oral sex from a woman or women. Stuart is addicted to illegal sex and doesn't care where or from whom he gets it. He solicits prostitutes and doesn't see any thing wrong with paying for sex. Stuart will probably not marry you because of his insecurities and immaturity. Every time Stuart has sex with you outside of marriage, he loses more and more respect for you, which makes him not want to pursue you emotionally. He follows the logic that if a woman was willing to sleep with him and not be married to him, who else has she been willing to sleep with. He doesn't want the responsibility of putting in the time and work to make a relationship or marriage successful with a woman he believes is a whore, even though he is promiscuous himself. If he does marry, because of his selfishness, he will more than likely never become a husband, only a married unfaithful man. It is very hard for him to charge a woman's emotional and spiritual battery using love because emotionally he doesn't respect her, so his eros love for her becomes conditional, inconsistent or nonexistent. Many women have been the victims of Stuart as he leads them down a road of deception and false dreams.

Unfaithful Frank. Frank is a person who has no self-discipline or self-control. He has not learned how to be faithful and loyal to God, so he struggles to remain faithful and loyal in secondary relationships. He has not learned how to say no to the things that are unhealthy to his well-being. Frank believes that one woman is not enough, so he is constantly unfaithful to his girlfriend or wife. Frank will never be able to "go the extra mile" because of his selfish behavior. He is the kind of person who not only has affairs with women, but also has affairs with other men. He hides his behavior from his wife and children and does things secretly. Frank does not value himself so he puts others at risk with his irresponsible behavior. He is also a guy who is addicted to pornography and masturbation. His habit of watching porn and masturbating to it is something he struggles with in his private life, and he hopes that no one finds out. Frank developed these habits long before he was married but had no idea of the repercussions it would have on his marriage. He is also addicted to strip clubs and wasting money to experience illegal sexual pleasure. Frank refers to them as "Gentleman's Clubs," but would a gentleman go there? Frank is a selfish person because in his mind, it is all about him and he is just having fun. He knows that he is supposed to be faithful, but the coward inside him tells him not to be. Is Frank homosexual or heterosexual? The man described here can be either, but it doesn't matter because in God's eyes he is being unfaithful if he is involved in any adulterous, illegal sexual acts. Many people bash and hate homosexual men and who they are as people, but God doesn't. It is the behavior of the unfaithful heterosexual and homosexual that God hates—not the person.

Party-Animal Allen. Allen is the guy who parties Wednesday through Monday. He is always out hanging with the guys, drinking and having what he thinks is a good time. Allen wants to be the life of the party and wants to be accepted by everyone. His ego is fed as he bar hops trying to pick up women. Allen does not value the fact that his partying habits bring stress and dysfunction to a relationship. He does not care because he is having so much fun being the center of attention. Allen is irresponsible and insensitive. Staying out indefinitely partying and drinking is what he wants to do, and he is willing to lose everything to have his fun.

Passive Paul. Paul has no backbone and is insecure. He has no definite plan or purpose in life. He is totally dependent on his girlfriend or wife and cannot make a decision without her. He is a weak man because he has no courage to stand up for himself or express how he feels because of the fear of rejection. He allows himself to be abused verbally because he is timid. He is afraid to assume the leadership and management role of the relationship. He is so indecisive that many times he defers to his woman, allowing her to lead the relationship. But if she is wrong in making a decision that he should have made, he is quick to point out her fault in the situation. He does not trust himself, so he becomes a doormat and his woman controls his every move. Paul is afraid to disagree with anything his woman says or does in fear that she will leave him. Passive Paul is a puppet who is controlled by his woman.

As a man, if you saw yourself described in any of the people just mentioned, there is still hope for you, if you want to change. However, you cannot just cross your fingers and say, "I don't like who I am, I sure hope things will change for me." I used to conduct myself like many of the men described as chauvinistic and cowardly. Then I heard Jim Rohn say, "In order for things to change for you, you must change. But if you don't change the next five years will be just like the last five years. Anytime you want to, you can learn from the last five years and make the next five years of your life totally different. If you get better, things will get better for you." When I heard Jim Rohn say this, I made up my mind that I would change. I started making small steps, exchanging poor habits for good habits until I got to this current point in my life. You can too!

The reality is that chauvinistic and cowardly men will not make effective husbands in their current state. When a man and woman get married, there is no magical wand that is waved over them during the wedding ceremony that will eliminate toxic habits and behaviors. Prior to getting married you must address and replace these habits and behaviors with new, positive, life-sustaining ones with the help of God and the resources available in books, people and support classes.

The Christ-Centered Man

There is another kind of man who I believe all men should strive to emulate. He is a Christ-centered masculine man, and we can describe him in two words: courageous and considerate. Jesus had courage, and he was considerate. A courageous man possesses the quality of mind and spirit that enables him to make decisions and face difficulties, danger and pain without fear. He is not a pushover. He knows how to say no to the wrong things so that he can say yes to the right things. He is a man who makes decisions based on godly principles and not on what is popular or preferred by the culture. The second characteristic of a masculine man is that he is considerate. He shows consideration by showing and demonstrating kindness, love, respect, and awareness of others, their circumstances or situations. A godly masculine man is dependable, loyal, has a positive mental attitude, has the ability to operate as a husband, goes the extra mile, and applies his faith.

Ladies, you know you've found someone special when you've found the kind of man who has the qualities on this list:

- He makes you feel relaxed. You are able to be yourself around him.
- He does not hold grudges and forgives.
- You are attracted to him mentally, to his personality and his spirit.
- He is loyal.
- He is responsible because he takes care of his business.
- He is not abusive in any way.
- He is a great listener. He listens to learn and not always to give advice.
- He is thoughtful and romantic. He understands it is the little things that count.
- He is affectionate. He knows your love language and he loves you accordingly.
- He appreciates you and does not take you for granted.
- He fits into your life. You value the same things. You complement each other.
- He will sacrifice for you because he loves you unconditionally.
- He is financially stable.

Chapter 11

What Is A Husband?

In the King James Version of Genesis 2:15, God gave the command to Adam to **dress** and **keep** the garden. God provided Adam with the framework of what type of leadership and management style He expected Adam to implement in marriage.

"And the Lord God took the man, and put him into the Garden of Eden to dress it and to keep it." Genesis 2:15

Leadership is different from management, which I will discuss later. People with leadership authority say, "This is my role, and these are my goals that I want to accomplish." God gave Adam his role and the goals He wanted him to accomplish. When you look at the words "dress" and "keep" they have very profound meanings. The word "dress" has many meanings, but the meaning used here is "to cultivate, or develop." The word "keep" means to protect. These two words have powerful meanings because they were God's instructions to Adam prior to him getting married. God also instructed Adam not to eat from the tree of the knowledge of good and evil. The word I would like to associate with this instruction is submission. As we look at these three words, dress, keep, and submission, we can apply them directly to the marriage relationship.

At this point, God is preparing Adam for marriage by using husbandry as a means to teach Adam how to become a husband to his future wife Eve. Husbandry is the physical action one does for the purpose of developing and producing edible crops for food or agriculture. It is also associated with the agricultural practice of breeding and raising livestock.

"And out of the ground the Lord God formed every beast of the field, and every fowl of the air; and brought them unto Adam to see what he would call them; and whatsoever Adam called every living creature, that was the name thereof."

Genesis 2:19

Understanding and applying the "principle of husbandry" was important and necessary in order to prepare Adam to become a husband. Adam was practicing husbandry in a garden in his private life by cultivating or developing edible crops for himself and for the animals God created. Before God made and brought the woman to Adam, he was in training performing husbandry. Unfortunately, there are many men who have not acquired the knowledge, skills, tools, and self-discipline to apply "the principle of husbandry" as single men but believe that they will be great and effective husbands.

It is wise for a man who desires to get married to have a clear understanding of what a husband is and how a husband should operate in a marital relationship. It is possible to be married but not be a husband. In summary, God was preparing Adam for a marriage relationship by showing and instructing him how to develop and protect a garden while submitting to Him. I believe God also wanted Adam to have success with himself before he introduced a woman to him. God knew that Adam would first need to develop himself as a man then as a husband prior to his introduction to Eve.

As a single person wanting to get married, it is vital that you are prepared for the responsibilities of marriage. Here are the 5 P's for marriage success. Proper, preparation, prevents, poor, performance in marriage.

For the married men reading this book, I have a question for you:

Are you a husband or just a married man?

I want to go into greater detail about what a husband is and how a husband must know what love is in order for him to operate in it as he interacts with his wife. A Christian husband is a male who operates underneath and is accountable to Christ. He is a male who has learned and made a conscious decision to submit his identity to the lordship of Jesus Christ. As a Christian husband are you in complete submission to Christ? Many Christian married men want their wives to submit to them, but are those women seeing the man they are married to submit to Christ? Before you can expect the woman you married to submit to you, Christ is saying submit to Him first.

If you are a man who wants to get married, it is important that you know exactly what your role as a husband will be so that you can prepare yourself to fulfill that role. It is equally important that a woman knows the true attributes and characteristics that a husband should have before they select who they will marry. Why? God commands a woman to submit to her husband in marriage as her husband submits to Christ and His principles for right living. This means that God gives the woman the power to select who she will submit to. Many women have selected the wrong man hoping that he would be the right husband and are miserable in their marriage. Knowing who a godly husband is allows a woman to enter a partnership with God to hold him accountable for the things that God has commanded him to be and do as a husband.

"Husbands love your wives, as Christ loved the church and gave himself up for her." Ephesians 5:25

Choosing to become a man and putting off childish ways is part of becoming a husband. Too often, married men still exhibit childish behavior. As a husband, a man must commit to loving despite what his wife does or does not do or who she is or is not. This takes maturity and a commitment to love her despite her character flaws and behavior.

"When I was a child, I spoke like a child, I thought like a child, I reasoned like a child. When I became a man, I gave up childish ways." 1 Corinthians 13:11

Unfortunately, many married men do not operate as husbands. A selfish, unloving married man and a husband have different roles and goals that they fulfill within the marriage relationship. A selfish, unloving married man is a man who is legally married but who is not interested in loving his wife, and if he does love her, it is conditional. He can be a manipulator and take advantage of her respect for him and his position in the home. He is a user and not a giver. He is not interested in meeting her needs and wants, and if he does, it is conditional on sex or selfish desires. This type of married man is interested in himself and uses the marriage to further his agenda and his personal interests. An unloving married man is a person who operates with a win-lose mentality. He wins, and the wife loses. It is a competition to him. He is a man who takes great pride in working apart from his wife and not with her. He does not utilize her gifts, talents, knowledge, and abilities when he makes decisions about the relationship or family. He operates in an "I win only" mentality and believes that as long as he wins, he is o.k. All he cares about is having his desires met. A selfish, unloving, married man can also be bitter, erratic, cold, unforgiving, unfaithful, prideful, controlling, demeaning, unappreciative, non-affirming, unsympathetic, disrespectful, destructive, verbally and physically abusive, emotionally abusive or angry.

As a married man, did you see yourself anywhere in that description? I hope not. As a single man, did you see yourself anywhere in that description? I must admit I was some of those things in my past relationships. What a horrible person I was.

However, I've learned that true values are very important. Humans are a special creation. All of the life forms are driven by instinct and the genetic code. A goose can only fly south in the winter, because he is a goose. He can't fly any other direction; he is driven by instinct and the genetic code. But humans are a special, unique creation. We are not like any other life form. We can go north, we can go south, we can go east, and we can go west. We can live one way for five years and tear up that script and live another way the next five years. We are not just driven by instinct and the genetic code; there is something special about human creation. I asked myself, "What could I really do if I learned the lessons, adopted the disciplines and read the books?" The possibilities are endless. I am amazed at the human spirit. People with the most enormous problems still manage to rise above them and do something noble, something powerful or something wondrous.

If we are not satisfied with the way things are or are going we can change. I made a choice not to be on the destructive behaviors list above. It did not happen over night but eventually I got there. The goal for me was to make progress, not become perfect.

So what is a husband? The definition of a husband is "a married man in relation to how he treats and responds to his wife." The English word "husband," is not a native English word. It comes ultimately from the Old Norse word *húsbóndi,* meaning "master of a house." The prefix "hus" refers to "house" and "band" means to put on or around something to decorate or identify it by or hold a number of things together in harmony. So a "house-band" is a married man responsible for connecting and keeping the marriage and family together. A house-band makes himself a sacrificial band around the marital relationship, responsible for its protection.

"Above all these put on love, which binds everything together in perfect harmony." Colossians 3:14

The word bind means, "to fasten or secure with a band." A man cannot be a husband or house-binder if he is not using love as a tool to keep the marriage in harmony. A husband must demonstrate love on a daily basis as he submits to God's provisions pertaining to biblical marriage. This allows a married man to become and remain a husband to his wife and the marital relationship.

The Meaning of Marriage

Joseph Murphy in his book, *The Power of Your Subconscious Mind* explains to the reader the meaning of marriage. I would like to share it with you. The following is an excerpt from his book *The Power of Your Subconscious Mind.*

"Marriage is the spiritual union of a man and woman who are bound together by love. Marriage to be real must first be on a spiritual basis. It must be of the heart and the heart is the vessel of love. Honesty, sincerity, kindness and integrity are also forms of love. Each partner should be perfectly honest and sincere with the other. It is not a true marriage when a man marries a woman for her money, social position, or to lift his ego because of her physical beauty; this indicates a lack of sincerity, honesty, and true love. Such a marriage is a masquerade. When a woman says, 'I am tired of working; I want to get married because I want security,' her premise is false."

Why Do You Want To Get Married?

Why do you want to get married? The right "why" will give you better clarity on finding the right "who."

Here are 8 things to look for that will lead you to the right "who" by Gary Thomas author of the book *The Sacred Search*.

What qualities should you look for in a spouse?

1. What kind of parent would they be? Find out!

2. How do they handle conflict? Are they abusive? Are they secure, anxious or avoidant?

3. Do they pray? Do they willingly pray with you and for you?

4. Do they forgive or hold grudges?

5. Do they have a good ability to communicate?

6. Humble- the worst thing is to be married to someone who thinks they are perfect. Do they serve or want to be served? Do they want to grow themselves every bit as much as they want you to change?

7. Are they a giver or a taker? Do they give to get? How do they treat other people? When you spend time with this person do you feel drained or energized?

8. Is the Holy Spirit active in their life?

According to Gary Thomas most people choose a mate based on the following criteria.

1. Infatuation.
2. Sexual attraction.
3. Getting along well on dates.

Gary Thomas mentions that having a **"shared purpose"** should be at the center of all marriage relationships.

Did you marry someone because of love? Love should not be the primary reason for you to get married. You should enter into a marital covenant for a **"shared purpose"** using both love and respect as tools to sustain and energize the marriage. Love is a tool you must use to bind or hold together a marital relationship. Love was not designed to be the deciding factor whether to marry or not.

Marriage was designed and created by God to fulfill a special purpose between a man and a woman, to achieve something greater as a team than as two separate individuals. Our society and the media have misrepresented the institution of marriage. Many people feel that love is the primary reason to marry, but such "love" in many circumstances is often confused with infatuation or lust. Couples tend to become sexually involved prior to marriage, and the act of sex distorts their emotions. Many couples get married with no "shared purpose" in mind, but were heavily infatuated or sexually involved with one another. When these things wear off so does the foundation of their relationship. You often hear people say, "We fell out of love." Many couples after only a few years of marriage don't see the purpose of staying together. This is because there wasn't a definite shared purpose to begin with. Love must be demonstrated through your actions. Love is a choice. Love is a tool used to make sure a husband and wife stay together so that the "shared purpose" ordained by God is fulfilled in the marriage. If one person were to leave the relationship because of the lack of agape love and respect, the couple's "shared purpose" would be in jeopardy of not being fulfilled. Love + Respect = Unconditional Service.

Marriage is the byproduct when a man or woman makes a choice to unconditionally serve their spouse for a "shared purpose." As they function as a couple to achieve this "shared purpose" they must operate in love, which binds everything together in perfect harmony.

Remember, God gave the command to Adam not Eve to keep [protect] the garden. Husbands are to protect the "shared purpose" of the marital relationship using love as the main tool. When a husband looks inside of his relational toolbox, he should find an assortment of love tools that he must use to bind the marital relationship and keep it bound. Here are six love tools he should always keep handy and ready to use at any time. They are the expression love tool, the sacrificial love tool, the beneficial love tool, the unconditional love tool, the judicial love tool and the emotional love tool.

The Expression Love Tool True love is always visual and expressed with actions not just words.

The Sacrificial Love Tool True love will sacrifice for the benefit of another. What have you sacrificed because of love?

The Beneficial Love Tool True love does not love to receive something in return but loves to benefit someone else.

The Unconditional Love Tool True love is unconditional meaning no one has to earn or pay for it; it is a free gift.

The Judicial Love Tool True love is judicial meaning it is not weak, but seeks out the truth to make sure everything is done in decency and in order.

The Emotional Love Tool True love is emotional; it is a longing to experience appreciation, affirmation, understanding, oneness and deep joy.

When a husband uses the tools of love, he is making a conscious choice to love. A husband's primary duty is to band together the marriage while also protecting it as he submits to God.

There are many married men who choose not to love unconditionally by not using these tools of love. This is because many married men have not made the choice to become husbands and therefore, do not operate in that capacity.

No wonder so many women are frustrated. They assumed that when they got married, the man was going to operate as a husband. To their surprise, many men never do.

Without applying love tools, a married man will not be able to unite together with his wife.

"For this reason a man will leave his father and his mother, and be joined to his wife; and they shall become one flesh." Genesis 2:24

Love, along with respect, forgiveness, trust and sexual intimacy is the glue that keeps the husband and wife bound to each other as one flesh. If a married man chooses not to love or bind his marriage, then his relationship will become unfastened and some form of divorce or separation will likely occur. He and his wife become two people not living as *one* but living as *two individuals* with only the title of being married.

When I think about all my failed relationships and the part I played in their failure, I realized that it was my counter-productive beliefs and choices that caused them not to be successful. It was the result of years of accumulating misinformation.

We sometimes hang around the wrong people and wrong sources and develop the wrong mindset when it comes to what a healthy marriage/relationship looks like. The decisions that we are making in relationships are not wrong based on the information we have, rather it is the information we have that is causing us to select the wrong people and make the wrong decisions in marriage or relationships.

I now realize that I had the wrong information about what a husband was and how to operate as one in marriage. With new information I can make different decisions and have a different outcome. The challenge of being a great husband is to be strong but not rude; to be kind but not weak; be courageous but not conceited; to be bold not a bully; be thoughtful but not lazy; be humble but not timid; be confident but not arrogant; have humor but without ignorance. These are characteristics that every wife desires from her husband.

Bobby L. Sneed Jr.

How To Attract The Ideal Husband

Joseph Murphy in his book, *The Power of Your Subconscious Mind* gives women advice on how to attract their ideal husband. The following is an excerpt from his book *The Power of Your Subconscious Mind:*

"Sit down at night on your couch, close your eyes, let go, relax the body, become very quiet, passive, and receptive. Talk to your subconscious mind and say to it, 'I am now attracting a man into my experience who is honest, sincere, loyal, faithful, dependable, happy, positive, considerate, courageous and prosperous. Theses qualities, which I admire, are sinking down into my subconscious mind right now. As I dwell upon these characteristics, they become a part of me and are embodied in me subconsciously. I know there is an irresistible law of attraction and that I will attract to me a man according to my subconscious belief. I will attract that which I feel to be true in my subconscious mind. I know I can contribute to his peace and happiness. He loves me unconditionally. He loves my ideals and I love his ideals. He does not want to make me over; neither do I want to make him over. There is mutual love, freedom, romance and respect. Amen.'"

Have a keen desire to give the best that is in you of respect, devotion, cooperation and love and I believe you will meet your ideal husband.

Part 1

Developing The Marriage Relationship

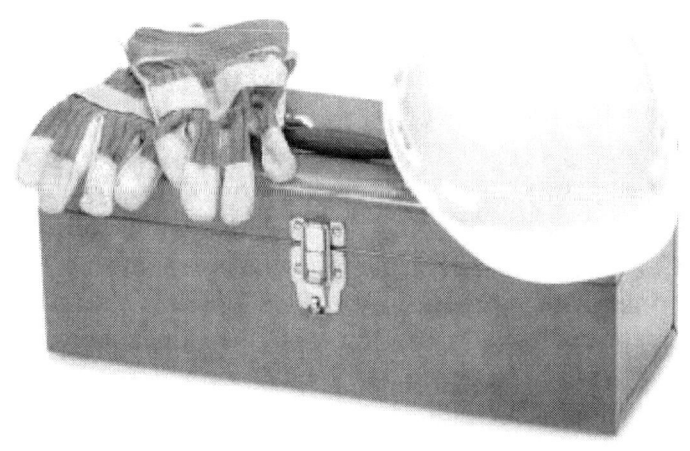

"The best time to prevent divorce is before marriage. It is not wrong to try to get out of a bad situation. But, why get into a bad situation in the first place?" –Joseph Murphy

Chapter 12

Development

Having a successful relationship or marriage is not an accident. Sadly, relational or marital failure is not an accident either. There are in my opinion three requirements for a successful relationship or marriage.

1. Decide what kind of relationship or marriage you want.
2. Determine the price you are going to pay to have that type of relationship or marriage.
3. Resolve to pay that price.

Honda Motor Company has a research and development division with the "mission to develop forward-thinking technologies that anticipate and satisfy the needs of people in the future." The latest Honda Accord looks very different from the first Honda Accord manufactured in 1976. The Honda research and development teams are committed to providing a product that will be reliable, safe and efficient while at the same time making innovative changes to improve the product. Every year Honda's research and development teams make improvements to the Honda Accord, making it more efficient, dependable, reliable, and safer. Similarly, developing a relationship is something that must be done throughout the life of the relationship. Over time, the relationship should not look the same. The communication should improve, love and respect should be even more evident, and the way the two of you interact with one another should improve. As the husband, you are primarily responsible for implementing the research and development initiatives that the marriage relationship will need to grow and flourish.

Marriage: It's in Your Hands

"Focus on God and His purpose for your life. So many people are looking for love, but emotionally they are not ready for it because there is some work that they still need to do on themselves. We oftentimes overlook the work we need to do because we are looking for someone else. What we don't realize is that when we focus on God and ourselves, God will bring that person into our lives."

-DeVon Franklin and Meagan Good on Finding Love

A person should not even begin to look for or expect a mate unless they are adequately prepared for the responsibilities of marriage and family, and are themselves spiritually mature, emotionally healthy, and financially secure. When emotionally needy, spiritually immature and financially fragile people get together in marriage, it is usually a disaster.

To know what you must do to properly develop your relationship, you need to have a basic understanding of what the word "development" means.

One of the definitions of development means to grow by degrees into a more advanced or mature state and to work out with great care and nicety of detail. Growth means to spring up and develop maturity. As time elapses in a relationship, the tendency to become complacent is inevitable. It is important that as men and women we continue to grow and mature with ourselves and with each other. This can be done in several ways, but seeking constant godly council throughout the marriage is one of the best ways to sustain it. As a couple comes together collectively, receives new information and adopts new ways of being interdependent through continued marriage counseling after the wedding, they are able to implement, evaluate and monitor progress to make sure that the relationship is growing and maturing.

Show me a relationship that is problem free, and I will show you two perfect people. The fact is that there is no perfect person, so there will be no perfect relationship. Even if you found a perfect person, the relationship would become imperfect as soon as you show up. There are, however, many successful and healthy relationships. The act of developing your relationship means that you are willing to elaborate the relationship in great detail. When an issue arises in the relationship, you decide that you will work it out with great care considering the other person's thoughts, feelings, and actions. This means that when faced with challenges or conflicts, you will choose to act kindly and with consideration.

As a man and woman grow together in a positive way and mature as a couple, they become a stronger unit. When God is the center of this union, they become a cord of three not easily broken. The divorce rate is 50% and higher for first-time marriages and even higher for second and third marriages because of emotionally underdeveloped or childish men and women. There will be times in a marriage where you will not be able to have it your way. I know that at the restaurant Burger King, you can have it your way all the time, but a marriage is not like a Burger King restaurant. Having childish reactions to situations due to a lack of maturity will inevitably poison the relationship. To make marriage work, you must be willing to end the childish behavior and replace it with a level of maturity that will meet the challenge of interacting in a spirit of harmony in a marriage.

A principle is a "rule, action or conduct." There are eight main principles that I believe men must develop before we can become authentic husbands. For a man, the first principle deals with love, which husbands are commanded to do. The seven remaining principles develop our private, personal and interpersonal being, allowing us to function and co-exist as effective husbands in marriage. Once we develop these principles of conduct within ourselves, we are to model and teach them to our wives, children, and families. Originally, I was unsure of how to explain how a man and woman should develop themselves into a person capable of sustaining a successful marriage. I prayed and asked God to show me what direction to take in explaining the development process. He led me to a book written by Dr. Stephen R. Covey: *The 7 Habits of Highly Effective People.* I began reading the book and discovered that highly effective people make highly effective marriage partners. I had my answer. It is a book that provides powerful lessons on personal change. Too often we enter into the marriage covenant immature and underdeveloped in our mindset, emotions, and spirit. This lack of fundamental maturity in these areas, I believe, account for many of the problems and frustrations that married men and women experience. Dr. Stephen R. Covey's book uses basic principles that I will focus on as we move from being dependent to independent to interdependent. Although his book is not about marriage, the seven habits or principles outlined in it can be applied to a marriage relationship to make it a successful one. I will be using the book *The 7 Habits of Highly Effective People* as a reference to describe the eight principles I believe a husband and wife must develop as their foundation to maximize and grow their marriage and make it a highly effective and successful one. I will not cover each habit in its entirety but will give you an overall view so that you may develop your marriage. Dr. Covey does a wonderful job of explaining and outlining these habits in great detail so that you can become an effective person and experience effective relationships with others. I suggest that you purchase his book for further and more complete development. It will transform your personal life and how you interact with other people. It has definitely impacted my life.

Over time, our bodies mature from children to adults. Although you may be a physically mature adult, this does not mean that you are mentally, emotionally, or spiritually mature.

Dependent People. Dependent people believe that someone else should and will take care of them. Someone else will make decisions for them, and someone else will come through for them. If someone else does not come through for them, they blame them for what happened. For them, love and respect are often measured by what people do for them or what they get out of the situation or circumstance. They take so that they will have whatever they want. This is selfish behavior. Dependent people do not make great team players or great spouses.

Independent People. Independent people believe that they can do things themselves and that they are responsible, self-reliant and can make their own decisions. They pride themselves on being able to do things alone without the help of others. They can be conditional givers and receivers. In many cases independent people express their independence by enabling the dependent person. Subconsciously, it is a way for independent people to control situations because they are the main providers or givers. This allows the independent person to call the shots and control the relationship. Normally, when two independent people date, and one or both of them discover what is taking place, they sever the connection. This is an unhealthy attachment because a donor gives so that he or she can get something in return or manipulate the situation for personal benefit. Again, this is selfish behavior. Giving in and of itself is not wrong, but giving for the wrong reason is unhealthy. Independent thinking alone is not suited to make a marriage successful. Independent people who do not have the maturity level to think interdependently may be great individuals but will not be great marriage partners.

Interdependent People. Interdependent people believe they can accomplish things on their own and cooperate together with other people. Andrew Carnegie described it as being a "Mastermind Alliance." They believe that two or more people can combine their talents and abilities and create something better together. An interdependent person does not allow selfishness to interfere in interaction with others. Interdependent people operate with a "we" mentality and not a "me" or "you" mentality. It is the philosophy of "not my way or your way but the best way for us." Interdependence is a far more mature, advanced concept than being independent. Life is, by nature highly interdependent. If I am physically interdependent, I am self-reliant and capable, but I also realize that you and I working together can accomplish far more that I could accomplish alone, even at my best. If I am emotionally interdependent, I derive a great sense of worth from myself, but I also recognize the need for love and respect, for giving, and for receiving love and respect from others. If I am intellectually interdependent, I realize that I need the best thinking of other people to join with my own. In marriage as an interdependent husband or wife, you have the opportunity to share yourself deeply and meaningfully with your spouse and benefit from the knowledge, skills, abilities, and talents that your spouse brings to the table. We live in an interdependent reality, and our most important accomplishments require interdependency skills well beyond our present abilities.

People do not maintain successful relationships or marriages, because they have tried to jump into them without first developing maturity, character, and integrity. You cannot be successful with other people if you haven't paid the price of developing success with yourself. If your life is chaotic, please do not create chaos in someone else's life by getting involved in relationship with them. Heal and rebuild yourself first. It means that you will have to start from the inside out. Examine your character, maturity and integrity. If you want to have a happy, successful marriage, become the kind of person who generates positive energy. This inside- out approach says that private victories precede public victories. Making and keeping promises to ourselves precede making and keeping promises to others. It is unwise to try to improve relationships with others before improving ourselves through personal development.

Chapter 13

The Four Kinds of Love

In Greek, the term "love" was expressed using different words with unique meanings. We typically don't use these distinguishing words anymore. Today we loosely use the term "love." Because of this, love can mean many different things to many different people.

What is the difference between love and sex? Love is spiritual and sex is biological. Are you spiritually plugged into the "source" to love?

"Husbands, love your wives, as Christ loved the church and gave himself up for her." Ephesians 5:25

Eros

The first kind of love was associated with the word eros. Eros is having one's sexual needs met. So when a man or woman would say, "I eros you," he or she was saying, "I want you in a sexual way."

Storge

Storge love also called familial love is the Greek word for natural affection- such as the love of a parent toward a child, "cherishing one's kindred, especially parents or children." This is the love one has for a family member or relative. It is used in a platonic way.

Phileo

The third Greek word for love was "phileo." Phileo describes the love of friends. The city of Philadelphia got its name from this word, meaning the city of brotherly love. When a man or woman said, "I phileo you," they were saying, "I love you as a friend." It had similar characteristics to the word eros in that it was tied to some degree of selfishness. The friendship was based on how the other person was treated. If you treated the other person right then they had a duty from your perspective to treat you right. So the attitude among friends was that, in order for your friend to be treated well, you must first be treated well. This friendship love is based on conditions.

Agape

This fourth word is different from eros and phileo because it expresses God's love and shows God's perspective on love. Agape is purged of all coldness. Agape is unique because, unlike eros and phileo, it has nothing to do with what the other person does or does not do. Eros is tied to having sexual needs met, and phileo is tied to how one treats another as a friend. But agape is taking the initiative to act and is not based on how someone else behaves, even at the person's own expense. It means to act on someone else's behalf for the improvement of the person or the relationship without anything in return. Paul is not saying, "Husbands, eros your wives," to look at them as sexual objects, or "Husbands, phileo your wives," defining them solely as friends. Paul is saying, "Husbands, agape your wives."

This is a specific term that God commands. Today we have a one-size-fits-all mentality of love, but that love is not the type that we find in the New Testament of the Bible; they had specific terms for love. As men, we are to love our wives in such a way that our mission is to meet their needs regardless of what we receive in return. Some of the problems many husbands face are that their wives may not phileo (befriend) them all the time or eros (sexually satisfy) them like they would want them to. This is where maturity and good communication of our needs come into play. A woman must interact with her husband with respect for his position as leader in the marriage and as a person. People who express agape love say, "I'm willing to love you and persevere through periods of mistrust, skepticism, or even hostility," to break through the protective shell that a spouse has built up. Agape love means that we need to take our cues from Christ. A husband must continue to love his wife regardless of whether she appreciates, affirms, or even deserves his sacrificial love. People who express agape love say, " I love you even when I allow you to make me upset, angry, frustrated, depressed, and tired." Ephesians 5:22 says, "Wives, submit to your own husband under the same conditions." This is where maturity comes into play because at times people in relationships desire everything to be about themselves and not what is best for the couple.

Jesus Is Love

What example should we follow as a couple to love and respect each other? The answer is in Jesus Christ.

"But God showed his great love for us by sending His son Christ to die for us while we were still sinners."

Romans 5:8

Are you looking for fulfillment in life? Do you desire to have the power to change? God created you with a God-shaped vacuum in your heart that only Christ can fill. Why don't you ask Him to come into your life today, thank Him for forgiving your sins and ask Him to direct your life from this day forward. If you desire to make Jesus your leader, the following is a suggested prayer:

"Lord Jesus, I want to know you personally. Thank you for dying on the cross for my sins. I believe you were buried and rose again on the third day. I open the door of my life to you and ask you to come in and be my Savior and Lord. Take control of my life. Thank you for forgiving my sins and giving me eternal life. Make me the kind of person you want me to be." Amen. Please read John 3:16.

God hates sin. He saw our negative attitudes and how we treated one another. Despite our rebellion, Jesus demonstrated His love for us. The reason why you and I can love people we don't like is because Christ's love is agape.

"Those who accept my commandments and obey them are the ones who love me. And because they love me, my Father will love them. And I will love them and reveal myself to each of them. Jesus replied, 'All those who love me will do what I say. My Father will love them, and we will come and make our home with each of them. Anyone who doesn't love me will not obey me. And remember, my words are not my own. This message is from the Father who sent me.'" John 14: 21, 23, 24

Husbands are commanded to love their wives. Agape love is demonstrable. If you say you love God but don't keep His commandments, the Bible says you are a liar.

Agape love is not concerned with what you say. Agape love is concerned with who you have become and what you do. What do you do that shows your agape love for others?

Chapter 14

Agape Love

Treat your wife as she is, and she will remain as she is; treat your wife as she can and should be, and she will become as she can and should be. When you as a husband operate by godly principles and treat your wife the right way, often times she becomes the right woman.

For the married man who has become a husband; everything starts with love. We are commanded to do it. With love as the foundation, it allows us to build on the seven principles that will be discussed in this book.

Ephesians 5:25 instructs husbands to love their wives. If you are a man who is contemplating marriage, you must adopt the principle of love and feed on it as part of your mental daily diet. The definition of a principle is "an acquired rule of action or conduct." Repeated actions make habits. As a man, demonstrating unconditional love may not come naturally to you. If this is the case you must create the habit of providing unconditional love. A habit is an acquired behavioral pattern that is regularly followed until it becomes almost involuntary. So how do you acquire this behavioral or action pattern?

"Let this mind be in you, which was also in Christ Jesus." Philippians 2:5

Here is how the process works and what the verse is saying. The quality of your life is determined by how well you choose the thoughts you think and words you speak. Our thoughts become our words. Our words determine our attitude. Our attitude determines our feelings. Our feelings determine our actions. Our actions determine our habits (good or bad). Therefore, our thinking determines our good or bad habits.

1. Faith
2. Belief
3. Thoughts
4. Attitude
5. Actions
6. Habits

Our faith is our core. Our faith powers our belief system and paints a picture of the way things are or the way things should be. The way we see the world, and the way we believe things should or should not be become the source of our attitudes and actions, which ultimately affects our relationships with others.

Be careful what you feed your mind. The mind has a way of feeding the heart. The type of music, videos or movies, settings, places, and people (with their negative or positive energy) that you entertain will affect your thinking. If you have a toxic mental diet, it affects the heart, showing itself in your actions and your habits. If you want to change your toxic habits it is best to start the process with small pieces at a time. It is best to substitute a toxic habit with a good habit. Maybe you want to quit smoking. Instead of making attempts to quit smoking, what about doing something positive that gets you so inspired that you start changing some of your negative habits and behaviors? This strategy has worked for many people.

A Heart That Beats For Love

The heart muscle is responsible for supplying blood to the vital organs. Blood is fluid, consisting of plasma, blood cells, and platelets that are circulated by the heart through the vertebrate vascular system, carrying oxygen and nutrients to, and waste materials away from all body tissues. The heart is an involuntary muscle. This means it beats independent of our will, not by our choice. As we engage in rigorous exercise, it beats even faster to supply oxygen and blood to the body. We have to love and operate like a heart muscle, loving involuntarily. When faced with difficult issues or challenges in a marriage, we have to be willing to love in a greater capacity. It is going to take more love than normal in these difficult situations, to survive the rigorous challenges a marriage will bring. Our love will be the deciding factor in whether the marriage will flourish or die. Once the heart stops beating, it goes into cardiac arrest.

Cardiac arrest is the sudden cessation of heartbeat and cardiac function, resulting in the loss of effective circulation. If the heart is not resuscitated then we cannot survive. If we as men stop loving in our relationships, they will eventually die because of the lack of love circulation. This is why we are commanded to love involuntarily.

Adopting and practicing a principle consist of six things: specific knowledge, skills, tools, strong desire, definite plans and self-discipline. So as men, we must adopt the principle of loving our wives into our minds. Knowledge addresses what to do. Definite plans and skills address how to do it and what tools to use. Self-discipline and a strong desire fuels and motivates you to do something even when you don't feel like doing it. Even if a man knows that to have a successful marriage he needs to love his wife, he may not possess the right information or plan to love her the way she desires to be loved. Knowing that he needs to love and knowing how to love are not enough. Unless he wants to love, unless he has a desire to love, he will not adopt the principle and practice of loving his wife because he doesn't have enough reasons to do so. Reasons make the difference. If you have enough reasons you will do just about anything.

The Formula For A Successful Marriage

I could, I should, I will!

I could love my wife, I should love my wife, and I will love my wife. This husband has made up his mind that he will love his wife no matter what happens. He understands that she it not perfect and will not always interact with him in a respectful way. He understands that he is responsible for what he thinks, says and how he responds to her. He has decided that he will give his wife a gift of love that she may not deserve when she acts disrespectfully towards him.

The Formula For Marriage Disaster

I could, I should, I don't!

I could love my wife, I should love my wife, but I don't love my wife because... Neglect has this person by the throat and the marriage will probably not last because he is lazy in his commitment to loving his wife unconditionally. He knows he should love her, but he just doesn't have enough reasons to do so. Luckily, he is a smart man and realizes that he has flaws too and decides to compile a list of reasons why he will now become an "I could, I should, I will" man and start loving his wife unconditionally.

I could, I should, I won't!

I could love my wife, I should love my wife, but I won't love my wife because.... Neglect also has this person by the throat and the marriage will probably not last because he is stubborn. It is one thing to be lazy but to be stubborn is really bad. Luckily, he is a smart man and realizes that his stubbornness and neglect to love his wife will cost him more than he anticipated. He also compiles a list of reasons why he will now become an "I could, I should, I will" man and begin loving his wife unconditionally.

There are many great books on the market that give their definition of what love is and what it means. In his book, *Love & Respect,* Dr. Emerson Eggerich says that the way you spell love to your wife is with the acronym C.O.U.P.L.E.

Closeness- She wants you to be close.

Openness- She wants you to open up to her.

Understanding- Don't try to "fix" her; just listen.

Peacemaking- She wants you to say, "I'm sorry."

Loyalty- She needs to know you're committed.

Esteem- She wants you to honor and cherish her.

I believe this is a wonderful acronym for spelling love to a woman. I highly recommend that you read the book *Love & Respect.* It is an extraordinary book for understanding how to build a foundation for marriage. I agree with Dr. Eggerich, but I would like to look at the description of love according to the Bible. It is found in I Corinthians 13: 4-7.

"Love is patient and kind. Love does not envy or boast or is prideful or rude. It does not demand its own way [uncompromising and inconsiderate]. *It is not irritable, and it keeps no record of being wronged* [does not hold grudges but forgives]. *It does not rejoice about injustice but rejoices whenever the truth wins out. Love never gives up, never loses faith, is always hopeful, and endures through every circumstance."*

So many single people are looking for the right person but are not willing to become the right person themselves. Part of the process of becoming a husband is understanding and applying love. Now I will go into more detail of what love is according to **I Corinthians 13: 4-7.**

Love Is Patient

The word patient means "the ability to endure or capable of enduring hardships, wrongs difficulties or inconvenience without complaining." Being patient means showing unruffled self-control and restraint under adversity. You are slow to retaliate or express resentment. A patient husband is a man who understands that his wife will not always interact with him in a respectful way, although she may desire to. A husband demonstrates love to his wife when he has a desire to want to love her by being patient with her. There will be times in marriage when hardship, wrongs, difficulties, and being inconvenienced will present themselves. When difficult things happen, choosing to exhibit self-control and restraint from retaliation allows one to diffuse the bullets of adversity. How does one develop patience?

"A fool is quick-tempered, but a wise person stays calm when insulted." Proverbs 12:16

Usually, when someone repeatedly annoys you or does something that you dislike, you tend to lose patience with that person. You feel like you do not want to invest any more energy in the person. They may have said that they were going to do something over and over again, but it never happened. When you are patient with someone, you make allowances for the person's wrongdoing and share the burden with the person. In other words, you extend grace and mercy. Why? God has been patient with you. I remember when I prayed to God to deliver me from the habit of watching pornography and masturbating to it. I prayed over and over to God, yet I found myself still struggling with this demonic stronghold in my life. I felt like I just could not stop watching it. Here God was being patient with me. What is patience again? Patience means "the ability to endure or capable of enduring hardship, wrongs, difficulties, or inconvenience without complaining." Being patient means showing unruffled self-control and restraint under adversity. You are slow to retaliate or express resentment. In my shortcomings and sins against God, I repeatedly shamed Him to His face with my sins. When I repeated the sins that I asked forgiveness for over and over again, God did not throw me away or become frustrated with me. His blood that was shed on the cross was for my wrongs against Him, difficulties toward Him, and me selfishly placing my personal agenda before His agenda for my life. Knowing that patience has been extended to me allows me to be patient with others. Being patient doesn't mean that you become a doormat to be walked on or that you enable other people. It means that you allow room for a person to grow in the necessary areas without condemning and ridiculing them for not growing at your desired pace. It means that you are supportive in your efforts to assist that person as he or she grows. One of the many ways you can assist someone in growth is to listen to the person without interrupting and judging. Listening takes patience because many times you may not want to hear everything that is being said. You may already have your solution, and to save time you would rather just present your solution. But it is about listening to learn instead of listening to reply. From my experience, I realize that many times a woman does not want her man to solve a problem unless she asks for his help. She just wants to talk about what is on her mind so that she can connect with him. Most of the time she just desires for him to listen to her. There is a difference between listening and hearing. Listening says, "I'm paying attention to you and what is being said, and I comprehend what you are saying." Listening means that I am not formulating a response before you communicate your ideas or thoughts. When I'm listening, I can repeat to you what you are saying. Hearing is simply the ability to perceive sound. That suggests that just because you hear someone speaking it does not mean that you are paying attention. You may just be hearing words or sounds but you are not internalizing what is being said to gain understanding. Effective listening takes patience.

What if the person does not see the need to change whatever it is that is challenging your patience? Let them know in a friendly, non-confrontational way what is bothering you. The other person then has to decide whether he or she will adhere to your concerns. Remember, you can't force anyone to do anything. But with prayer and patience, God and the Holy Spirit can. Choosing to be patient is choosing to obey God. God's love is patient.

Love Is Kind

How the Grinch Stole Christmas is a children's book written by Dr. Seuss. The Grinch is a bitter, cave-dwelling, catlike creature with a heart "two sizes too small" who lives on snowy Mount Crumpit, a steep, 3,000-foot-high mountain just north of Whoville, home of the merry and warm-hearted Whos. The Grinch is a "Whoville-hating" grouch and is always out to ruin something. He comes down to Whoville only on holidays to cause mischief for the Whos. His only companion is his faithful dog, Max. Max is loyal to his master despite the Grinch treating him like a nuisance and being abusive towards him.

Are you a Grinch? Do you act like a bitter, cave-dwelling creature with a heart "two sizes too small?" The second way to show love is by being kind. Being kind means having or showing a friendly, considerate, warm-hearted and helping nature. Being kind means showing sympathy or understanding and being gentle. Many men come across as the opposite, which is cruel and mean. God has called husbands to be kind to their wives. When a person is kind, he or she chooses to interact with you in a way that breeds love. A considerate husband is a man who will show regard for his wife's feelings; he is thoughtful. Too many times when unkind men interact with their wives in cruel ways, the wives then tend to react disrespectfully. Many married men have no remorse about how their hurtful words and actions suck the life and love out of the relationship. Many married men see their wives as property and not as a gift from God or the daughters of God. Sometimes married men place unrealistic expectations on their wives and treat them as if they are slaves, and they themselves are the masters.

Sympathy, which is connected to kindness, is a social affinity in which one person stands with another person, closely understanding their feelings. Thus, the essence of sympathy is that one has a strong concern for the other person. Domestic violence, also known as domestic abuse, spousal abuse, child abuse, or intimate partner violence, can be broadly defined as a pattern of abusive behaviors by one or both partners in an intimate relationship such as marriage, dating, family, friends, or cohabitation. Domestic violence has many forms including physical aggression (hitting, kicking, biting, shoving, restraining, throwing objects) or threats thereof, sexual abuse, emotional abuse, controlling or domineering behavior, intimidation, stalking, passive/covert abuse (e.g., neglect), and economic deprivation. If you are displaying acts of domestic violence, you are not being kind and therefore are not being loving.

If your spouse or partner took the following survey, how would they rate you?

1. My partner talks down to me with his words.
2. My partner treats me harshly with his actions.
3. My partner is not supportive and encouraging
4. My partner is not sensitive to my needs and feelings.
5. My partner is not helpful with the daily tasks that we share.
6. My partner is not faithful and is sexually promiscuous.
7. My partner is abusive physically, mentally, or emotionally.

If they said yes to any one of the statements above then you are not practicing kindness.

How do you show kindness towards others? As a man, what if I have a girlfriend, fiancée or wife who is disrespectful? Ephesians 5:33 says to love her. What if she shuts me out and won't talk to me? Ephesians 5:33 says to love her. The way you love her is by not allowing her to dictate what you do. You do not play the tit-for-tat game. You must make a choice to be kind even if she does not show you the respect you deserve.

When you get married it is for better or for worse, sickness and in health. Ladies, he may not earn a 9 figure income, drive a Ferrari, or look like Idris Elba or Brad Pitt. But if he is dependable, loyal, responsible, committed, loving, forgives, doesn't hold grudges, encourages you, cares for you, makes you smile, effectively communicates, praises you, and is committed to taking care of you if your health fails , I suggest that you hold on to him. Choosing to be kind is choosing to obey God. God's love is kind.

Love Does Not Envy

A married man who is envious is not binding his marriage with love. If you were to take a look in the mirror and ask yourself, "Am I an envious person?" What would be your answer? The third way to demonstrate love is to not envy. The hardest thing for a man or woman to do is to be open and honest with themselves about themselves.

Are you the type of person who holds everything in, or are you a person who chooses not to tell the truth for fear of being rejected? What is the difference between jealousy and envy? Jealousy is not the same thing as being envious. Jealousy is reflective of a person's feelings or attitude toward another person, whereas envy expresses a person's feelings or attitudes toward another person's advantages or accomplishments (covetous behavior). Jealousy pertains to emotional rivalry, while envy is resentment of a more fortunate person. Being envious is something that cripples many men from being loving husbands to their wives. Envious people tend to begrudge others or wish they did not have what they have. Envy says, "I want what you have." Jealousy says, "You don't deserve what you have, but I do." Insecurity rests at the heart of being envious and jealous in both men and women. You can demonstrate love in your relationship by not being envious. The way you practice not being envious is by first being content with yourself and confident in yourself as a person. Many people are envious out of fear. It is fear that cripples them into behaving this way, causing them to be apprehensive of losing affection or position. Fear will cause you to be irrational and erratic. It is the fear of being cast aside, replaced, or abandoned that causes many people to envy. If you are an envious person, know that fear and insecurity lie at the heart of the matter, manifesting themselves as envy. God does not operate in fear but in faith.

You and I can be secure in God because of His love for us. God's arm is not short and God's love is not envious. You may be saying to yourself, "Well I thought God was a jealous God." I hear you. God, in fact, is a jealous God, but remember that being jealous and envious are two different things. Everything starts and stops with God. He is the creator of the heavens and earth. No one is bigger than Him. God does not tolerate unfaithfulness or rivalry. There is nothing you can compare with God. There is nothing you can place over Him that has more value than Him. When we attempt to place created things over the creator of all things, we are not showing love to God. God is not to be compared with a created thing, and he becomes jealous when we attempt to do so. God's love for mankind, however, overrides the jealousy He feels when we place created things above Him. Jesus is the reason God's love overrides His jealousy. Jesus paid the sin debt for all mankind when He died on the cross.

"For God so loved the world, that He gave His only son that whoever believes in Him shall not perish but have eternal life."
John 3:16

If you say you love someone, then envy toward them cannot be found in your heart.

Love Does Not Boast

A married man who is boastful is not binding his marriage with love. A boastful person is conceited, cocky, or egotistical. They tend to speak with exaggeration and excessive pride, especially about themselves. The fourth way to demonstrate love is by not being a boastful person. Boasting usually refers to a particular ability or possession that may be one of such kind as to justify a good deal of pride. What you are doing is glorifying yourself or placing yourself on a pedestal, so to speak. As men, we have to be careful not to become conceited or have an excessively favorable opinion of our own ability, importance, or intellect. This will shut down the communication lines because it makes you unapproachable. Who can approach someone so perfect and holy?

"For all have sinned and fall short of the glory of God."
Romans 3:23

The Bible says that all have sinned and come short of the glory of God. This means that we have nothing to boast about because we are all imperfect. It is almost as if you become a god to yourself when you are boastful. We know what happened to Lucifer when he thought he was bigger and better than God. It takes being humble, not boastful in a marriage to relate to your spouse, because you must take into account that person's feelings and desires. You must be willing to be open to your spouse's opinions and needs. The opposite of being boastful is being modest. Modest behavior is having or showing a moderate estimation of one's own talents, abilities, and value. This does not mean that you minimize your talents and abilities; you just do not brag about them. When you boast about yourself, you are trying to gain the approval of someone or attempting to make someone feel less important than you. Being modest when you have the opportunity to boast, demonstrates love. God's love is not boastful.

Love Is Not Full of Pride

"All who fear the Lord will hate evil. That is why I hate pride, arrogance, corruption, and perverted speech." Proverbs 8:13

A prideful person is like a full glass of water. Nothing else can be added to it. The fifth way to demonstrate love is to not be full of pride. Are you a know-it-all? Do you know more about this life than God? Have you reached a point in your life where you have acquired more knowledge and wisdom than God and therefore cannot be instructed, directed, or corrected by Him? A prideful person would answer yes to these questions. Being prideful is having a high opinion of oneself that is not within reasonable limits in the manner in which you conduct yourself. Your attitude and actions have the residue of arrogance. Being arrogant is the offensive display of believing that you are of greater worth than others and that your thoughts, feelings, and actions are all that matter because you are your own god, and no one measures up to you. A prideful person is one who cannot be taught because he or she already has all the answers.

"Pride leads to arguments; those who take advice are wise." Proverbs 13:10

Prideful people reject meaningful information and instructions because in their minds it does not apply to them. Prideful people do not see their shortcomings because they don't think they have any. This type of mind set will lead you down a path of destruction.

"Pride goes before destruction and haughtiness before a fall." Proverbs 16:18

Well, what then would be the opposite of pride that would allow us to love? The answer is humility. When you show humility, you carry yourself in a way that says, "I do not have all the answers, intellect, or always know what decision to make." People with humility say, "I am willing to learn from others." Humility describes a person who is willing to yield his thoughts, feelings, and decisions to God's plan for their life and marriage. Humility says, "God, I know your way is the best way. Teach me your ways, and then demonstrate them to me so that my thoughts and actions match your thoughts and actions."

"Pride ends in humiliation, while humility brings honor."

Proverbs 29:23

Agape love is not prideful. You are demonstrating love when you exercise humility instead of pride in your marriage.

Love Is Not Rude

A rude person is someone who exhibits unkind behaviors or words. It is important to know the general characteristics of rude behavior and rude people. The sixth way to demonstrate love is by not being rude. Rude people often expect you to cater to them and their every need. They make inappropriate comments at inappropriate times, lack basic etiquette, take things you do for them for granted and treat people with no respect. Your mouth can be a helpful tool or a lethal weapon. You are not operating out of love if you do not control the negative things you say. What we say probably affects more people than any other action we take. It is no surprise that the book of Proverbs gives special attention to words and how they are used.

Rudeness in marriage is something that will always create separation between a husband and his wife. There is an old saying: "Sticks and stones will break my bones, but words will never hurt me." Well, I would say it depends on what is being said and who is saying it. Inappropriate comments at inappropriate times do not demonstrate love. Many married men complain or make sarcastic comments about their wives' physical appearances in a joking manner. So as husbands, you must be careful not to make unloving comments or practice inappropriate behaviors towards your wives, tearing them down. Remember, a woman has a strong desire to feel loved. When she is not receiving the love from you, which you are commanded to give, you make it very easy for someone else to offer it to her. As a man, how long can you go without receiving respect from your wife?

Having great etiquette simply means having great manners and being polite. When you are in public, there are certain behaviors that are inappropriate. It is not wise to discuss concerns or issues in public that are meant to be discussed in private. There is a time and place for everything. Having great manners and being polite says that even if I have a concern that I need to discuss with you, I will not be rude in addressing the concern.

Another form of rudeness shows up in the area of taking a person for granted. Rude people tend to not be appreciative of what you have done, are doing, and will do for them. When you operate out of love instead of rudeness, you value your mate and you are grateful for him or her. As a husband, your speech should be controlled and caring.

The Controlled Tongue

A husband with a controlled tongue is a wise man. Men with this speech pattern think before speaking. They know when silence is appropriate and when to give wise advice. Husbands that use this speech pattern operate out of love.

"Gentle words bring life and health; a dishonest tongue crushes the spirit." Proverbs 15:4

"Whoever belittles his neighbor lacks sense, but a man of understanding remains silent." Proverbs 11:12

"A gentle answer deflects anger, but harsh words make tempers flare." Proverbs 15:1

Men, when—not if—you have a disagreement with your wife, be aware that gentle words bring life and health. There is a saying: "fight fair." Disagreements are a part of any relationship. If you make a decision to not use harsh words when you have a disagreement, you demonstrate love.

The Caring Tongue

A husband with a caring tongue is also a wise man. Men with this speech pattern speak truthfully while seeking to encourage. What you have is a man who understands how powerful his words are and uses them to build up, not tear down, his wife. When he speaks to her, his words nourish her soul. Husbands who use this speech pattern operate out of love.

"The Godly speak words that are helpful, but the wicked speak only what is corrupt." Proverbs 10:32

"Worry weighs a person down; an encouraging word cheers a person up." Proverbs 12:25

Stress causes people to worry and become fearful of the unknown. When a person is feeling this way, it is good to know that an encouraging word has the power to cheer that person up. We as men have to be willing to use encouraging words in our conversations.

Love Does Not Demand Its Own Way

The definition of selfishness is a person devoted to or caring only for oneself. Selfish people are concerned primarily with their own interest, benefits, and welfare, regardless of others. The seventh way to demonstrate love is to not be selfish. Are you ready and willing to serve your spouse? Are you ready and willing to not demand your own way? Love says, "How may I serve you?" People with lust say, "How will you serve me?" In today's culture, we have gotten love and lust mixed up. We say we love, yet we are not willing to serve. If we do serve, we serve with the wrong attitude. Within our relationships, we should be willing to serve and meet the needs of our spouses. A selfish person is not concerned about meeting the needs or finding out the needs of the other person because to him or her, the other person's needs are not important. Selfish people do not take into consideration how their actions and words will affect another person. Someone who has an affair is a selfish person because he or she is concerned with meeting his or her own needs in an unauthorized way. What I mean is that there are boundaries in a marriage relationship. For example, in basketball and football they have out-of-bounds lines. If you step on the line, you are out of bounds. The game is meant to be played within the boundaries to prevent chaos. Just imagine if an NBA player on offense could elude a defender by dribbling the basketball out of bounds into the stands, enter the court from the opposite end, and score the shot. That would be a chaotic scheme. As a married man, I made a decision to have affairs with several women. My reasoning was that I felt my ex-wife was not meeting my needs the way I wanted her to.

Another reason is that I compared my wife to the images and the things that I saw in pornographic videos and wanted her to be and do the things I saw on those videos. That is a warped definition of what love is! Instead of being patient with her and developing legitimate and authentic intimacy, I chose to be unfaithful multiple times with multiple women. I was driven by lust and I wanted it my way. I was very selfish in my actions. I could have given a sexually transmitted disease to my wife; I could have fathered a child with another woman while I was still married to her. I was not thinking about all the possible consequences and how I was crushing her heart because I was being selfish, demanding my own way. Being selfish does not demonstrate love.

The second part of selfishness is being inconsiderate. An inconsiderate person is insensitive to others. Many professional athletes develop corns and calluses on their feet and toes. This is a hardened or thickened part of the skin usually caused by excessive rubbing. The skin in this area begins to lose sensation or feeling. Have you allowed life and circumstances to form a callus over your heart so that you have become insensitive to others?

If you look at the word sin, you will discover that the middle letter in sin is "I." Eavesdrop on your conversations. Do you start your sentences by saying things like " I'm not happy, I want this, and I want it to go my way?" In a marriage, it is not what is best for you; it is about what is best for the marriage. It could be that you are selfish with your money. Maybe you are selfish with your time. You may be a selfish person with your communication because you do not share your thoughts, feelings and the decisions you make for the family. You have to make a conscious decision not to be self-seeking but to be selfless because as a couple you are a team. As husband and wife, you have to do what is best for the marriage and that takes being mature. In every marriage, there must be a funeral to your selfish ways for the betterment of the marriage. If you are not willing to do this, you are not ready to be married. If you are a married man and you are inconsiderately demanding your own way you are not operating as a husband, or house-binder. A true husband is not selfish because God's love is not selfish.

Love Is Not Easily Irritated

I was watching a movie called *Are We There Yet?* The main protagonist, Nick Persons, played by Ice Cube, is a bachelor who specializes in sports collectibles. He finds himself attracted to the bright, stunning Suzanne Kingston, played by Nia Long, until he realizes that she has two children.

When Suzanne is stuck in Vancouver on a business trip, she is unhappy because she misses her children. Furthermore, Frank, their father, who was supposed to be looking after the children for the weekend cancels at the last minute, saying that he was sick. Later in the movie, it turns out that Frank has lied to them and they discover that their father has another wife and newborn baby.

Seizing the opportunity to win Suzanne over, Nick offers to transport the children from Portland to Vancouver, despite the fact that he finds the kids very annoying and described them as "snot-nosed runts and cockroaches that you can't squish." The children do their best to make their trip with Nick as nightmarish as possible.

In the movie, the kids are attempting to annoy Nick to the point that he gives up trying to pursue a relationship with their mother. But he is determined to persevere through their antics.

That's the way love operates, it's not easily irritated. Being irritable means you are easily annoyed or bothered. It can often push you to a point of becoming angry or distant.

"Fools show their annoyance at once, but the prudent overlook an insult." Proverbs 12:16

When you allow others to annoy you or you become bothered by their antics, in a sense, you short-circuit your love.

We have been discussing the characteristics of love and how as a tool it binds a marital relationship in perfect harmony. But when you become irritated, you are not operating in love. This is because in your annoyed or bothered state, your frustration normally comes in the form of anger or resentment. Provoking behavior can incite someone to anger or resentment. When this happens, it makes it really difficult to love and want to love. The first two characteristics of love mentioned in 1 Corinthians 13 are patience and kindness. When you feel annoyed or bothered because of what someone is doing or not doing, you must exercise patience and kindness. To harass or disturb someone by repeated attacks is not right, but unfortunately, it happens in many relationships.

Addressing the offense by using patience and kindness without becoming annoyed is how you demonstrate love in a situation where someone is annoying you. A loving husband is a person who is operating out of patience and kindness even when they are being irritated or annoyed.

Love Does Not Hold Grudges

What is a grudge? A grudge is defined as "resentment strong enough to justify retaliation." Everyone has, at some time or another, allowed himself or herself to be deeply hurt by someone close. Bitterness toward a person or situation leads to holding a grudge. The ninth way to demonstrate love is by not holding grudges. Personal injustice ignites resentment in the heart, which turns into a grudge. Since a grudge is a form of resentment, a person who bears grudges may become revengeful. Instead of focusing on what they need to do to solve a problem, for instance, they may spend most of their time thinking of ways to get back at whomever they resent. This can be dangerous, because there is a possibility of physical harm. When we allow someone to hurt us, a natural human reaction is to hurt him or her back. Our very nature spurs us to settle the score, to get even. Usually, we forgive the offender over time as the intensity of the infraction weakens. If we do not forgive the offender, the only alternatives are to try to get revenge or decide to hold a grudge. The person who hurt us might not even know how angry and bitter we are. Our emotions of hate and anger continue to aggravate at their supposed indifference. Isn't it ridiculous that in our efforts to supposedly get even with others that the only ones we hurt are ourselves? With this unhealthy behavior, we place our physical, spiritual and emotional health at risk. A grudge pours its corrosive bitterness into us, arrogating our entire being. Soon the door will be open for envy, malice, jealousy, animosity, gossip, and slander to come and visit and ultimately take up residence in our soul. Anger weakens the liver, grief weakens your lungs, worry weakens your stomach, stress weakens your heart and brain and fear weakens your kidneys. The price of holding a grudge is too much. Holding a grudge will only devour you from the inside out, eventually turning you into an acrimonious person. All this happens when a person refuses to forgive the person who they allowed to hurt them. The price to pay is too high. Holding a grudge keeps life running on rewind, preventing us from moving on with life and looking forward to the future. We recall how awful it was and keep dwelling on the experience. A grudge handcuffs us to the negative past, causing us to irrationally focus on the past and blame our present setbacks on past misfortunes.

There is a song by Israel Houghton called *Moving Forward*. Read the lyrics:

What a moment

You have brought me to

Such a freedom I have found in You

You're the Healer

Who makes all things new

Yeah yeah yeah

I'm not going back

I'm moving ahead

Here to declare to You

My past is over in You

All things are made new

Surrendered my life to Christ

I' m moving moving forward

Chorus

You make all things new

Yes

You make all things new

And I will follow you forward

You cannot change the past so stop dwelling on it. Stop abusing yourself with negative thoughts of yesterday's past. Forgive yourself! Forgive others! Smile because God is still good and keep moving forward.

This is a powerful song about putting the past behind you and moving forward with life. How do I get past holding a grudge?

Releasing a grudge can bring happiness and peace. Carrying a grudge pokes holes in your energy bucket. You will constantly feel weary or lethargic. It takes a great amount of unconscious energy to maintain a grudge. Releasing a grudge through forgiveness will result in a brand new surge of emotional and physical energy.

It is conceivable that you can remember everything that has ever occurred in your life, especially painful experiences, or more so, the feelings resulting from these experiences. Therefore, we cannot forget an offense; however, we can choose not to think on past injustices, once they have been forgiven.

True, authentic loves does not hold grudges. God's love does not hold grudges.

Love Forgives

Fear is three times stronger than greed, according to research cited by Professor Daniel Kahneman, a Nobel Prize-winning behavioral economist. Most of our irrational and erratic decisions are fear based and anger is a secondary response to fear. Who are you angry with? Who do you need to **forgive** so that you can stop being afraid of the future?

When you have been hurt or wronged, it is human nature to want to hold a grudge. The tenth way to demonstrate love is by forgiving but not enabling. Many people hold the idea that forgiveness is for the other person. Actually, forgiveness is for you. Here is what I mean. Forgiveness searches out the emotional cancer in the form of bitterness, hate, resentment, grudges, fear, and anger in your soul and eradicates them. Forgiveness allows you to live peacefully and orderly with yourself. You may feel like someone does not deserve your forgiveness. This person may have hurt you in a way that has shaken and turned your world upside down.

Why Should I Forgive?

In Romans 12: 19-21, Paul's command to not repay evil for evil sounds impossible when we listen to it with our carnal mind. Forgive those who I have allowed to hurt me? You may be telling yourself that this is too hard to do. You could be thinking: "This person who has hurt me does not deserve my forgiveness. Also, to add insult to injury, the person is not even apologetic for his or her actions, and I am the one who has to forgive!" The key to forgiving others is remembering how much God has forgiven you as a believer. Very often we forget how many times God has forgiven us, as a result, we then become hesitant to forgive others. Realizing and experiencing God's infinite love and forgiveness can help you and I forgive others.

How Often Should I Forgive Someone?

Then Peter came to Jesus and asked, "Lord, how many times shall I forgive my brother when he sins against me? Up to seven times?" Jesus answered, "I tell you, not seven times, but seventy-seven times." Matthew 18:21, 22

Wow! We are instructed to forgive a person seventy-seven times for a single offense. Peter had a definite rationale for saying "seven times." The Jews had ruled that one could only be forgiven three times, but never a fourth. Realizing Jesus would show more mercy than the Jews, he must have thought seven times was more than fair.

Christ's response shows how important forgiveness is. *"I tell you, not seven times, but seventy-seven times."* He means we are not to limit our forgiveness to a specific number of times. As often as someone offends us and asks to be forgiven, we should forgive them and treat them properly, setting the right example.

"Make allowance for each other's faults and forgive anyone who offends you. Remember, the Lord forgave you, so you must forgive others." Colossians 3:13

In marriage, when you forgive your wife for being disrespectful and/or unloving, you give up the right to hold a grudge and to be disrespectful and unloving in return. By forgiving, you can gain strength and freedom.

Forgiveness means canceling the debt. If a person owed you $100.00 dollars and never paid it to you, and you decided to forgive them, you would cancel the debt owed. This means that you would still treat them kindly and loving within your interactions. You would not bring up that they once owed you money because forgiveness was extended to them. You remember the debt, but you do not hold the debt against that person. You simply say, "If I had the opportunity to do to you what you did to me, I would not do it nor would I attempt to get even with you by retaliation."

When you respond in this manner you allow that person to see that their debt was forgiven, but more importantly, you choose not to put it in their face that they once owed you. When a person with good will has experienced forgiveness, something strange normally happens. The person knows the one they have wronged remembers the debt, but when you do not hold it against them (not to be confused with accountability), it allows that person to see Christ in you. When that person sees Christ in you, Christ can begin to work on their soul and convict their spirit.

Too many times we attempt to do God's job of convicting and

changing people. God created men and women in His image. It is going to take the power of God to change people to line up their beliefs, feelings, and actions with His. You and I have no such power to change the soul and spirit of a man or woman.

When we are hurt deeply, instead of giving people what they deserve, Paul says that we should befriend them. We must forgive those who have betrayed, abandoned, hurt, and treated us unkindly for the following reasons:

1. Forgiveness may break the cycle of retaliation and lead to mutual reconciliation.
2. It may make the other person who has hurt you feel ashamed and change his or her ways toward you and others they have hurt.
3. Repaying evil for evil hurts you just as much as it hurts your enemy. By forgiving the people who have hurt you, you free yourself from bitterness that can act like a cancer to your inner being and ultimately cause you to hurt and treat others harshly.

Lastly, Paul is stating that when we choose to forgive someone it is done with our attitude and actions. This can be done with acts of kindness toward that person. It could be sending an e-card through e-mail saying, "I forgive you." The point is that we are willing to act to demonstrate our forgiveness.

Listen, you are too worthy to be upset by someone else and their silly, controlling, abusive, negative behavior. Forgive, live and move on. But you say, "That is easy for you to say Bobby. That person hurt my feelings and I can not help the way I feel." Well I would say that you can help the way you feel, but you have chosen to be upset because of your thoughts towards that person. Have you ever wondered how Jesus was able to remain in control of his feelings despite his haters and enemies? Your feelings got hurt because of what you told yourself about the way they reacted or didn't react to you. We can choose happiness or at least not choose unhappiness at any given moment. Learning not to be unhappy is a tough assignment. We have grown up in a culture, which has taught us that we are not responsible for our feelings. The truth is we are responsible for our thoughts and feelings.

As believers in Christ, will we forgive the people who we have allowed to hurt us, knowing that Christ has forgiven us and given us eternal life even though we have repeatedly hurt Him? God's love forgives.

The Prayer Of Forgiveness

Forgiveness of others is essential to mental peace and radiant health.

Quiet your mind, relax and let go. Think of God's love for you and then affirm, " I fully and freely forgive (mention the name of the offender); I release them mentally and spiritually. I completely forgive everything connected with the matter in question. I am free, and he/she is free. I release anybody and everybody who have hurt me or who I have allowed to hurt me and I wish for each and everyone health, happiness, peace, and all the blessings of life. I do this freely, joyously, and lovingly, and whatever I think of the person or persons who hurt me, I say, 'I have released you, and all the blessings of life are yours.' I am free and you are free. It is wonderful. Amen." Once you have forgiven someone it is unnecessary to repeat the prayer. Whenever the person comes to your mind or when the particular hurt comes to your mind, wish that person well and say, "Peace be to you." Do this whenever the thought comes to your mind.

Love Does Not Rejoice In Injustice

A husband who operates out of love does not enjoy or celebrate when injustice takes place. A husband does not participate in injustice. The eleventh way to demonstrate love is to not celebrate when injustice takes place. The definition of injustice is the violation of the rights of others or unfair action or treatment towards others. Being unjust is not considering or doing what is right in a situation. Often in marriage men tend to act unjustly. Some men violate or knowingly allow someone to violate, treat unfairly, or abuse their spouse. It could be how your family treats your spouse when you attend family functions together. Maybe, you are a man who brags to your friends about how you mistreat your wife. It could be that you have double standards and operate out of selfishness. Either way, love does not rejoice about injustice. A loving husband will defend his marriage and wife and not allow injustice in their marriage. God's love is just. True love rejoices when the truth wins out. True love is fair. Fairness is free from bias, dishonesty, or injustice. When a husband is acting in an unbiased manner he implies a kind of fairness that comes about especially because he does not desire a selfish advantage. He has decided that he will be fair even if being fair will hurt him. He has decided to sacrifice his agenda for the betterment of the relationship. True love rejoices about equality or when the truth wins out.

Love Never Gives Up

Love is persistent. Many marriages fail because of the lack of persistence. If a loved one was drowning and you dove in to save them from drowning but realized once that person was out of the water that he or she needed CPR, would you perform CPR? How long would you perform CPR on that person?

The final way to demonstrate love is by persevering and not giving up. Love never gives up, never loses faith, is always hopeful, and endures through every circumstance. It never throws in the towel. There are a lot of married men who quit too soon on their relationship. They are not persistent. A man who is a house-binder must understand that it takes time to become united to his wife. The reality is that many men have wives who appear to be disrespectful at times. Yes, your wife may be wrong in how she interacts and relates to you. As a house-binder using love to keep the family together, you must decide to separate what she is doing to you from the feelings of giving up. How? This is done by interacting with her using love. So you loving her has nothing to do with her respecting you. You do not take on the attitude of "if she does not respect me, I will not operate out of love." That is immature behavior. When I was married to my first wife, my love was based on whether I felt respected. When I felt that she was acting in ways that came across as disrespectful to me, I reacted in ways that came across as unloving to her. I allowed her to dictate my behavior. This is because I did not know what a husband was. I did not know I was supposed to respond, not react. I did not know I was supposed to be proactive, not reactive. I write this book as a divorced man. As I write, God continues to mature me and mold me into a future husband—a future house-binder. If I have the opportunity to once again become a house-binder, I have grown and matured and God will continue this process in my life until I die. Men, please learn from my mistakes and ignorance and make the necessary adjustments to become a real authentic husband not just carry the title. Men who desire to become house-binders, please understand that love is the tool that we as men must use to band together the marriage and keep it united until death do us part. Whatever the issues you face, know that love does not give up and the problems can be worked through by using patience, kindness, confidence, faithfulness, humbleness, consideration, caring/giving, niceness and forgiveness.

Unconditional Love

A wife is to receive unconditional love from her husband. When a wife feels unloved, it is especially hard for her to respect her husband. Without love she reacts without respect. God has very high standards when it comes to the treatment of His daughters. There are dire consequences for men who choose not to love their wives as Christ loved the church.

"But if any provide not for his [speaking to married men] **own, and** *especially for those of his own house, he hath denied the faith, and is worse than an infidel." I Timothy 5:8*

Paul is stating that a man who does not take care of his wife and family is worse than an unbeliever. Now Peter chimes in on the topic of challenging married men to demonstrate love to their wives.

"In the same way, you husbands must give honor to your wives. Treat her with understanding as you live together. She may be weaker than you are, but she is your equal partner in God's gift of new life. If you do not treat her as you should, your prayers

will not be heard." 1 Peter 3:7

This is profound. Peter is saying if a man is not patient, kind, faithful, humble, considerate, caring/giving, nice, forgiving and respectful to his wife, his prayers will not be heard by God. A living relationship with God should be reflected in the marriage relationship.

Chapter 15

Self-Control

To have an effective marriage, you must first develop yourself into an effective man or woman so that you can operate as an effective husband or wife. It is the understanding that private victories precede public victories. You have to be willing to work on yourself.

"You have control over three things: what you think, what you say, and how you behave. To make a change in your life, you must first recognize these gifts are the most powerful tools you possess in shaping the destiny of your life." – Sonya Friedman

Noble men tend to make great husbands. They are proactive men. Proactive husbands do more than take the initiative, they operate out of positive value-based influences. They recognize that they are responsible for their own choices and have the freedom to choose based on principles and values rather than on mood, feelings or conditions. Proactive husbands are agents of change in their marriage.

Ineffective men make ineffective husbands. They are reactive men. Reactive men don't take responsibility for their own lives and the lives of others. Ineffective married men operate out of an anxious or burdened state of mind. They feel victimized—a product of circumstance, their past and other people. They do not see themselves as the creative force of their lives.

When something causing or regarded as causing a response in you shows up, you have the freedom to choose how you will respond. Self-control and self-discipline play a major role in how you respond or react to people and circumstances. At the end of the day whatever comes your way in the form of circumstances or situations, you have the freedom to choose how you will respond to it. Our behavior is a function of our decisions, not our conditions. We can choose to place our values over our feelings when responses, choices, and difficult decisions have to be made.

There are four human capacities that give you the freedom to choose. They are self-awareness, imagination, conscience and independent will.

A noble, loving husband activates all four human capacities and goes through each progression before he responds to a situation or circumstance. Because I have self-awareness, imagination, and a conscience, I can evaluate my core values. I can self-assess and realize that either I am or am not living congruently with my core values. A noble husband is a man who is responsible. When you look at the word responsibility—"response-ability"—it means you have the ability to choose how you will respond to people or situations. Reactive people build their lives around the behaviors of others and their environments. Their choice or ability to choose is controlled by what happens to them. If someone yells at them, they yell back. If someone curses at them, they curse back. Their choices and the way they react to people are based on feelings or the situation. They do not base their decisions on positive values or principles. I'm not saying that the actions and words of others will not affect you mentally, emotionally, or spiritually, especially if they are disrespectful and rude. But how you respond to what another person does or doesn't do is your choice. It takes self-control and self-discipline to respond and act in a loving manner to your wife who is coming across as disrespectful and unappreciative. When you respond out of love, which as a husband is part of your core value system, you have adopted the principle of love. As a husband you do it involuntarily instead of out of the negative feelings from the condition or situation you are facing. You do not empower the weakness of your wife's disrespect and rudeness to control you and your responses. Your ability to choose your response is not based on people, circumstances, or conditions but based on your decision to operate out of your core value system: **Love.**

Noble husbands are aware of where they focus their time and energy. They focus on the things that they can do something about. Reactive married men focus their energy on the weaknesses of others, the challenges they face in society and on the situations and circumstances which they have no control over. These men become occupied with blaming and accusing others, using negative language, and claim to be the victim instead of being the victor. When a husband loves his wife unconditionally, he helps her feel secure, safe, validated, affirmed and appreciated in her essential worth, and identity. When a married man does not love, or places conditions on his love for his wife, he encourages her to react from a defensive position where she feels that she has to prove that she matters as a person. In this emotional state many women become vindictive and disrespectful. When a woman rebels against her husband, it is a knot of the heart, not of the mind. Love massages the knots out of the heart.

"When your honor becomes greater than your mood or feelings, you develop self-control and integrity, which gives you the power to make and keep commitments to yourself and others. Marriage is a great commitment. Be proactive."

–Bobby L. Sneed Jr.

Chapter 16

Having a Vision

Having a vision means to start with a clear understanding of your destination. It means to know where you're going so that you better understand where you are now. This ensures that the steps you take are always in the right direction.

"Where there is no vision, the people perish."

Proverbs 29:18

What makes a single man a great leader, which will ultimately allow him to lead effectively in a marriage?

Leadership is a process by which a person influences others to accomplish an objective. Leaders carry out this process by applying their leadership attributes such as beliefs, values, ethics, character, knowledge, and skills. Great leaders respond and make decisions based on values and principles. There are four life support systems that allow us to govern our responses. These four life support systems give us the ability to follow the values and principles that we hold as "truth." When all four of these support systems are developed you are operating proactively and out of a principle-centered-life. The four factors are security, guidance, wisdom, and power. They range from low to high. Low means you are operating as a dependent person, and high means you are operating as an independent person.

1. Security represents your sense of worth, your self-esteem, your identity, and your emotional capacity. It is your personal strength in having well-founded confidence in yourself. Your security can range from

being firmly secure to extremely insecure.
2. Guidance represents your desire to choose or be led in a certain direction. It allows you to avoid the dangers and take advantage of the opportunities. It is your internal decision-making compass used in accordance with your internal maps of how you interpret the world around you. Your guidance can range from being lead by situations, circumstances, or people to having a stronger inner direction being led by God.
3. Wisdom represents the knowledge you have attained and how that knowledge is appropriately applied to each individual person, situation, or circumstance. It is the ability to make a decision based on the combination of knowledge, experience, and intuitive understanding. Your wisdom can range from a total misapplication of the knowledge that you have attained to accurately applying it to fit each situation or circumstance.
4. Power represents your ability to do or act. It is your mental, emotional, and spiritual capability of doing or accomplishing something. Power is the means by which you make choices and decisions. It gives you the ability to break destructive habits and replace them with positive life-sustaining ones. Your power can range from having no power, allowing others to make your choices for you, becoming their puppet, reacting to circumstances and situations to operating highly proactively and operating out of your values and principles.

These four life support systems when developed, will allow you to lead and manage an interdependent marriage relationship.

Having a successful relationship or marriage is not an accident. Sadly, relational or marital failure is not an accident either. There are in my opinion three requirements for a successful relationship and marriage.

- Decide what kind of relationship/marriage you want.
- Determine the price you are going to pay to have that type of relationship or marriage.
- Resolve to pay that price.

Do you have a mission statement or a vision for your relationship or marriage? Most marriages fail because they are not clearly defined with a vision or a mission statement. It is a good idea to have both.

Before a man can operate as a noble husband he must develop effective personal leadership skills. A man who desires to get married should have a personal mission statement for his life that aligns with God's purpose for his life. Effectiveness to lead the marriage and your family is directly tied to your personal mission statement. How can you lead your wife and family if you are unable to lead yourself? You must first know where you are going and what you want to accomplish before you can know where the marriage is going and as a couple what the two of you will accomplish. Too often men and women merge together as one only to realize that they have different agendas. Marriage is about operating as one unit. Many times both parties are operating in different directions, so functioning as an interdependent couple is challenging. It is important to know what you are called to accomplish and what your spouse is called to accomplish in life so that you can compare mission statements. You must know your purpose prior to marriage. You may discover that your paths are not in the same direction. Or could it be that as the man, you have no set goals or definite purpose to accomplish, so what do you really need help with? Why do you desire a wife? Before you can function as a husband you must first be able to function as an effective, proactive successful single man.

If you are having difficulty defining your purpose and identifying what it is you are to accomplish for the greater good of mankind, I suggest praying and asking God for guidance. I also suggest reading the books *The Purpose Driven Life* by Rick Warren and *Think and Grow Rich* by Napoleon Hill. They are powerful books that may help you identify your purpose.

Here are a few questions to help you get started. Take some time to pause from reading and write out your mission statement, roles, and goals, for yourself. Make a list of priorities in your life.

1. If you could do anything without being paid one cent, what would it be. What are you passionate about?
2. Identify an influential person who knowingly or unknowingly had a positive influence on your life. What qualities do you admire in them? What qualities did you gain from this person?
3. Who do you want to become? What do you have a strong desire to do? What do you want to have? How can you help others?

What is important to you? What do you live for other than yourself? List ten things that are most rewarding to you.

Chapter 17

Personal Management

Personal management is not so much how you manage your time, but how you manage yourself with respect to time. Leadership identifies what I or we will accomplish. Personal management is identifying and applying what is the best way to efficiently and effectively accomplish it. As a husband, before you can manage the marriage relationship you must first be a great manager of yourself.

"Then the Lord answered me and said, 'Write the vision and make it plain on tables that the one who reads it may run with it.'" Habakkuk 2:2

As a man or woman desiring to get married, knowing how to manage a relationship is vital to the success of it. Knowing what direction the relationship is heading in is the first step. Devising a plan to get there is the second step. When you identify your destination or what you want to accomplish for your marriage, it is important to understand that to get there, you must be willing to say no to some people and things in order to say yes to each other and what you wish to accomplish together as a couple. Life has many distractions, and it is easy to get off track and begin to focus on the things that are not priorities.

Practice makes progress, so as a single person you must practice managing yourself so you are prepared to manage a marital relationship. It is very important to list your priorities and manage yourself around those priorities. One thing that every man, woman and child has in common is that we all get 24 hours in a day. It is not so much what we do with our time; it is what we do with ourselves with respect to time. It is called putting first things first. In marriage you have different priorities, and your ability to identify them and prioritize them based on their importance will be the deciding factor whether the relationship is harmonious or chaotic. Often times we put first things second, fifth, twentieth, and so forth, but not first. Using and applying this principle of putting first things first as a single person will allow you to implement it in your marriage relationship.

Many things in our life can be classified as urgent or important. Urgent matters require our immediate attention or action. Important matters strongly affect the course of events or the nature of things; they are significant. Urgent matters, while they require our attention, may not be important. In your marriage and everyday lifestyle, you must determine how you manage yourself and others with regard to urgent and important matters. The way we manage others and ourselves in our everyday lives fits into one of four categories.

1. Urgent/Important matters consist of dealing with crisis after crisis. You deal with pressing problem after problem. You are reactive to what is happening to you with other people, circumstances, or situations. When you operate like this you do not take time to think about and plan how to minimize the repeated crises or problems.
2. Not Urgent/Important matters consist of prevention, maintenance, and planning to reduce and prevent a crisis or problem. The questions you should ask yourself today are: "What action steps can I take before things go sour in my relationship?" "What will I need to do to prevent an affair or divorce from happening to me?" "How do I need to start managing myself now, so that I'm prepared to face the

challenges of a marriage?" A proactive person asks themselves these questions and then searches for the answers before chaos breaks out, so that if it does, a plan is in place. A proactive person is a crisis/problem prevention specialist.
3. Urgent/Not Important matters are the things that you may feel are urgent and important, but they are not important. The reality of the matter is that many times other people's priorities are believed to be urgent and important when they are not important. Because they are urgent and important to them, we accept it as well. An example is someone calling you with the latest gossip. These activities consume our precious time, causing us not to focus on our priorities. The result is that we are delayed in accomplishing our goals.
4. Not Urgent/Not Important matters are called "time wasters." These are the activities that have nothing to do with accomplishing what you have set out to accomplish. Many times when you operate in this category, you move in the opposite direction of achieving your goals.

As you prepare yourself for marriage, understanding how you manage yourself and where you spend the majority of your energy and time will allow you to know where you need to make adjustments to become the effective spouse you desire to be. Now that you understand that you must become an effective manager of yourself prior to marriage, I would like to share with you the reader, an effective strategy on how to accomplish this. Becoming a self-manager requires that you use specific tools to manage yourself. These management tools consist of identifying roles, selecting goals, scheduling and daily adopting. These same tools can be applied to managing a marital relationship.

1. Identify roles. What is your role? First, write down the key roles in your life. For example, you may want to list taking on the role of a husband, teacher, or consultant.

2. Selecting goals. The next step is to brainstorm and come up with ideas about what you want to accomplish associated with each particular role.

3. Scheduling. Now look at your schedule for the upcoming week, and with your goals in mind, begin to schedule in times to achieve them throughout the week.

4. Daily Adopting. After you have assigned your goals to the days you want to accomplish them, you are now ready to execute the plan. Each morning wake up and review what you have set to accomplish for that day as a priority, understanding that unanticipated things or situations may occur and you must be flexible.

When priorities are identified, it makes it easier to manage your life around them. As you and I proactively place our plans on paper for the week, we in turn become more aware of how we are managing ourselves.

Chapter 18

Marital Interdependence

In most cell phone devices there is an indicator that lets you know when your battery is low and needs recharging. As men, we have a respect battery that energizes and provides power to our personality. A woman has a love battery that energizes and provides power to her personality. Has the respect or love low battery indicator light come on in your relationship? When a man loves a woman, he acts like a battery charger that charges up her love battery, so she feels energized and motivated to respect him. When a woman respects a man, she acts like a battery charger, which charges his respect battery so he feels energized and motivated to love her.

Without love, she has a tendency to react negatively, and without respect he has a tendency to react negatively as well. Wives are made to love, want to love and expected to love. Husbands are made to respect, want respect and expect respect. Without love from him, she reacts without respect. Without respect from her, he reacts without love. This is a cycle that many marriages go around and around on. Dr. Eggerichs, in his book *Love & Respect,* calls this cycle the "Crazy Cycle."

"So again I say, each man must love his wife as he loves himself, and the wife must respect her husband."

Ephesians 5:33

Love and respect are the key solutions to any problem in a marriage. How the need for love and respect play off each other in a marriage has everything to do with the kind of marriage you will have. In other words, a husband is to obey the command to love his wife even if she does not obey the command to respect him. A wife is to obey the command to respect her husband even if he does not obey the command to love her. To take it a step further, a husband is called to love a disrespectful wife; a wife is called to respect an unloving husband. We keep each other's batteries charged by showing unconditional love and respect.

Before You Say I Do

"Don't break your promise to the wife you married when you were young. I hate divorce says the Lord God of Israel." Malachi 2:15

There is a difference between a great marriage and a working marriage arrangement. A great spouse who is dependable, loyal, has ability, has a positive mental attitude, is willing to go the extra mile and applies their faith is a virtuous person. All six must be present in the choosing of a spouse for a harmonious great marriage to exist.

Great marriages are the by-products of great people as they cooperate with each other, being faithful in their agreements. Your marriage is an agreement about who you will be to your spouse and who they will be to you. When two people decide that they want to be married they are agreeing to certain terms and conditions within the marriage. The problem that many people face is that they have not become the person capable of fulfilling that agreement or they choose not to for selfish reasons. What many marriages face are broken agreements. A broken agreement exists whenever you fail to tell the other party that you've changed your mind about who you are or who you have become. If your spouse is still under the impression that the original agreement is still in place because of your lack of being honest with them, you are being unfaithful. Unfaithfulness is being false to duty, obligations, or promises, by which we break our agreements. We can solve broken marital agreements by confessing that we are no longer who we had originally agreed to be in the relationship. When you change your mind about who you will be and what you will do in a marital relationship, and those changes have an adverse affect on the other person, that is unhealthy. When agreements are broken, you must communicate it to your spouse so that a new agreement can be discussed and formed.

"You have broken your promise to her. You did it even though she's your partner. You promised to stay married to her and the Lord was a witness to it." Malachi 2:14

One night as I was cleaning out the guest room of my house, I found a VHS copy of my first marriage, and I began watching it. During the ceremony, it came to the point where my ex-wife and I exchanged our marital agreements. Here is a synopsis of what was said.

"I, Bobby Sneed, take you, (name), to be my lawfully wedded wife, my constant friend, my faithful partner, and my love from this day forward. In the presence of God, our family, and friends, I offer you my solemn vow to be your faithful partner in sickness and in health, in good times and in bad, and in joy as well in sorrow. I promise to love you unconditionally, to support you in your goals, to honor you and respect you, to laugh with you and cry with you, and to cherish you for as long as we both shall live."

These are the vows that I made when I got married. I stood before my pastor, my wife to be, and God and made those vows. The drawback was that even though I agreed to those vows, I did not own enough of myself to follow through with them and be faithful to the marital agreements. You have to ask yourself the question: "Am I capable and willing to follow through with these agreements? Have I been developed in my private life and have I addressed and overcome those unhealthy addictions, habits and behaviors that will allow me to be faithful in marriage?" There will be times in a marriage when agreements have to be revised because we do change. Changing for the betterment of the relationship is a positive thing and it will benefit the relationship. Revising agreements is not the problem. It is when the other person is not informed that an agreement has been broken because of deviant behavior and it needs revision, which creates dishonesty. People do not typically fall out of love; they choose to stop loving. When the marital relationship stops working it is because someone or both people have broken their agreement. This is why it is so hard to regain trust when an agreement has been broken without notice; it has been broken from the person who broke it. A marriage agreement that has been broken will only be rectified once it is cleaned up with the truth.

So many people claim that they are this particular person who will do this or that particular thing when they get married, but often these are just empty words. Many people are in love with the idea of marriage, not the sacrifice that comes with it to make it work. Are you mature enough or do you own enough of yourself to make such an agreement? Many married couples do not want to be held accountable to their agreed duties, obligations, and promises. So, as a single man or woman, before you say "I do," please understand that by doing so you are agreeing that you have become someone in your private life who is willing and able to do what is necessary and honorable with your future spouse, to have and experience a successful marriage. Please don't say "I do" to something you won't do. If you have broken an agreement, the way to amend it is to accept responsibility, show empathy, and agree with God.

"People who conceal their sins will not prosper. But if they confess and turn from them, they will receive mercy."

Proverbs 28:13

It seems to be human nature to not want to admit or resist being responsible for our wrongdoings. In a marital relationship, if you have not been the person you agreed to be, you must admit that you are wrong and change your plan and actions. The first step that leads to forgiveness and reconciliation is confession and repentance.

1. Accept responsibility.
The first step in mending a broken agreement is to accept responsibility for your actions and take the necessary steps to make things right. Have you apologized for your ill-advised behavior?
2. Show empathy. Do you regret what you did or did not do to break the agreement? Are you truly apologetic? Showing that you are truly apologetic for what was done shows remorse.
3. Confessing to God. What does God's Word say about your behavior? Have you asked God for forgiveness for breaking agreements with Him?

"But if we confess our sins to him, he is faithful and just to forgive us and to cleanse us from every wrong." 1 John 1:9

As we approach God with a humble spirit and acknowledge our sins, He is just to forgive us of our sins.

Attachments Styles

A loving relationship is not a barter system. A barter system is when you give to get.

Relationship - the way in which two people talk to, behave toward, and interact with each other.

Attachment - strong feelings of affection or loyalty for someone or something.

There is a difference between a marital relationship and a marital attachment. If you cannot be yourself in a marital relationship, you are living a lie in that relationship. You don't relate in truth with each other because you are attached by living a lie. You are afraid of being the real you out of fear that the person attached to you will detach himself or herself from you if he or she found out the real truth about who you are or who you have decided to become. This is why before marriage, many people become professional actors in an attempt to deceive you into believing that they are someone they are not. In these dating attachments, you tend to do a lot of role acting, being whatever the other person wants you to be. This toxic, unhealthy living is at the expense of your integrity, religious affiliation, and character. Many times, what people demand from us as the requirements to interact with them in an unhealthy attachment does not line up with who we are or want to be. Living a lie and lying to others as well as to yourself is unhealthy and destroys your inner soul. In the process you damage your inner being. By allowing yourself to remain attached to an alliance that no longer serves you, you will eventually, subconsciously sabotage the connection mentally, emotionally, or physically by withdrawing yourself or pushing the other person away. This is why divorce is so common after the first two and a half years of being married. Sooner or later, you must detach yourself and be free. Ultimately, we should desire to grow individually and collectively and that can't take place in the environment of a non-working marital or dating attachment.

Who are the participants in a dating or marital attachment? They are people who operate at the lowest level of human conscience. They are codependent, dependent, and selfish independent people I call "keepers." Another term for codependent and dependent people is "human leeches." Human leeches are people who have the following mindset: " How can I get what I want and not have to give anything to get it?" What can this person or situation do for me?" If I do participate or contribute, what is in it for me? Human leeches, men or women, seek out relational attachments looking for those they can use for their own personal gain and agenda. They attach themselves to people who will offer benefits to them without receiving hardly anything in return from them. *So as long as I can manipulate you and that person allows himself or herself to be manipulated, or long as you possess and freely give me the resources, needs, and wants that I desire, I will stay attached to you. When all resources have been used up and I can no longer receive from you what I want, I will detach myself from you.*

Most human leeches are not attracted to other human leeches. This relationship would not work because you have two selfish-minded dependent individuals looking to capitalize on the other person. Human leeches are attracted to donors. The donor's role is "What can I do for you?" The human leech's mindset is, "What do you have for me that I want and need from you?" The donor says, "If I give you what you want and need, you will give me the love, approval and acceptance that I need." This is not a healthy relationship because love and respect are not present, and love and respect must be present to have a legitimate relationship. True agape love and authentic respect create space in a dating or marital relationship to be who you are without compromising your character, integrity and maturity.

If you want to have a great marriage it starts with you learning how to be a great husband or wife and knowing what your attachment style is. What is your attachment style? What is your partner's attachment style?

According to John Gray, Amir Levine, M.D., and Rachel S.F. Heller, M.A., in their groundbreaking book *Attached*, which redefines what it means to be in a relationship, we rely on science to tell us everything from what to eat to when and how long to exercise, but what about relationships? According to Dr. Amir Levine and Rachel Heller, there is a scientific explanation for why some people seem to navigate relationships effortlessly, while others struggle. I agree with them. In *Attached*, Levine and Heller reveal how an understanding of adult attachment—the most advanced relationship science in existence today—can help us find and sustain love. This book drastically changed my life. It is a must read for anyone desiring to experience a healthy relationship. Pioneered by psychologist John Bowlby in the 1950's, the field of attachment posits that each of us behaves in relationships in one of three ways:

Secure - (the best option) people who are comfortable with closeness and intimacy and won't push you away. They are very consistent and reliable and won't send mixed signals. They are usually warm, respectful and loving. They know how to reassure you. They feel comfortable telling you how they feel, very early on, in a consistent manner. They bring out the best in you.

Life With A Secure Person

- Great conflict busters—During a fight they don't feel the need to act defensively or to injure or punish their partner, and so prevent the situation from escalating.
- Mentally flexible—They are not threatened by criticism. They are willing to reconsider their ways, and if necessary, revise their beliefs and strategies.
- Effective communicators—They expect others to be understanding and responsive, so expressing their feelings freely and accurately to their partners comes naturally to them.
- Not game players—They want closeness and believe others want the same, so why play games?
- Comfortable with closeness, **unconcerned about boundaries**—They seek intimacy and aren't afraid of being "enmeshed." Because they aren't overwhelmed by a fear of being slighted or the need to deactivate, they find it easy to enjoy closeness, whether physical or emotional.
- Quick to forgive—They assume that their partners' intentions are good and are therefore likely to forgive them when they do something hurtful.
- Inclined to view sex and emotional intimacy as one—They don't need to create distance by separating the two.
- Treat their partners like royalty—When you've become part of their inner circle, they treat you with love and respect.
- Secure in their power to improve the relationship—They are confident in their positive beliefs about themselves and others, which makes this assumption logical.
- Responsible for their partners' well-being—They expect

others to be responsive and loving towards them and so they are responsive to others' needs.

Anxious - come off as needy and are preoccupied with their relationships, are sensitive to any form of rejection, have a hard time saying what is bothering them and are very impulsive and erratic. They feed on closeness and intimacy and when that is threatened they act out in irrational protest behaviors and will try to reconnect at any cost. Anxious people often times jump to conclusions. They shoot from the hip and they are all over the place making misjudgments and hurting themselves. When they feel their partner pulling away, they activate their "activating strategies." Activating strategies are any thoughts or feelings that compel you to get close, physically or emotionally, to your partner. Once he or she responds to you in a way that reestablishes security, you can revert to your calm, normal self.

"Activating Strategies"

Thoughts and Feelings That Compel you to Seek Closeness with Your Partner

- Thinking about your mate, difficulty concentrating on other things.
- Remembering only their good qualities.
- Putting them on a pedestal: underestimating your talents and abilities and overestimating theirs.
- An anxious feeling that goes away only when you are in contact with them.
- Believing this is your only chance for love, as in
    1. "I'm only compatible with very few people—what are the chances I'll find another person like him or her.
    2. "It takes years to meet someone new; I'll end up alone."
- Believing that even though you're unhappy, you'd better

not let go, as in
1. "If they leave me they will turn into a great partner for someone else."
2. "They can change."
3. "All couples have problems—we're not special in that regard."

Protest Behaviors

Letting Your Anxieties Get The Best of You

Excessive attempts to reestablish contact:

- Calling, texting, or emailing many times, waiting for a phone call, loitering by your partner's residence or workplace in hopes of running into him or her.

Withdrawing:

- Sitting silently "engrossed" in the computer, literally turning your back on your partner, not speaking, talking with other people on the phone and ignoring him or her.

Keeping score:

- Paying attention to how long it took them to return your phone call or text message and waiting just as long to return theirs; waiting for them to make the first "make-up" move and acting distant until such time.

Acting hostile:

- Rolling your eyes when they speak, looking away, getting up and leaving the room, while they're speaking (acting hostile can transgress to outright violence at times).

Threatening to leave:

- Making threats—"We are not getting along, I don't think I can do this anymore," "I knew we weren't really right for each other," "I'll be better off without you"—all the while hoping he or she will stop you from leaving.

Manipulations:

- Acting busy or unapproachable. Ignoring phone calls or text messages, stating you have plans when you don't.

Making him or her feel jealous:

- Making plans to get together with an ex for lunch, going out with friends to a singles bar, telling your partner about someone who hit on you.

Avoidant -When things start to get serious they withdraw mentally and physically. They send mixed signals and play games. They are bad at reading nonverbal cues and focus on a person's weaknesses never their strengths. They equate intimacy with a loss of independence and constantly try to minimize closeness. They prefer to keep things fuzzy. Even if the relationship is very serious, some question marks still remain. If you're avoidant, you connect with romantic partners but always maintain some mental distance and an escape route. Feeling close and complete with someone else is a condition they find difficult to maintain. Avoidant people use deactivating strategies to keep their partner at arm's length. A deactivating strategy is any behavior or thought that is used to squelch intimacy.

Some Common Deactivating Strategies

- Saying (or thinking) "I'm not ready to commit"—but staying together nonetheless, sometimes for years.
- Focusing on small imperfections in your partner: the way he or she talks, dresses, eats, or (fill in the blank) and allowing it to get in the way of your romantic feelings.
- Yearning after an ex-girlfriend or boyfriend.
- Flirting with others—a hurtful way to introduce insecurity into the relationship.
- Not saying "I love you"—while implying that you do have feelings toward the other person.
- Pulling away when things are going well. (e.g., not calling for several days after an intimate date)
- Forming relationships with an impossible future, such as with someone who is married.
- "Checking out mentally" when your partner is talking to you.
- Keeping secrets and leaving things foggy—to maintain your feeling of independence.
- Avoiding physical closeness.

If you are an avoidant person, these small everyday deactivating strategies are tools you unconsciously use to make sure that the other person you love or will love won't get in the way of your independence.

Recognize and Rule Out Avoidant Prospects Early On

- Sends mixed messages—about his or her feelings toward you or about his or her commitment to you.
- Longs for an ideal relationship—but gives subtle hints that

it will not be with you.
- Desperately wants to meet "the one"—but somehow always finds some fault in the other person or in the circumstance that makes commitment impossible.
- Disregards your emotional well-being—and when confronted, continues to disregard it.
- Suggest that you are "too needy," "sensitive" or "overreacting—thus invalidating your feelings and making you second guess yourself.
- Ignores things you say that inconvenience him or her—doesn't respond or changes the topic instead.
- Addresses your concerns as "in a court of law"—responding to the fact without taking your feelings into account.
- Your messages don't get across—despite your best efforts to communicate your needs, he or she doesn't seem to get the message or else ignores it.

Levine and Heller guide readers in determining what attachment style they and their mate (or potential mate) follow, offering a road map for building stronger, more fulfilling connections with the people they love. Let me reiterate that this book is a game changer for having successful relationships and marriages. I highly suggest you read the book *Attached*.

True agape love and authentic respect create space in a dating relationship to be who you are without compromising your character, integrity, and maturity. The key to having a successful, effective interdependent marital relationship is when each of you can live in truth, love and respect unconditionally, and like yourselves when you are together as a couple. If every married person lived by these principles, then there would be no divorce.

Here is how to know if you are in an unhealthy relationship.

1. I break my commitments and agreements or do not operate within them. These exist when I am no longer who I agreed to my partner that I would be.
2. When I do not tell the truth about a situation or circumstance, I am not telling the truth about who I am. Telling the truth and being open and honest are necessary to establish trust. If my partner knew the whole truth about who I really am, would that person still want to marry me?
3. If I can't be myself in the relationship, the real me is no longer there.
4. Undelivered communication or assumptions are the norm.

Here is how to know you are in a healthy dating or marital relationship.

1. I can openly and lovingly communicate my needs and wants to my spouse as well as to others.
2. I can be honest in expressing my hurts, fears, insecurities, dreams, aspirations, and goals.
3. I am encouraged to develop my relationship with God.
4. I do not feel vulnerable sharing my needs and wants with my spouse.
5. I can speak the truth in love and receive the truth in love.
6. I can be the "real me" and I am accepted, loved, and respected for who I am. I am affirmed, appreciated and understood.

Most failed relationships are due to self-sabotage. Why? Because people have the prodigious ability to lie to themselves and avoid seeing the truth about themselves. It hurts to look within yourself for the cause of a failed relationship. Most people rationalize that they don't have a problem and there is no need to learn new strategies for having a successful relationship. What most people do is blame others, bad luck, or anything else instead of taking responsibility for their actions. Most people are in such a rush to find love that they act like impulsive children rushing into relationships without knowing who they are or who they are dating.

The mental baggage from childhood is another factor that prevents many relationships from blossoming. You have to identify your weaknesses and work on them to change. For me it was fear, worry, and insecurity that kept me very unstable and unbalanced in past relationships. That is not attractive and I decided I was done living like that. Look for the patterns; they are there, and then go to work on yourself. Don't search for someone who is better than your ex. A better you will attract a better next.

Love, Respect, Sexual Intimacy, and Romance

Marriages that lack unconditional love and respect, properly balanced and proportioned with sexual fulfillment cannot be happy ones and seldom last. Love and respect alone will not bring lasting happiness in a marriage, nor will sexual fulfillment alone. But when all three are present, love, respect, sexual fulfillment, and a fourth is added in the area of romance, you experience a spiritual reality that one may never know while on earth! When a husband and wife totally understand, and implement love, respect, sex and romance on an ongoing basis, they never will lose interest in each other. This is the key to sustaining a healthy great marriage.

"It is true that no woman has as great an influence on a man as his wife unless he is married to a woman totally unsuited to his nature. If a woman permits her husband to lose interest in her

and become more interested in other women, it is usually because of her ignorance, or indifference toward the subjects of sex, love, respect and romance. This statement presupposes, of course, that genuine love and respect once existed between a man and his wife. The facts are equally applicable to a man who permits his wife's interest in him to die. Married people often bicker over a multitude of trivialities. If these are analyzed accurately, the real cause of the trouble will be found to be indifference, or ignorance in the application of Love, Respect, Sex and Romance." -Napoleon Hill

How To Attract The Ideal Wife

Joseph Murphy in his book, *The Power of Your Subconscious Mind* gives men advice on how to attract the ideal wife. The following is an excerpt from his book *The Power of Your Subconscious Mind.*

"Affirm as follows: 'I now attract the right woman who is in complete accord with me. This is a spiritual union because it is divine love functioning through the personality of someone with whom I blend perfectly. I know I can give to this woman, love, respect, light, quality time, affection, peace and joy. I feel and believe I can make this woman's life full and complete, and wonderful. I now decree that she possesses the following qualities and attributes: She is spiritual, kind, loyal, faithful, considerate, dependable, patient, forgiving, honest, and self-sacrificing. She is harmonious, peaceful, and happy. We are irresistibly attracted to each other. Only that which belongs to love, truth, and beauty can enter my experience. I accept my ideal companion now. Amen.' As you think quietly and with interest on the qualities and attributes, which you admire in the companion you seek, you will build the mental equivalent into your mentality and you will meet this woman in divine order."

Pursue The Right Woman

"A wise woman builds up her house, but a foolish woman tears it down with her own hands." Proverbs 14:1

"A successful marriage begins with the intelligent choice of a partner. Let me explain what I mean by an intelligent choice. In the first place, a man should test his prospective partner in marriage through a series of frank and intimate talks with her. He should tell her how he intends to make a living and be very sure she is on board with him, both as to his chosen occupation and his method of achieving it. Her response here is very important. It will be of priceless help to a man if his wife becomes so enthusiastically sold on his occupation, and his method of achieving it, that she is willing to help him achieve it by any ethical means necessary. Failure to have an understanding on this subject has destroyed the possibility of having a successful marriage." -Andrew Carnegie

On the bus a man noticed that the man sitting next to him had his wedding ring on his right finger. So he said to the man, "Excuse me, did you know you have your wedding ring on the wrong finger?" The man replied, "I know. I married the wrong woman."

Marrying the wrong person can be one of the most devastating experiences in life. According to Napoleon Hill, one of the most common causes of personal failures and set-backs in life is **the wrong selection of a mate in marriage.** Why? The relationship of marriage brings people into intimate contact. Unless the relationship is harmonious, setback after setback is likely to follow you wherever you go. Moreover, they will be a form of setbacks that are marked by misery and unhappiness, destroying all signs of ambition, the driving force of success. Conversely, the presence of the right woman has the power to lift a man to new heights of success, which he could not otherwise experience on his own. There are many men who try to take all the credit for their unique success but truth be told, if it wasn't for their wives' encouragement, support, belief, faith, drive and persistence they would have never accomplished what they did. An amazing wife has faith and is honest. She is humble with character that rises above the stress of life's surprises. She has a magnetic personality and she is generous. She has a loving heart that is real and true.

Martin Luther King, Jr. was an American Baptist minister, activist, humanitarian, and leader in the African-American Civil Rights Movement. He is best known for his role in the advancement of civil rights using nonviolent civil disobedience based on his Christian beliefs. King adhered to Mahatma Gandhi's philosophy of nonviolence and was awarded the Nobel Peace Prize in 1964. He was married to Coretta Scott-King who was the kind of wife who brought unique value to their marriage. She helped Martin achieve a high level of personal and national success, which he otherwise would not have been able to achieve on his own.

Almost everyone who knew of Henry Ford's plans for automobiles condemned and criticized them in one way or another. The defining moment that gave him the courage to move forward was when his wife Mrs. Ford said to him, " Go ahead and do it no matter who criticizes you." After Henry Ford became ridiculously rich and successful, he later said, "I called her 'the Believer', because my wife was the only one who believed in my idea of a Motor Carriage." Henry Ford passed away in 1947, having accumulated $199 billion dollars (inflation adjusted)

Marriage: It's in Your Hands

Ross Perot has a net worth of 3.7 billion dollars (2015). How did he do it? After he got out of the Navy he got a job working for IBM, but IBM had a ridiculous sales quota policy and Perot didn't think it was fair. He had a great idea for expanding IBM's computer service division but was denied. He figured the only solution was to go into business for himself. Upset with the quota, he went to get his hair cut at a local barbershop and read a quote from Henry David Thoreau that was printed in a Reader's Digest magazine. The quote said, "The mass of men lead lives of quiet desperation." He made up in his mind that would never be him and quit IBM. On his 32nd birthday, he incorporated EDS, by borrowing $1000 dollars from his wife's saving account because he didn't have the money. What if his wife didn't believe in him? What if she wasn't supportive of his dream to start a business? He sold EDS to General Motors for 2.25 billion dollars. A $1000 dollar investment was turned into a 3.7 billion dollar net worth. Ross Perot and his wife have been married for 59 years.

Don't rush the selection process of choosing a mate. It takes time to get to know someone and your wanting to know them should not be based solely on how they look physically, but who they are and who they will be to you.

The Founder of Marriage

According to the Bible, God created the heavens and He created the earth. God created the marriage institution and defined what it was. He also established a spiritual hierarchy, which created roles for the husband and wife in marriage.

"But I want you to understand that the head of every man is Christ, the head of a wife is her husband, and the head of Christ is God." 1 Corinthians 11:3

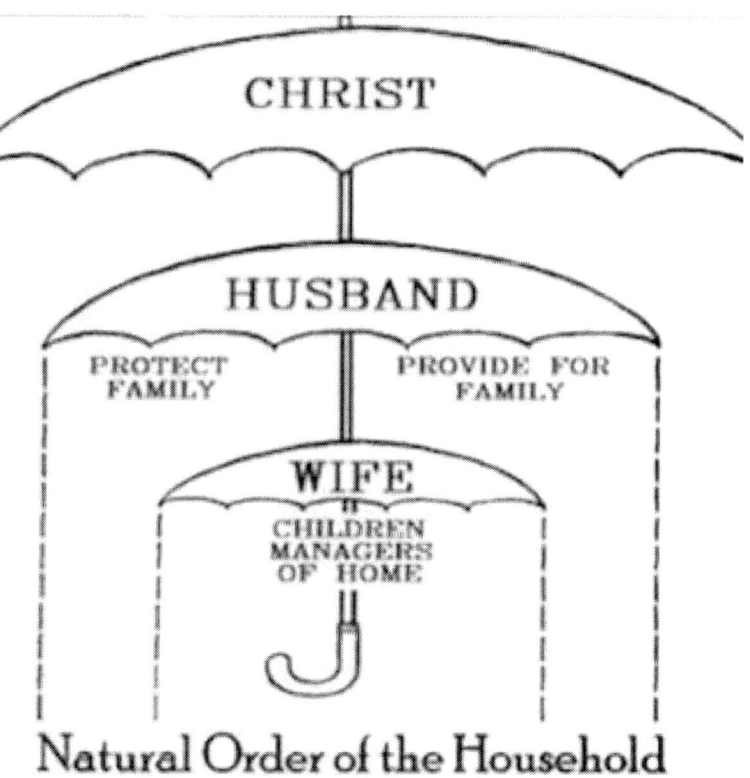

Natural Order of the Household

God appoints the husband the primary leader and manager of the marriage, so he bears most of the responsibility for the care of the marriage. The husband's responsibilities include but are not limited to...

- Being of sound mind, body and spirit as he leads and manages the marriage.
- He has acquired specialized marital and relational knowledge and applies this knowledge to the marriage as he submits to God's instructions pertaining to marriage.

- Makes sure that the marriage relationship stays healthy and positive.
- Loves his wife unconditionally, respects her, romances her and emotionally/sexually satisfies her.
- Protect the marriage relationship from danger, divorce and destructive behaviors.

The wife's responsibilities include but are not limited to…

- Helping and encouraging her husband to achieve his God ordained purpose.
- Respecting him unconditionally and his position as the husband, loves him, romances him, and sexually/emotionally satisfies him.
- Assisting him with important decisions that have to be made that affect the marriage.
- Being an accountability partner and friend to him.
- Not distracting him by complicating, complaining or comparing. She is to cooperate, compliment and care for him.

God is the founder of marriage, so he owns it. In marriage, God appoints the husband as the leader and manager and appoints the wife as his suitable helper. The husband has someone who supersedes his authority in marriage and that is God. God allows the husband and wife the freedom to communicate, cooperate, interact in their respective roles as long as they do not disobey His instructions and guidelines found in the Bible. A married man as a husband cannot lead or manage with legitimate God ordained authority unless God is leading and managing him. God appoints one person, the husband, to lead and manage the marriage. So does that mean that a woman has no voice, no say in the relationship or its direction? Absolutely NOT! That is ridiculous. God instructs a husband to listen to the wise counsel of his wife before he makes a decision in marriage. They are to submit to each other as unto the Lord. According to God, a biblical God ordained marriage on earth between a man and woman consist of a husband and wife. A biblical God ordained marriage does not consist of two husbands or two wives leading and managing together. A woman who is married to a man is supposed to function as his wife and be a helper to him, suited solely to help her husband. She must be suited to help him lead and manage their marriage relationship. He cannot lead and manage effectively and efficiently without her help.

"The presence of the right woman has the power to lift a man to new heights of success he could not experience on his own. The pages of history are filled with the records of great leaders whose achievements may be traced directly to the influence of women who aroused their creative minds through the stimulation of sex desire. If time would permit, we might easily mention thousands of men, well known to the American people, who climbed to great heights of achievement under the stimulation influence of their wives, only to drop back to destruction after money, fame, pride and power went to their heads and they put aside the old wife for a new one. Thousands of men have discovered afterwards that sex influence in marriage, from their wives, accounted for their unique successes. The person you marry must create a "Master Mind Alliance" with you. The human mind is a form of energy, a part of it being spiritual in nature. When the minds of two people are coordinated in a spirit of harmony, the spiritual units of the energy of each mind form an affinity or like-mindedness, which constitutes the 'psychic phase of the Master Mind Principle.' Great power and a great marriage can be accumulated and

acquired through no other principle."

-Napoleon Hill

So as a man, it is imperative that you choose the right woman to be your wife because part of the success or failure rest in how well she interdependently relates to you.

"Better to dwell in the wilderness, than with a contentious and angry woman." Proverbs 21:19

The author Solomon is saying that if you pursue and marry a contentious or angry woman, it is better to live in the wilderness with the wild animals than to live at home with her. A contentious woman is a woman who acts in opposition to you. She can be argumentative, belligerent, combative, and disrespectful towards you. By choosing to hate someone or have anger towards him or her, you build a fire in your heart for him or her. Forgive and LIVE! Now there is a difference between a woman disagreeing with her husband respectfully and being contentious. In marriage, a wife with her own opinion will not agree with everything her husband does or says because she is not supposed to. She is to give him her honest opinion, perspective, and advice. This is accomplished through effective cooperation, and he then should take what she says into consideration as he makes the final decision that will result in a win-win outcome. Many men, when choosing their wife, did not seek wise advice before pursuing her. Many men have chosen the wrong woman to help them lead and manage and have suffered dire consequences for their poor selection. If a woman has not developed herself, she is not qualified to help her future husband lead or manage the marriage. In my opinion it may take anywhere from 12 to 18 months to determine whether she is capable of being the wife you need her to be. My point here is not to rush. Many Christian men have chosen a woman as their wife based on their pretty face and smile, on her butt and breasts, not her inner beauty, on her high sex drive not her salvation, life purpose and dedication to Christ—and they are miserable.

"Don't team up with those who are unbelievers. How can goodness be a partner with wickedness? How can light live with darkness?" **2 Corinthians 6:14**

The Bible warns against being unequally yoked or teamed up with those who do not share your same values, morals, life principles or religious view. You should not pursue a single woman who is not qualified to help you lead, manage and provide solid, competent advice.

20/20 Vision

"Can the blind lead the blind? Will they not both fall into a pit?" **Luke 6:39**

The main function of the eye is to work with the brain to provide us with vision. The eye and brain translate light waves into a sensation we call vision. Do you see the vision for your marriage relationship? Do you see how your actions affect others? The sad reality is that many women and men have figuratively closed their eyes in their marriage and are walking around blind. With closed eyes you have no sense of direction in your marital relationship. When your eyes are shut, you have the tendency to bump into things you may have avoided if they were open. In a marriage, there are many pitfalls and distractions along the way. There are also many opportunities that will present themselves, which will be a benefit to the relationship. Therefore, it is wise to prepare yourself to receive these opportunities when they present themselves. It is better to be prepared for an opportunity than to have an opportunity become available but not be prepared to seize it.

As a man when you look at your wife, what do you see? Opportunity? Do you see a gift from God?

"He who finds a wife finds a great thing and obtains favor from the Lord." Proverbs 18:22

Many of us have been trained to view marriage through the lens of a secular world. The goal is to view marriage the way God views it. The reality is that we all have had poor eyesight and are in need of spiritual Lasik surgery. God is so precise and detailed about correcting poor vision through His Word, He gives us precise literature to read to encourage, instruct, and correct our misconceptions and misperceptions on marriage. Building interpersonal leadership through effective interaction involves cooperation—not competition. It involves two people working in harmony, side by side with their identified roles and goals, who come together to develop common goals to accomplish something together that would not have otherwise happened if they operated as individuals. They are in agreement. Many married men and women do not have a road map in place to lead themselves, which ultimately leads to not having set goals or plans that they plan to accomplish together. Having success in marital relationships first starts with having success with thyself. What is success you might ask? Success to me is the steady progress toward your predetermined goals, ultimately achieving those goals. So marriage success would then be the steady progress the couple makes toward their predetermined goals for the marriage, ultimately achieving those goals. Being proactive and having a vision allows a man and woman to identify their roles in the marriage and create their marital goals. A husband and his wife then can begin the steady progress toward achieving those predetermined goals, walking together toward marital success.

Chapter 19

Marital Interdependent Leadership

Interdependent leadership relates to how you interact with another person. Interaction in a marriage is often approached with an independent mindset. The question is: How do we operate interdependently when it comes to the leadership of our relationship? How do we base our marriage on cooperation instead of competition?

"A person standing alone can be attacked and defeated, but two can stand back-to-back and conquer. Three are even better, for a triple-braided cord is not easily broken." Ecclesiastes 4:12

There are six human interaction philosophies. The basis and foundation of interdependent leadership is to think Win-Win.

Six Human Interaction Philosophies

Win-Win is the foundation that supports interdependent leadership and management. It is the most effective way to successfully interact with another person. The alternatives to Win-Win would be Win-Lose, Lose-Win, Lose-Lose, Win, and No deal.

"Each of you should look not to your own interest, but to the interest of others." Philippians 2:4

Win-Win. Win-Win is a frame of mind and heart that constantly seeks mutual benefit in all human interactions. In the marriage relationship, it means that agreements or solutions are mutually beneficial or satisfying. With Win-Win all parties feel good about the mutual decisions that have to be made and are committed to the action plan in place. The mentality is that we can find options that will be acceptable for everyone. The foundation of a Win-Win agreement is based on harmonious cooperation—not destructive competition. It is the philosophy that it is not my way or your way but the best way for us. If you choose to operate with a Win-Win mentality, then you must exhibit maturity. Hrand Saxenian gave the definition of maturity in a *Harvard Business Review (January-February, 1958)*. Hrand said maturity is: "The ability to express one's own feelings and convictions balanced with consideration for the thoughts and feelings of others." To operate with a Win-Win mentality, you must have high consideration and high courage. It requires that you are nice and tough. When you operate with that kind of mentality, you are considerate to take into account the thoughts, feelings, and desires of others, but you also have the courage to confront in love and not be a pushover. You focus on the positive, but provide constructive feedback on improvement areas. Adopting the Win-Win philosophy is a necessary tool for establishing and maintaining a long-term interdependent marriage. A Win-Win agreement consists of five key elements that must be identified and implemented for it to work. The five key elements are desired results, guidelines, resources, accountability, and consequences.

1. **Desired results.** The outcome is defined by what we want to accomplish. Everyone involved envisions the same outcome, which is mutually beneficial to both parties.
2. **Guidelines.** The identified rules, policies, or specifications involved in our agreement.
3. **Resources.** The physical, financial, and medical resources we will need and their availability.
4. **Accountability.** Who will do what and when will it happen? What will we use to measure our success?
5. **Consequences.** What will happen when we are finished? Is

the desired outcome connected to positive or negative consequences?

When building Win-Win agreements, it is vital to incorporate all five elements into that agreement. When you develop a Win-Win agreement you will notice that your relationship will operate smoother and more effectively.

Win-Lose. If you are high on courage but lack consideration, you mainly operate from a Win-Lose mentality. Win-Lose says, "I win and you lose." The Win-Lose mentality is "I get my way; you don't get your way." People with a Win-Lose mentality have high courage to ask and get or even demand what they need or want but lack the consideration to take into account the needs, feelings, thoughts, or wants of the other person. Many people feel that they must win every discussion and be right and win in every situation. Their relationship is a competition and losing is not an option for them. Being an effective team means that instead of competition there must be healthy interaction, understanding that no one wins in a Win-Lose approach. If both people are not winning, then both people are losing.

Lose-Win. If you lack courage but are high on consideration, you mainly operate from a Lose-Win mentality. You are considerate of others' thoughts, feelings, wants, and needs, but you do not have the courage to express your own. The people who operate in Lose-Win agreements have no standard, no demands, no expectation, no vision. They are quick to please and appease. They have little courage to express their convictions and are easily intimidated by the dominating ego-driven personalities of others. In times of negotiation and decision-making, they tend to give into what the other person wants to do, even at the expense of their well-being. People with a Win-Lose mentality love people with a Lose-Win mentality because they feed off their weaknesses and take advantage of them.

Lose-Lose. This is when two people with Win-Lose mentalities get together. Both are high on courage to demand what they want and need, but low on consideration for what the other person wants and needs. In the end, both will lose. In most cases, in a Lose-Lose situation both people become vindictive and seek revenge on the other person. Many times each person's objective is to make sure the other person loses, even if it means that they lose themselves in the process. It is the thought process of "if I cannot win, then no one can win." Many people have been hurt or even killed because of this type of thinking. "If I can't have you, nobody can have you." There are also people who operate from the mentality of scarcity. They believe that there is not enough to go around for everyone to mutually enjoy. They have a very hard time sharing recognition or credit for achievement, power, or profit from their position, even with people who may have helped them get to the place they are. They tend to harbor a secret desire for misfortune for others that would prevent success. Often times they surround themselves with people who are emotionally weaker so that they won't be challenged. People with this mindset will not make great marriage partners because of their selfishness. The key to having a great marriage is to operate from an abundance philosophy versus a scarcity philosophy. When you operate out of an abundance philosophy, you operate from a Win-Win mentality. You believe there is plenty out there and enough to go around for everyone. You are excited by the success of others and celebrate their achievements. You recognize and appreciate their unique attributes, talents, and gifts.

Win. With this mentality you operate with courage but really do not have any consideration for the other person. You really are indifferent if someone wins or loses at the expense of your winning. If the other person should win or lose, it does not matter; all that matters is that you get what you need and want. Your mentality is, "I'm going to secure the things I want and need, and it is up to you to do the same. Good luck."

Win-Win or No Deal. An alternative option of Win-Win is No Deal if a Win-Win outcome is simply not an option. No Deal means that if we cannot find or come up with a solution or agreement that will benefit everyone, then we will agree to disagree—agreeable No Deal. When you have a No Deal as an option, you do not have to manipulate others so that you can get what you want at their expense. You can be open with them about what you desire and seek to understand their concerns as well. With No Deal as an option, you interact with your partner in a way that says, "We are aiming for Win-Win." People with this mentality think, "I would not want to get my way and have you not feel good about it because you lose in the deal. If we cannot come up with a Win-Win, then let's not make a deal at all because it would be better to not deal than to make a decision that was not right for the both of us."

Win-Win is the only real way to operate in the marriage relationship. No Deal is always an option as well or you may elect to go with a lesser form of Win-Win, which is compromise. There are some guidelines to having an effective Win-Win outcome that will be mutually beneficial to both parties. The idea when negotiating is to not focus on the person but on the problem or situation. It is easy to allow emotions to take your focus away from the problem or symptoms. Address the root of the problem—not the fruit. There is a four-step process in negotiating a Win-Win agreement.

1. See the problem from the other person's point of view. There is an old saying: "Put the shoe on the other foot." This simply means look at it from the other person's perspective. Here you really seek to understand their needs and concerns, and you empathize with them.
2. Identify the key concerns or issue. What is the root of the problem—not the fruit of the problem? Here you do not focus on the person with the problem but on the problem that is affecting the person and you.
3. Determine what results would constitute a reasonably acceptable solution.
4. Seek out new possible options that would achieve the desired results.

The Win-Win philosophy is a human interaction tool that, when used effectively, will achieve harmony within the marriage relationship.

Chapter 20

Marriage Systems

For the Win-Win agreement to work, you must have systems set up to support it. A relationship system is an organized set of interrelated ideas or principles that can be used in a marriage or dating relationship. How do you plan to function on a day-to-day basis? Who will be responsible for what? Here are eight systems that a couple should consider implementing in order to have a successful marriage.

1. The Spiritual System
2. The Marriage System
3. The Family System
4. The Household System
5. The Financial System
6. The Career/Domestic System
7. The Personal/Social System
8. The Ministry System

Many times the problem in relationships or marriages is the lack of systems in place—not the people. If you put good-natured people in bad or non-existent systems, you will get unfavorable results. As a couple begins to operate within these systems of the Win-Win agreement, they become more cooperative and experience harmony in their relationships.

To make a marriage successful, you must first define what goals you want to accomplish within each system in your Win-Win interpersonal relationship. Once identified, the goals of the relationship must be prioritized. Interdependent leadership is what we want to accomplish together, and interdependent management is coming up with detailed plans for the best way we should accomplish it.

Before you say I do, it is a good idea to first become proactive and independent. Before you decide to get married, it is wise for a man to first sit down to discuss whether he as an independent man will be able to form an interdependent relationship with the woman he wants to marry. If either person still operates as a dependent person, more than likely they will not be a great spouse to each other until they make the necessary personal changes.

A man and a woman who are considering marriage must agree that the current and future goals they have and want to achieve are congruent. Many times people who are considering marriage are not compatible in their individualized unique "life purpose or purposes" they are called to accomplish in this life. A proactive man/fiancé will put on paper his mission statement, roles, goals, and what he believes he is called to achieve for the greater good of humanity. He will then ask the woman to put on paper her mission statement, roles, goals and what she believes she is called to undertake for the greater good of humanity. Once the data is compiled and compared, a mutual, logical decision can be made about whether there should be a merger of the two independent, individual lives. I seriously doubt that Payless Shoe Source Corporation would merge with Discount Tire Corporation. Although they are two independent corporations, a merger would not make sense nor would it allow them to maximize their corporate strengths because they have different mission statements and provide different products and services. There is no "shared purpose" that ideally links these two corporations together.

If you do decide that there should be a merger or marriage, then during the engagement period, the man and woman must develop a marital mission statement that they can agree on prior to the wedding date.

What should be in the marital mission statement? Here are a few questions you should ask each other.

1. What will be the role(s) of the husband?
2. What will be the role(s) of the wife?
3. What does God want us to accomplish for him as a married couple?
4. What are your expectations for your husband within the 8 marriage systems?
5. What are your expectations for your wife within the 8 marriage systems?

Discovering the answers to these questions is being proactive—not reactive. With collaboration from each other define and discuss what your roles and goals will be. Overtime your roles and goals may change but your mission statement should remain the same.

If you are contemplating marriage, you are operating proactively by taking the necessary actions to create a collaborative marital mission statement. When marital roles are established and goals identified, it lays the foundation for effective decision-making. Life consists of countless decisions. It is important to have an agreement on how two independent individuals operating as one unit interdependently will make those decisions together. There must be a vision/mission statement established for the marriage and family.

"Where there is no vision, the people perish."

Proverbs 29:18

The Hebrew word for "perish" can be translated to mean, "going unrestrained each to his or her own way."

What a tragic reality that many married men and women are not walking as one. Married men and women pursuing their own agendas, not functioning as a coupe but as separate individuals. We all have a choice to perish or flourish, to wonder aimlessly or to work together with a shared purpose and vision.

"Can two walk together, except they be agreed?"

Amos 3:3

Agreeing on where the relationship should and is going is necessary to achieve oneness. A great place to start in a marriage is to agree that no one will make a time commitment involving the other without first discussing and agreeing on the matter with a Win-Win outcome. As a couple identifies each system and develops goals within those systems, that couple begins the process of walking together. Without established systems and related goals, confusion, contradiction, and conflict will abound. Having established systems and goals, a couple or family faced with a decision can simply ask, "Will this choice further accomplish our marriage and family goals, or hinder them?" Depending on the answer, you can proceed or decline. There are 8 individual systems. Within these systems a man and woman who want to get married must formulate goals related to each marital system. How you function within these marital systems as a couple will have a profound impact on the "two walking as one." As we discuss goal setting within these systems, it is important to understand the "what" approach to formulating a goal.

The what approach asks, "What do we want to see accomplished?"

The key here is to be as specific as possible when making the goal measurable and attainable. What is our objective to accomplish? For example saying, "we want to become more spiritual" is too vague, "establishing a morning devotional time to read our Bible together" is more defined and workable. We will now take a look at each individual system and how each system will help you maximize your marital relationships' full potential.

The Spiritual System- Within the spiritual system, you set the spiritual goals for the relationship. Here you decide together what direction you would like the marriage to go or where you'd like to be spiritually in 3 months, 6 months or 9 months. You decide as a couple what you will focus on for the next several months to make this possible. It will help to keep your spiritual goals short and attainable.

Here are some sample spiritual goals to prompt your thinking.

1. We will pray together before we go to bed and when we wake up.
2. Purchase a couple's devotional Bible and have devotions daily.
3. Attend a spiritual renewal conference twice a year.
4. Attend church service weekly.
5. Read through the book of Proverbs each month, one chapter per day.

Come up with five specific spiritual goals as a couple that the two of you would like to undertake in your spiritual life during the current year and following year.

The Marriage System- Within the marriage system, you set the marital goals for the marriage relationship. The marriage system consists of two people: the husband and wife.

How you interact will determine whether the marriage grows or dies. How you communicate, your agreements on intimacy, sexual expectations, and conflict resolution are goals to be identified here. Here is where you plan and decide what you will focus on for the next several months that will bring "oneness" to the marriage relationship. Here are some sample marital goals to prompt your thinking.

1. Set aside specific time during the week for talk time without distractions.
2. Attend marital counseling every quarter for the duration of the marriage. Everything by longevity tends to get off course.
3. Schedule a date out together alone once a week.
4. Speak the truth in love and do not play marital games.
5. Express daily praise and appreciation to your spouse.

Come up with five specific marital goals as a couple that you will undertake in your marriage during the current year and upcoming year.

The Family System- Within the family system, you set the family goals for the marriage relationship. This is where the parents decide what direction they would like the family to proceed in or what they would like to accomplish as a family. Here is where the two of you discuss the guidelines and principles for the children and for yourselves as parents. Ask yourselves the following questions as parents when you begin to create goals for the family.

- Could we benefit from more time together, planning our parenting approach?

- When would we discuss this?
- What would we discuss?
- What additional support would we like from each other in parenting?
- What are some activities that we could do as a family?
- What specific goals would we have for each of our children in their development of maturity, integrity, and character?

These questions can possibly generate goals for the family. Here are some sample family goals to prompt your thinking.

1. Begin weekly fun nights for family fellowship and conversation.
2. Eat five meals a week together as a family without television.
3. Have weekly meetings with spouse about rules, discipline and parenting ideas.
4. Attend a parenting workshop yearly.
5. Pray as a family before meals.

Come up with five specific family goals as a couple that both of you would like to undertake in your marriage during the current year and following year.

The Household System- The household system encompasses how you will plan to deal with the challenges of operating a household.

- What goals do we need to establish that will make our household run smoothly?
- What types of eating habits will we develop?
- What home improvements will we undertake?
- How will we divide up the chores and cooking?

From these questions you get a good idea of what goals need to be formulated for the household system to work. Here are some possible goals for the household system.

1. We will not make any major decisions without the consideration of the other person.
2. We will have a family meal schedule and prep meals weekly to avoid spending money on fast food.
3. Develop and agree on a list of all household chores.
4. Develop a landscape plan and schedule for the yard.
5. Develop a plan to lead and manage the children's activities.

Come up with five specific household goals the both of you as a couple would like to undertake. If your children are old enough and would like to contribute to the list I would encourage you to get their feedback. Plan out the current year and upcoming year.

The Financial System- In the financial system you establish goals for your budget finance. This includes personal spending, saving, budgeting, paying off debt and items you purchase together.

- Is money being spent where it should be?
- Have we established a family budget?
- If something were to happen to me, do I have a life insurance policy and is it adequate to take care of my family?
- How will we handle debt, credit card, student loans, and other expenses?

Maybe your lifelong financial goal is to become financially independent. My definition of being financially independent is the ability to live off your personally invested resources. Would you like to experience financial freedom? Here is some advice in the form of a quote from Jim Rohn on how to achieve financial independence.

"Work harder on yourself than you do on your job. Working on your job will earn you a living which is fine, but working on yourself will earn you a fortune which is super fine." – Jim Rohn

Here is a list of tools, techniques, and resources that when implemented will allow you to work harder on yourself than you do on your job.

- Read the Books *Think and Grow Rich* by Napoleon Hill
- Audio listening programs
- Documentaries of Successful People
- Asking questions
- Interactive learning (find out how things work)
- Become more valuable (we get paid for the value we bring to the market place)
- Study and Attend Seminars
- Facing fears
- Learning to lead others

Goals established within the financial system answer all these questions and many more. Here are some possible goals for the financial system that might trigger some ideas for possible financial goals.

1. Develop a family financial statement that tracks monthly savings and spending. We need to know where it all goes.
2. Save 10% for investing, 10% savings, and 10% benevolent offerings and live off the remaining 70%. If we are in real financial trouble then we will implement 1% for investing, 1% for savings, and 1% for benevolent offerings and live

off the remaining 97% until we can do better.
3. Give a certain amount each month to nonprofit organizations.
4. Complete a family will and or living trust.
5. Pay off all credit card debt and student loans.

Now list the goals that both of you would like to establish as a couple for the financial system to become effective for the current and upcoming year.

The Career/Domestic System- The time you spend on your career and domestic responsibilities will have a great impact on the marriage relationship.

- Is your career interfering with your marriage or family in a negative way because of neglect?
- Do you spend excess time on your career that could be devoted more to your marriage and family?
- How can you and your mate be more supportive of each other?
- What ways can you encourage and support your mate?
- Have you asked your spouse or children whether they feel neglected by your absence?

Here are some sample goals to get the thought process going for goal development for the career/domestic system.

1. We will only say yes to those things in our careers that warrant a yes, and no to all the others.
2. We will make our marriage and family a priority by leaving our work at work whenever possible.
3. We will delegate responsibilities, so we have more time for our marriage and family.

4. We will read articles and books on delegation and implement this in our home.
5. We will not place unreasonable expectations on the marriage with work-related situations.

Now indicate five goals that both of you would like to establish as a couple in the career/domestic system for the current and upcoming year.

Personal/Social Systems- There are certain goals and objectives that you should want to accomplish as independent people operating interdependently in a marriage. It is important to work together on the goals that you as a couple have identified, but it is also important to have personal social goals for yourself. It is equally important to be supportive of your partner's personal or social goals. When the two become one, what is important to him or her becomes important to you. As long as personal/social goals do not bring harm or neglect to the marriage or family, it is healthy to have these goals. This system is designed to assess your personal and social life.

- What are some areas you feel confident in?
- What are some areas in your life that you need to pay more attention to? (i.e. health, wealth or relationships)
- What are some of your personal dreams?
- Does your mate know your dreams and aspirations?
- In what ways can you become supportive in the effort to help your mate achieve his/her personal goals?

Here are some examples to get your thoughts activated so you can come up with five personal/social goals for this year and next year.

1. Join a health club or gym and workout three days a week

alone or with your spouse.
2. Lose or gain a specific amount of weight in a certain time frame.
3. Learn to play tennis or basketball or join a sports league.
4. Enroll in a German or French cooking class.
5. Eliminate one irritating habit by replacing it with a more life sustaining one.

After discussing these questions with your partner, take some time to establish five personal/social goals and list those that you wish to implement during the next several months.

Ministry System- Ministry is something that is not always affiliated with a church or spiritual organization. Ministry means the act of service. While it is tied to the church and other spiritual organizations, you do not have to be a part of these organizations to serve. Part of Christ's message was to go out and minister to people outside of the church. In establishing goals for the ministry system, answer the following questions.

- What special gifts, talents or abilities do I see in my spouse that could be a blessing to others?
- What are some of my dreams that God has placed in my heart that will allow me to serve others?
- What ideas do I have for ministry that together as a couple we can impact and serve others?

Maybe you and your spouse want to volunteer at a local middle school as mentors. Or maybe volunteer with the Red Cross once a month. The idea is to serve together with a glad heart, touching and altering lives with your service and love. Couples who minister and serve together have less than a 10% divorce rate. You can help and nourish yourself when you serve and help others. Here are some sample ministry goals to provoke thinking for goal formulation.

1. Become a mentor to a couple with a troubled marriage or to an engaged couple.
2. Volunteer as a Sunday school worker.
3. Volunteer at a high school mentoring at risk youth.
4. Spend a week of vacation doing mission work in your community.
5. Volunteer to babysit a married couple's kids for free so they can have a date night out.

Write down your five ministry goals as a couple you wish to accomplish during the current and upcoming year.

Now that you have completed the eight sections on setting specific goals within the various marriage systems for yourself, marriage and family, you are ready to develop an action plan that will lead to successful implementation of your goals within each marriage system.

Chapter 21

Marital Interdependent Management

Once a marital destination has been determined, the next step is the formulation of an effective plan using a marital map.

Developing interdependent management skills as a couple addresses the aforementioned statement. After you have identified your systems in which to operate your marriage and formulated your goals as a couple, it is now time to sit down and plan out how the two of you will execute them. It is wise to set aside time during the week to reflect and determine how productive, effective and efficient the systems and goals you have implemented are. During this time you talk and discuss how you will implement each of your goals within each system, the estimated time frame in which they will be reached, and the progress you are making with each goal. You may choose to be responsible for four systems each. The point is that each system and the goals associated with them are discussed and the progress is assessed. As a couple you must progress monitor your goals so that you know if you are headed in the right direction or if you need to make mid course corrections. As you work together managing the marriage, you will discover how much smoother it will operate. The next step is to take the systems and goals you developed and formulate a goal setting worksheet.

Goal Setting Worksheet

"With No Vision the People Perish"

System Areas	What (Goals)	How (Plan)	When (Schedule)
Spiritual			
Marriage			
Family			
Household			
Financial			
Career			
Personal/Social			
Ministry			

"Most people don't plan to fail; they fail to plan."

- John L. Beckley

It is best to plan what you are seeking to accomplish on a weekly basis. As effective managers, it is how you manage the relationship as you manage yourselves that determine success or failure within that relationship. It is recommended that you have a weekly planning schedule for yourself that coincides with your spouse. This allows you to know where you are spending your time. Remember that it is not time that you want to manage but the relationship. The major point being stressed and discussed in this chapter is making sure that you are *putting first things first*. Managing the relationship in regard to what is important and urgent will have a profound effect on whether the relationship is successful.

Marriage Maintenance Plan

A marriage maintenance plan will alleviate most unexpected marital breakdowns. Many couples in marriage are reacting to problems instead of being proactive to them because there is no plan in place to address the emergencies. Having a **"Marriage Maintenance Plan"** and **"Marriage Emergency Plans"** are a must in order to have a harmonious marriage.

"Marriage Emergency Planning" must be done prior to the emergency happening. After the honeymoon is over, reality will set in. The reality is that you will have conflict and experience setbacks in your marriage.

"But those who marry will face trouble in this life."

1 Corinthians 7:28

What is your plan for resolving conflict as a newly married couple or as an established couple? What is your plan for effective communication when as a man you feel disrespected or as a woman you feel unloved? How long will you avoid the problem and each other and not communicate with one another? Most good willed couples experience disaster early on in marriage, because they are careless and neglect to put a marriage disaster recovery plan in place that fits their situation. Learn to provide marital care in the form of marriage maintenance before you call the pastor or marriage counselor and have a **"Marriage Maintenance Plan"** and **"Marriage Emergency Plans"** in place.

Haynes Corporation in conjunction with the American Honda Motor Co., Inc. developed a repair manual for all of Honda's vehicles dating as far back as 1983. While each car or truck has many similarities, there are also many differences. Honda Accord repair manuals help you get the best value from your vehicle. It does this in several ways. It can help you decide what service must be performed and if it can be done by you or serviced by a certified mechanic, it provides information and procedures for routine maintenance and offers diagnostic and repair procedures to follow when trouble occurs. Do you have a repair manual for your marriage?

The first chapter in the manual does not begin by offering information about diagnostic and repair procedures. The first chapter is titled "Tune Up and Routine Maintenance."

Automakers know that 85% of all problems that you have with your vehicle can be traced back to the neglect of providing the proper routine maintenance. What many people do is just get into their automobiles and drive. It is a known fact that dealerships make the majority of their money not from selling new vehicles but from performing expensive maintenance procedures that could have been avoided by simply doing routine maintenance. When automakers designed cars and trucks, they were designed to last. When God designed marriage, He designed it to last. Here is an example of a list of routine checks to perform on your vehicle to keep it properly maintained, maximizing the life of your vehicle.

Honda suggests that when your vehicle is new that you should follow the maintenance schedule to the letter and record the maintenance performed in your owner's manual, keeping all records.

Every 250 miles or weekly, whichever comes first:

- Check engine oil.
- Check the engine coolant.
- Check the windshield washer fluid.
- Check the brake and clutch fluid.
- Check the tire pressure.

Every 3,000 miles or 3 months, whichever comes first:

All items listed above plus:

- Check the power steering fluid level.
- Check the automatic transaxle fluid.
- Change the oil and oil filter.

Every 7,500 miles or 6 months, whichever comes first:

All items listed above plus:

- Inspect and replace, if necessary the windshield wiper blades.
- Check and service the battery.
- Check and adjust, if necessary, all under hood hoses.
- Check the cooling system.
- Rotate the tires.
- Have the brake system inspected.

Every 15,000 miles or 12 months, whichever comes first:

All items listed above plus:

- Seat belt check.
- Replace the air filter.
- Have the fuel system inspected.
- Check the manual transaxle lubricant level.
- Have the suspension, steering components, and drive axles inspected.

Every 30,000 miles or 24 months, whichever comes first:

All items listed above plus:

- Check and replace, if necessary, the spark plugs.
- Inspect and replace if necessary, the spark plug wires, distributor cap, and rotor.
- Check and adjust, if necessary, the engine idle speed.
- Service the cooling system. (drain, flush, and refill)
- Replace the brake fluid.
- Change the automatic transaxle lubricant.
- Check and replace, if necessary, the air-conditioning filter.

Every 105,000 miles or 72 months, whichever comes first:

- Replace the timing and balance shaft belt.

Do you have a weekly, 3-month, 6-month, 12-month, 24- month and 72-month maintenance schedule for your marriage?

If it takes this much routine maintenance to extend the life of your vehicle, know that it is going to take routine maintenance to extend the life of your marriage. Cars and trucks, and all other vehicles are very complex, and if not routinely maintained they will not operate as they were designed to. The marriage relationship is very complex, and if not routinely maintained, it will not operate as it was designed to either. Are you experiencing a marital breakdown? You may think it is your spouse or kids, but it could be that you have neglected the marital relationship in the area of routine maintenance. Many people get frustrated with expensive repairs that have to be done to their automobiles and just want to trade them in for a new one to avoid paying for the maintenance that is needed. But even if you decide to go out and purchase a new, pre-owned, or a more expensive automobile such as a BMW, Ferrari, or Mercedes, it still will require routine maintenance. Marriage is the same way. No matter who you marry or are currently married to, the marriage relationship will not operate efficiently if it is not properly maintained, resulting in a marriage breakdown. If by neglect you have been the cause or contributed to not keeping your marriage maintained, be willing to make the repairs no matter the cost. Sure, it may be time consuming and costly, but a great benefit is that you already have records of what has been serviced.

Starting over with a new person should be the last resort. It may seem like a good idea until you find out that in the new person's previous relationship there was neglect in properly maintaining that relationship, now you will have more problems with your new partner than you did before. Your next relationship most certainly does not always end up worse than your previous one but often times it can. Either way you choose to proceed, a routine maintenance plan must be implemented to have a successful lasting marriage relationship.

A very important aspect of marriage maintenance is having marriage staff meetings. They are a set time during the week that you discuss the status of the relationship. It is an opportunity to talk about and share with your partner successes or concerns of the relationship. It is not a time for finger pointing or playing the blame game, but a time to review the marriage maintenance plan that you have established. In these meetings as a couple, you perform a "marital systems diagnostic check" on the marriage and make adjustments if necessary.

From the research I have compiled, there are eight main reasons why couples divorce. As an interdependent couple, you must be proactive about managing your relationship and addressing these concerns. Having goals in each of your systems to address these concerns is being proactive and having a solution before the crisis occurs. As we look at these eight main reasons that contribute to divorce, you will see that there is a marital system to prevent these events from happening in your marriage. Whether your marriage flourishes or perishes is in your hands.

1. Lack of commitment toward marriage, sexual incompatibility, and infidelity.
   (Spiritual, Marriage, and Family Systems)
2. Lack of communication or ineffective communication.
   (Spiritual, Marriage and Family Systems)
3. Abandonment, addictions, and substance abuse.
   (Spiritual, Marriage and Family Systems)
4. Physical abuse, sexual abuse, and emotional abuse.
   (Spiritual, Marriage and Family Systems)
5. Inability to manage or resolve conflict.
   (Spiritual, Marriage and Family Systems)
6. Differences in personal and career goals.
   (Spiritual, Marriage, Career, and Personal/Social Systems)
7. Different expectations about household tasks and financial challenges.

(Spiritual, Household, and Financial Systems)
8. Religious beliefs, cultural, and lifestyle differences. **(Spiritual and Ministry Systems)**

There is a system in place for each of these eight reasons why couples divorce. Having these systems in place and goals to support them, along with your maintenance plan make you a proactive couple—not a reactive couple. As you plan proactively to address the eight reasons why couples divorce and incorporate that plan into the management maintenance plan of the marriage, you can prevent divorce from happening to you.

Chapter 22

Marital Interdependent Communication

How would a woman from France who speaks French effectively communicate with a man from America who speaks English if they met each other in a coffee shop? How will they mutually understand one another? It is difficult to communicate and mutually understand someone who does not speak or understand your language. Often times in relationships men and women speak a different language. To effectively communicate and relate to your spouse, you must learn to speak and understand his or her language. I recommend reading *The Five Love Languages* by Gary Chapman for further development in this area.

"In the same way, you husbands must give honor to your wives. Treat your wife with understanding as you live together." 1 Peter 3:7

Peter is giving husbands some valuable game-changing advice on how to communicate with their wives. His overall message is to seek to first understand and then be understood. People really do not care how much you know until they know how much you care. Next to survival, the greatest needs for a human being are to be affirmed, appreciated, and understood.

"Wisdom is the principle thing; therefore get wisdom and in all of your getting, get a good understanding." Proverbs 4:7

Solomon, one of the wisest men who ever lived, is saying in this proverb that to gain knowledge and wisdom from interdependent communication with someone in a situation, you must first *understand* that person or situation. Many times when conflict arises in the marriage or just in platonic relationships and someone is seeking advice, most people react by habitually rushing in to offer their advice as to what the person should or should not do. They do so without really understanding what is being said or what that person is feeling. To have interdependent, effective communication, you must desire to understand first and then be understood. What it means to understand someone is to perceive and comprehend the nature and significance of or to grasp what that person is communicating. There are four ways to communicate with someone. This is done through reading, writing, listening, and speaking. The ability of the husband or wife to do them well will have a great impact on their ability to effectively communicate with each other. To effectively interact with your spouse, you must sincerely desire to understand them and create an environment where they feel safe opening up to you. If a person is not comfortable opening up to you because you are a criticizer, judger, hypocrite, or a person who just does not listen, then you will not be able to effectively advise or council that person. Your partner wants to be understood first before they receive counsel from you. The reality is that most people do not listen with the intent to understand but listen with the intent to reply. Usually as a person is speaking, we are listening only to certain words because we are preparing what we are going to say and the questions we are going to ask as a response. We compare what is being said with our belief system without fully understanding what the other person is attempting to convey. We prematurely give advice that was not asked for or that was inappropriate because we do not fully understand what is being communicated. When someone is speaking to us, we are doing one of four things. We are *ignoring* them, which is not listening to them at all, *pretending to* listen where we are really ignoring them but we act like we are not, *selectively listening* where we only hear certain parts of the conversation, or *attentively listening* where we are paying attention and are focused on what is being said. We can repeat to the person what was said with clarity.

The highest form of listening is *empathic listening.* Empathic listening is listening with the intent to learn—not reply. There is a major difference between listening and hearing. We can hear many things, but to gain wisdom and knowledge in what we are hearing, we are required to listen. You desire to understand how the other person feels and the logic behind that feeling. You are not analyzing why they feel the way they do or analyzing why they did what they did. Your desire is to forget about yourself and what you would have done or said in that situation and focus on gaining insight into their soul. When you listen in this manner, you make psychological deposits into their emotional bank account in the forms of appreciation, affirmation, and comprehension. When you listen to understand and not just to reply, you acquire accurate information to work with. Instead of guessing or assuming and using your thoughts, feelings, motives, or interpretations, you are able to get a clear inside look into another person's mind and heart. Being empathetic does not necessarily mean being sympathetic. Sympathy is a form of agreement and judgment. When you seek to really understand, you are not agreeing or disagreeing with a person or his or her situation. Your intent is to understand them and their unique situation as you connect with them emotionally and intellectually without judging, criticizing, or comparing. You may be saying, "Hey, I'm only seeking to be helpful and relate to the other person by drawing from my own personal experiences. What is wrong with that?" You may be sincere in wanting to share and advise, but there is a time for everything. Again, you must first understand and then be understood. I will explain what it means to be understood a little later. Most people respond before they have a deep understanding. We tend to respond in one of four ways.

1. Evaluate. You either agree or disagree.
2. Probe. You ask questions, not to understand the other person's thoughts or feelings but to validate from your own frame of reference or perspective.
3. Advise. You give advice or solutions to problems based on your own experiences.
4. Interpret. You try to figure people out. You explain motives and behaviors based on your motives, experiences, and behaviors.

Most married couples are so used to responding to each other in one of these four ways that, out of habit, they are not even aware that they do it. If this describes you, it is crucial that you recognize how you are reacting and realize that your partner may not even want a response from you. As men we sometimes have a tendency to go into "problem solving solution mode," and we interrupt and force our responses on our partners, because we know that we are going to have to listen to them talk for at least two hours. In order to bypass all of that listening, we would rather save ourselves an hour and forty-five minutes and give our response before they can finish expressing themselves. When this happens, we are perceived by our women to be intrusive, unloving, and unwilling to understand them, which can cause women to shut down. Even if your intentions are to help, giving advice or evaluating without being asked to do so may backfire on you in the long run.

So how do you listen with the intent to understand and learn not reply?

When you or someone else speaks, the meaning of what is being communicated comes from three sources: word choice, body language, and tone. When you are focused visually, you are able to pick up on nonverbal cues that are being communicated through the body language of the person. When you listen with your heart, you listen to the tone and inflection of the person's voice to identify how they are feeling or what they felt. When you listen with your ears, you comprehend the words that are being said. Ten percent of what people communicate is verbal, while the other ninety percent is nonverbal.

There are three skills that enhance empathic listening.
1. Rephrasing content.
2. Reflecting on feelings.
3. Asking questions for clarity.

When you rephrase what is being said, you take the meaning and put it into your own words. When you reflect feelings, you concentrate on how the other person feels or felt. When you

combine rephrasing content and reflecting feelings, you gain a deeper understanding of what is being communicated. Finally, when you ask questions for clarity, you are not probing but seeking to clarify what is being said to reach mutual understanding.
After you have been successful in understanding the other person, the next part of effective communication is being effectively understood. To have influence with other people, they must first feel that you understand them. Once they are understood, more than likely they will be open to listening to your ideas or receive advice or counsel from you. Effective understanding and then being effectively understood is part of the foundation of having successful Win-Win relationships. In order to be understood it is imperative that you have the vocabulary, the insight, the knowledge and skills to effectively communicate so you can be understood. You have to be willing to go through the laborious process of gathering and extracting the information. In order to be fully understood you must use brevity. Brevity is so important because the human attention span is so short and you don't have long to say what you need to say before you lose their attention. Trust is at the center of being understood by someone else. When someone is open to listening to you and receive advice from you, it is usually because they perceive you to be credible. It takes having a strongly developed character, competence, emotional sensibility and great reasoning skills to become credible. Every relationship will have challenges in the area of communication. As a married couple, you may have different communication styles that you are comfortable with. If there is a breakdown in the marital communication lines you do not have to let it be a stumbling block but instead, let it be a stepping-stone to effective marital communication as you make the marital adjustment and begin to start seeking to understand the other person before you are understood.

Here are eight ways to becoming a better empathic listener in a marriage relationship.
- Start off by saying, "You have my undivided attention; I'm listening."
- Set your own agenda aside and focus on the other person.
- Learn to appreciate the other person's point of view, even if you disagree.
- Listen without interruption. Do not be in a hurry to take over the conversation.
- Place yourself in the other person's situation.
- Rephrase, reflect and ask questions for better clarification.
- Be sensitive to the other person's feelings.
- Do not offer your advice or recommendations until asked to do so.
- Ask the person, "Are you looking for a listening ear or advice from me?"

Chapter 23

Marital Interdependent Cooperation

Men and women are different. Not wrong, just different.

As a man, to effectively cooperate with your girlfriend/fiancée/wife, you must bring yourself to the realization that she is not you. She is different from you. Cooperative interaction is being synergistic. When you have synergy between you and your spouse, you have effective cooperation.

"Two people can accomplish more than twice as much as one; they get a better return for their labor." Ecclesiastes 4:9

Synergy is the interaction of two or more people working in a spirit of harmony where their combined effort is greater than the sum of their individual efforts. In marriage, it simply means that two people working together effectively will produce a greater result than by attempting to reach the same result individually. The principle of cooperation is applying synergy to your marital relationship. The way you become a synergized couple is by first accepting and valuing each other's differences. As a man I must understand and realize that my girlfriend, fiancée or wife may not see the world in the same way I do. She may not see the circumstances or situations the same way I do, and I must accept it and value it because I accept and value her. She is not wrong, just different. She is pink and I am blue. It takes being humble to recognize that as a man I do not know it all and I have limitations. My humility and respect for differences allows me to appreciate the knowledge, skills, and intellect that will be available through interaction with my future wife. Some married men can be so narrow minded that they believe that it is their way or the highway.

This limited way of thinking can put you, your family and loved ones in an unfavorable situation because of your stubbornness to listen to rational ideas and the advice of others. An intelligent husband will embrace his wife's thinking even if it is different from his. He will cooperate with her as he values her opinions and ideas. When faced with a difference of opinion, you can respond in the following ways.

1. **Attack** -You put down the other person's ideas and become defensive because of fear.
2. **Tolerate-**You put up with the idea but do not accept its legitimacy.
3. **Value-**You value and see the opportunity in having new information from a different perspective.
4. **Celebrate-**You seek out and embrace individuals with different ideas, learning from those differences. A noble husband understands and values the differences his wife has because he knows that it adds value to his life. It is possible for two people to perceive the same picture but see something completely different. What do you see? Do you see an old lady or a young woman?

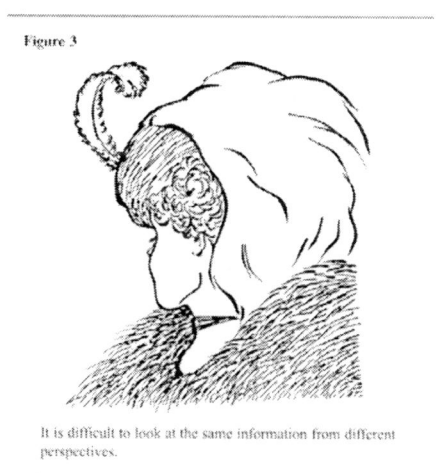

Figure 3

It is difficult to look at the same information from different perspectives.

If you take a glass of water and fill it halfway, is the glass half full or half empty? It just depends on who is looking at the glass of water. When I value and respect your perceptions and differences and understand that we may be both right, I'm open to the fact that life is not always an either/or. There is almost always a third alternative, but I must be willing to embrace the differences in people that make them unique. The glass may be half full or half empty but a third alternative is that the water is taking up half of the glass.

Once you believe and change your thinking to understand that differences are strengths and not weakness, you will be open to finding new alternatives. You move from the mentality of "my way or the highway" to "It's not my way or your way but a better way for us."

Here are five steps to finding a better way.

1. Define the problem or opportunity.
2. Listen to the other person. Seek first to understand then to be understood.
3. Share your views in love and with a respectful tone.
4. Brainstorm ideas and options together.
5. Find and agree on the best solution together for everyone.

It is possible to value the differences in other people. You do not have to agree with a person; you merely affirm that that person's opinion is just as valuable as yours. Synergy in a relationship allows you to look past your two alternatives, my way and the wrong way, to a third alternative, a better way, where everyone wins. In a marriage, coming together is the beginning, staying together is a process but cooperating as you make steady progress toward your goals as a married couple is marital success! Couples who pray together tend to stay together.

Pray Together Stay Together

The book of Ephesians 4:26 and 27 gives married couples advice pertaining to anger. It says, **"And don't sin by letting anger control you. Don't let the sun go down while you are still angry. For anger gives a mighty foothold to the devil."**

A foothold is a firm or secure position that provides a base for further advancement. In marriage unresolved anger gives Satan a mighty secure position in the marital relationship. When a foothold is present it allows Satan to further advance his program and implement his strategy, which is to bring shame to God by manipulating your thinking, emotions, and will with the goal of the separation and divorce of your spouse.

Joseph Murphy in his book, *The Power of Your Subconscious Mind* outlines three steps on how to keep harmony in the marriage by praying together as a couple.

The following is an excerpt on prayer from his book *The Power of Your Subconscious Mind*.

1. The First Step: Never carry over from one day to another accumulated irritations from little disappointments. Be sure to forgive each other for any sharpness before you go to sleep. The moment you awaken in the morning, claim that God is guiding you in all your ways. Send out loving thoughts of peace, harmony, and love to your marriage partner, to all members of the family, and to the whole world.

2. The Second Step: Say grace at breakfast. Give thanks for the wonderful food, for your abundance, and for all your blessings. Make sure that no problems, worries, or arguments shall enter into the table conversation; the same applies at dinnertime. Say to your wife or husband, "I appreciate all you are doing, and I radiate love and good will to you all day long."

3. The Third Step: The husband and wife should alternate in praying each night. Do not take your marriage partner for granted. Show your appreciation and love. Think appreciation and good will, rather than condemnation, criticism, and nagging. The way to build a peaceful home and a happy marriage is to use a foundation of love, mutual respect, romance, sexual fulfillment, harmony, faith in God and all things good. Read the 23rd, 27th, and 91st Psalms, the 11th chapter of Hebrews, the 13th chapter of I Corinthians, and other texts of the Bible before going to sleep. As you practice these truths, your marriage will grow more and more blessed through the years.

Chapter 24

Self-Renewal

To execute the seven previously listed relational principles, you must be physically, spiritually, mentally and socially/emotionally healthy. These four dimensions of your being give you the power to practice and execute the seven principles that will lead you to marital success. Personal renewal is the act of making sure you are staying strong physically, spiritually, mentally, and socially/emotionally. This is important because it will allow you to be alert, sharp and effective in your personal life as well as in whatever relationship you involve yourself in.

Self-renewal is vital in maintaining balance. Living an effective life is about balance. Life and its demands have a way of draining our energy. The challenges that a marriage brings will inevitably cause wear and tear on you physically, emotionally, spiritually and socially. Renewal and revival allow you to recharge yourself so that you can continue to operate at a high level within the marriage relationship. There are four areas where you and I need renewal. These four areas are physical, spiritual, mental, and social/emotional.

Physical Renewal. Physical renewal consists of having a nutritious diet, adequate fitness, and getting sufficient amounts of rest and relaxation. The foods you eat provide the energy your body needs to function. Just like you need to put high quality fuel in your car for optimal performance, your body needs to be fed healthy energy-producing foods every day for optimal performance. The types of foods you eat or don't eat will have a profound effect on your mood, mental state, and overall body functions.

Our body has fifteen systems that carry out different functions. They are:

- Circulatory system
- Cardiovascular system
- Digestive system
- Endocrine system
- Immune system
- Integumentary system
- Muscular system
- Nervous system
- Reproductive system
- Respiratory system
- Skeletal system
- Urinary system
- Excretory system
- Sensory system
- Lymphatic system

When you become more aware and pay greater attention to your diet, you increase the vitality of these systems, which equate to a longer, healthier life. What if you should walk around the block everyday for your good health, but you don't? Most people have heard the saying, "An apple a day keeps the doctor away." What if it were true? Would it be worth it and easy to eat an apple a day to have great health? Physical renewal is having a great exercise regimen. It also deals with flexibility, endurance, and strength. Your heart is a muscle that you can't exercise directly. It can only be exercised through the large muscle groups. This is why it is important to perform exercises like rapid walking, running, biking, or swimming. Not everyone will have the same exercise workout plan. It should be tailored to the type of lifestyle you have.

Finally, getting plenty of rest is important to maintain a physically healthy body.

The sleep requirements for each person depend on many factors, including age. For example, in general:

- Infants require about 16 hours a day.
- Teenagers need about 9 hours a day.
- Most adults need 7 to 8 hours a night to feel recharged, although some people may need as few as 5 hours or as many as 10 hours of sleep each day.

However, experts say that if you feel drowsy during the day, even during boring activities, you haven't had enough sleep. The amount of sleep a person needs also increases if he or she has been deprived of sleep in previous days. Getting too little sleep creates a "sleep debt," which will demand that the debt is paid.

Too little sleep may cause:

- Memory problems
- Depression
- A weakening of your immune system, increasing your chance of becoming sick. When you are well rested and you incorporate a healthy diet with the right amount of exercise, you have more patience and are a friendlier person. Be proactive and develop a diet and exercise program that you can adapt to your life.

Spiritual Renewal. The spiritual dimension is our core. It is who we are when no one else is around. It is the real you. What you hold as your core values and beliefs lie within your spirit. The essence of spiritual renewal is to refocus and or meditate on your purpose in life and what is important to you. We sometimes get confused or sidetracked about what is important and urgent and what is not. When you spend time renewing your spirit, you get in touch with your innermost thoughts, feelings, desires, and reexamine your value system to determine whether you are living what you believe. It is realigning your beliefs to your actions through whatever process you feel comfortable engaging in. For me, it involves prayer, reading the scriptures from the Bible, and listening to other influential religious and motivational speakers. I also find that reading inspirational books provide a type of spiritual renewal for me. When I have a deep understanding of my core beliefs, I have self-awareness of where I excel and where I come up short. Before you can win and have success outwardly, you must first win the battles within the mind. Within the mind is where the battles of the life are won and lost. As I renew my spirit inwardly I feel renewed, strengthened, and refocused to serve outwardly.

Mental Renewal. Every day we are exposed to all sorts of stimulus ranging from the television to the radio and Internet. The information we receive is not always positive or conducive to having a sound mind.

"And do not be conformed to this world, but be transformed by the renewing of your mind, that you may prove what is the good, acceptable, and the perfect will of God." Romans 12:2

We must be careful what we allow into our minds. What we spend the majority of our time thinking about has a way of showing itself through our actions.

Mind renewal consists of exercising the mind. To exercise the mind and to keep it sharp and alert, it is highly recommended that you enroll yourself in a continuing educational program where books become the weights you use to strengthen your mind. Not only is reading very beneficial but journal writing as well strengthens and renews the mind. When you read, you have access to new information, and it allows you to keep up with the ever-changing world. It also gives you the opportunity to expand your experiences through others. It is said that the person who does not read is no different than the person who cannot read. Set realistic goals for yourself to read one book a month, and then move to one book every two weeks and so forth. Make it a point to set aside one hour a day to renew yourself in the three mentioned areas. Decide that you will wake up an hour earlier and start your day off stretching for 10 minutes and then doing a light aerobic exercise for 10 minutes. Next meditate and envision what kind of day you are going to have. Pray for 10 minutes. Finally, read for 30 minutes. Spending an hour each day renewing your body, spirit, and mind will improve every aspect of your life. It will give you clarity and the energy and strength you will need to handle the difficult challenges of life.

Social/Emotional Renewal. A socially and emotionally stable husband is a person who can operate in an interdependent relationship with his wife. Being social means seeking or enjoying the companionship of others by being friendly and gregarious. Being emotional is the part of the consciousness that involves feelings and sensibility. Many times we can become socially and emotionally drained, where we do not seek the companionship of others by being friendly or gregarious. We can become numb to the feelings of others, which makes us insensitive. To carry out Win-Win agreements and to effectively communicate and cooperate, you must be socially and emotionally stable. An effective spouse is a person who renews himself or herself daily, not allowing negative emotions and situations to make them unloving or disrespectful.

Here's what emotionally stable people don't do:

1. They don't take other people's behaviors personally.
2. They don't get caught up in petty arguments and drama.
3. They don't just react (they respond mindfully).
4. They don't get stuck thinking the world is ending.
5. They don't tie their present emotions to past negativity.
6. They don't try to escape change.
7. They don't try (or pretend) to be perfect.
8. They don't spew hate at themselves.

Investing in our emotional wellness helps us get the most out of life. When we are emotionally stable, we feel more balanced and we are able to effectively operate interdependently in a marriage relationship. We become more productive, better at making decisions, more attentive, and more fulfilled.

Part 2

Protecting The Marriage Relationship

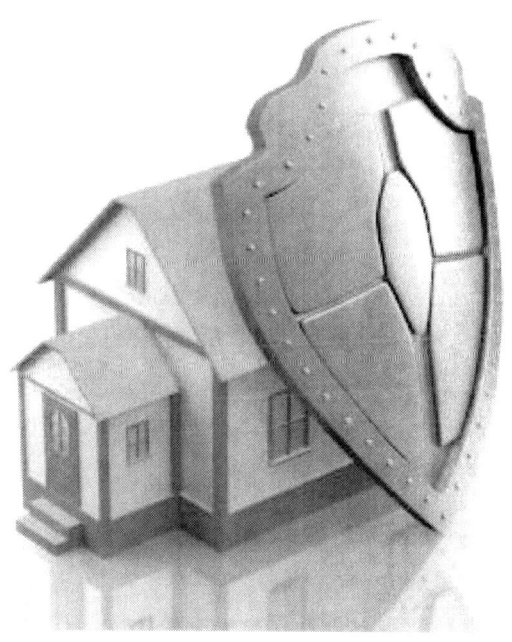

All great things will be attacked. – Jim Rohn

Chapter 25

Protection

The responsibility of the husband in a marriage relationship is to defend or protect the marriage against anyone or anything that seeks to attack, bring danger or dismantle it. This includes himself. The wife is to assist him in this effort.

Together as a team, a husband and wife must be willing to consistently protect and look out for each other.

A husband is similar to a law enforcement officer. The two main responsibilities of a law enforcement officer are to serve and protect. A successful husband maintains order, prevents and detects misconduct, and enforces the laws. Men and women do not have biblical authority to make laws pertaining to biblical marriage. God has already done that. He has defined what biblical marriage is and how a man and a woman are to function in marriage. A husband is called to serve and protect his wife, family and the community.

"You can not play with the animal in you without becoming wholly animal, play with falsehood without forfeiting your right to the truth. He who wants to keep his garden tidy doesn't reserve a plot for weeds." - Dan Hammarskjold

When God placed Adam in the garden, He instructed him to not only develop it but to keep it. The word "keep" means to protect. God instructs Adam to protect the garden from Satan because God recognized Satan's nature was to bring confusion, destruction, and death to the environment that God placed Adam in. If you look at the majority of failed marital relationships today, they have the residue of confusion, destruction, and death on them.

Weeds In The Marital Garden

Every gardener's dream is to have a garden free of pesky weeds that threaten the health of vegetables, fruits, and flowers. Maintaining a garden free of weeds takes consistency and dedication, but the effort is certainly worth it. Weeds come in various forms, so it is important to be able to distinguish them from your vegetables, fruits, and flowers. Weeds are a serious agricultural problem. They rob vegetables, fruits, and plants of sunlight, water, and nutrients. They also provide hiding places for insects and serve as a source of vegetable and fruit diseases. It is important to control weeds while they are small and before they get out of control. Most weeds can be controlled and kept from becoming serious problems in the garden. Methods of control include hand-pulling, mulching, and ***cultivation***. Remember Adam was to cultivate or develop the garden and provide a garden full of abundant fruit. Just as there are weeds in a garden, there are weeds that tend to sprout up in marriage relationships.

"And God blessed them, and God said unto them, be fruitful, and multiply, and replenish the earth." Genesis 1:28

You cannot be fruitful or have a functional family in a marriage full of weeds. They will rob the marriage of love, respect, trust, joy and all other life producing attributes necessary to sustain a healthy, fruitful relationship. They provide hiding places for additions and serve as a source of emotional, spiritual, social, and physical diseases. The good news is that just like weeds in a physical garden they can be controlled and kept from becoming a serious problem in the marriage garden. Please understand it is very likely that your marriage will have weeds sprout up from time to time, so do not despair. Having knowledge about weeds in your marriage garden is a start, but it will not be enough to stop their destructive course of action. You must be willing to do something about it and not let them get out of control. If you are willing to make a conscious and consistent effort to eradicate them whenever they show themselves, you will allow your marriage garden to flourish and be healthy, bearing abundant fruit.

Chapter 26

The Weeds Of Sexual Immorality

Paul the Apostle, who wrote much of the New Testament of the Bible, gives numerous warnings to avoid sexual immorality. He writes and describes in 1 Thessalonians chapter four how believers of Christ should conduct themselves as it pertains to sexual fulfillment.

Thessalonica is a city northeast of Greece on an inlet of the Aegean Sea. Today, it is a major port and the second-largest city in Greece. The church established at Thessalonica during Paul's ministry had a very young congregation. These were young believers who had just recently accepted the message of Jesus Christ. Because they were young Christians, they needed to mature in their faith. Paul established the church of Thessalonica during his second missionary journey at about 51 A.D. He wrote Thessalonians a short time later to encourage and support the young believers who lived there. Paul strongly desired these young believers of Christ and us to understand that our conduct should match our faith. If we say we are Christians, then we should act like it and live a Christian lifestyle. Paul wanted them to also understand that being a Christian was more than just having good intentions and good resolutions; it meant making the right actions and choices. Paul understood that when we accepted Jesus as our Savior we entered into a continuing education program. The more we know about Christ, the more we are being changed to be like Him. Paul knew this would be a life-long process and that inappropriate sexual conduct is detrimental to spiritual growth. So in Chapter four, Paul challenges the Thessalonians to live a sexually pure life by pleasing God in their daily living by avoiding sexual immorality.

"One final word, friends. We ask you—urge is more like it—that you keep on doing what we told you to do to please God, just as you learned from us. You are aware of the guidelines we laid out for you from the Master Jesus. God wants you to live a pure life. Keep yourselves from sexual promiscuity. Learn to appreciate and give dignity to your body, not abusing it, as is so common among those who know nothing of God."

1 Thessalonians 4:1-5

God created sex and had several things in mind when He did. Consider the following:

1. To propagate the race
2. To provide mutual pleasure in marriage.
3. To reduce sexual temptation.
4. To create mutual ownership.
5. To produce a unique union and means of communication, cooperation, and interaction between a man and woman that is not possible on any other level.

The standard of being faithful in your sexual lifestyle starts with Jesus. Before you can be faithful to your spouse in marriage, you must demonstrate faithfulness to Christ. Choosing to be faithful to Him in the decisions and actions you make, pertaining to how you interact with yourself and others, shows faithfulness to Him. By choosing to reject what Christ has called you to do by not keeping yourself holy, you turn your heart against Him even before you turn your heart against your spouse.

In the book *The Act of Marriage,* Tim and Beverly LaHaye share a powerful message concerning the sacredness of marriage. The following is an excerpt from their book. "Marriage is really a sexual contract exclusively between two people of the opposite sex who have made this promise: 'to keep you and only you unto me so long as we both shall live.' That is why it is not something to be done hurriedly or without careful consideration but deliberately and in the will of God. For it involves giving your body to another person as long as you both shall live. This exchange of ownership of one's body with another is a decision that should last a lifetime. God obviously had many purposes in mind when He deliberately created our sexual capabilities, from reproduction to pleasure to unique union. Like all things He created, it is all very good. As with many of His wonderful gifts to humankind, it is only when we distort it and misuse it that it becomes twisted and ugly. Sex in marriage is beautiful, enriching, and fulfilling when practiced as He directed—but only in marriage. Adultery, fornication, homosexuality, promiscuity and other forms of sexual abuse become ugly, harmful, and life shortening. All people have the same choice about the use of their sex drive. They can obey God and confine its expression to marriage, which He calls sacred, or they can adopt the standards of the world and become promiscuous." I strongly recommend purchasing and reading this book. *The Act of Marriage* has sold over 2,500,000 copies and is a must-read for anyone desiring to educate themselves on how to have a great marriage.

"Don't you realize that your bodies are actually parts of Christ? Should a man take his body, which belongs to Christ, and join it to a prostitute? Never!" 1 Corinthians 6:15

Well, as followers of Christ, Christ is spiritually attached to us through his death on the cross for our sins. Our bodies are the members of Christ. Knowing this, we should not indulge in sexually immoral acts because Jesus is right there when or if we decide to participate. In a sense we say, "Jesus, I want to have sex outside of the boundaries that you have assigned and established. I could care less that you call it a sin. I don't see it that way. I also want to continue to watch porn and masturbate to it. I just hope my boyfriend/girlfriend, fiancé/fiancée or husband/wife doesn't find out. I know you are against porn and premarital sex, but this is what I want to do. I want to stop, but then again I kind of don't want to stop. I know it hurts you that I am disobedient and I know you feel some kind of way because of all you have done for me but I just don't care. I am horny and I want to have sex with whom ever I choose, period! I don't want to sacrifice my sexual desires and operate with self-control. Who does that these days? I don't want to sacrifice and honor you the way you have sacrificed for me and extended endless grace and mercy to me. I want to be selfish and I will continue to be selfish, but I still want you to love me unconditionally and bless me abundantly." How many people think like this and have a mindset that resembles this scenario?

God hates sin and cannot stand to be in its presence. He will judge all sins and the world. So before you can be faithful in a marriage relationship, you must be faithful to Christ in your salvation.

During the time when Paul was writing this letter to the Thessalonians, sexual standards were very low. It was common to have multiple sexual partners because this was the norm. In some cultures sexual encounters were part of the worship experience. Thus the new believers in Thessalonica shared some of these beliefs about sex, and Paul was challenging them and teaching them about what God had to say about being sexually pure as a single person and in the marriage relationship. Paul was teaching the benefits of sexual purity and the consequences of sexual immorality.

The Weed of Adultery and Illegal Sex

"Drink water from your own well. Share your love only with your wife. Why spill the water of your springs in public, having sex with just anyone? You should reserve it for yourselves. Don't share it with strangers. Let your wife be a fountain of blessing for you. Rejoice in the wife of your youth."

Proverbs 5: 5-19

To drink water from your own well is symbolic of faithfulness in marriage. In desert lands, water was and is the most important resource you can have. It was considered a crime to steal water from someone else's well, just as it is a crime to commit adultery or an illegal sexual act. Solomon is stating that a man or woman should only engage in sexual activity with their spouse to prevent danger to themselves and family.

What is adultery or an affair? It is a form of extramarital sex. It is sexual infidelity to one's spouse. What is fornication or unauthorized sex? It is sex that takes place outside the boundaries of biblical marriage. These acts include oral sex, masturbation, pornography, anal sex, dry humping (*grinding on each other with your clothes on*) penile/virginal penetration, stimulating or kissing of genital areas or erotic areas, fore play, twelve play and intimate tongue kissing. Sex with animals and relatives is also considered unauthorized sex inside or outside of a marriage covenant. Please note that masturbation and pornography are not permitted within the boundaries of a marriage covenant. The weeds of adultery and unauthorized sex have been damaging and killing dating and marriage relationships for centuries. This particular weed never seems to go away no matter what you do to prevent it from appearing in the marriage garden. Know that it is a pesky weed, and you have to be on constant guard and be willing to protect your marriage garden from it. This weed will show itself anytime and anywhere in your marriage garden and must be eradicated before it matures into a weed that consumes and kills the entire marriage garden.

We were created to be dependent on God, independent of other human beings but operate interdependently with them. Within our independence we are to function interdependently with other people to achieve that which we would not be able to achieve alone. God is the only entity who can solely operate independently without the need of another person to achieve a greater level of success operating interdependently. According to the Bible, God created the heavens and the earth.

God created marriage and He created sex. God does not forbid sexual sins to be mean or difficult. He does not get upset that two warm bodies are coming together sexually. His issue is that something so sacred and holy is being viewed and treated so cheaply. God is all-knowing, and He knows the power it has to destroy us physically, emotionally, and spiritually and the benefits it brings to a man and woman in a monogamous marriage. God does not take this lightly and neither should we. God is well aware that unauthorized, unhealthy sexual habits, addictions, and actions have destroyed families, marriages, churches, businesses, communities, and even nations. He desires to protect us from hurting and injuring others and ourselves. So He offers to take our loneliness, voids, and desires and meet these needs with Himself. God created sex primarily to inaugurate a covenant between a man and a woman in the marriage relationship. You have the inauguration, or consummation after you become a married couple—not before. As a married couple—not a dating couple—it was used as a reminder of the covenant established by the man and woman when they exchanged their marital vows, much like the purpose of communion is to remember Jesus and the covenant He has established with us through the cross. Sex was also created for procreation and for pleasure as an expression of love and synergy between a husband and his wife—not with a partner in a dating or casual relationship. Sexual fulfillment is to be reserved for the marital relationship only according to God's instructions found in the Bible. Everything God does, He does for a purpose. In doing so, when we obey Him, it brings order and stability to our lives. God does give us the choice to go against how He has said we are to live, but you or I will not experience the order and stability that comes from being obedient to Him. Having sex outside the boundaries of marriage is like using a credit card; its fun until you get the bill and then have to pay the compound interest. Authentic and holy sexual experiences must be limited to the marriage relationship to avoid injuring ourselves, our relationship with God, and our relationship with others.

"The person who has self-discipline understands the emotion of sex, respects it, and learns from it to control it and converts it into constructive activities." –Napoleon Hill

Negative Consequences Due To

Over-Indulgence of Sex

- The greatest damage is that it depletes the source of a man's greatest driving force, and wastes, without adequate compensation, man's creative force.
- It dissipates energy needed by nature to maintain physical health. Sex is nature's most useful therapeutic force.

- It depletes the magnetic energy, which is the source of an attractive personality.
- It removes the sparkle from one's eyes and set up discord in the tone of one's voice.
- It destroys enthusiasm, subdues ambition, and leads inevitably to the habit of drifting on all subjects and endeavors.

Sexual Energy Transmuted

Controlled sex supplies the magnetic force that attracts people to one another. It is the most important factor of a pleasing personality.

Sex is a virtue when it is controlled and directed constructively in a monogamous marriage. It becomes a liability when it is directed towards acts of lust. Here are some of the advantages of exercising self-control in the area of sexual expression.

- It gives quality to the tone of voice and enables one to convey through the voice any feeling desired.
- It gives motive-power to one's desires.
- It keeps the nervous system charged with energy needed to carry on the work of maintaining the body.
- It sharpens the imagination and enables one to create useful ideas.
- It gives quickness and definiteness to one's physical and mental movements.
- It gives one persistence and perseverance in the pursuit of one's major purpose in life.
- It is a great antidote for all fear.
- It gives one immunity against discouragement.

- It helps master laziness and procrastination.
- It gives one physical and mental endurance while undergoing any form of opposition or defeat.
- It gives one the fighting qualities necessary under all circumstances for self-defense.
- In brief it makes winners and not quitters.

The Weed of Masturbation

The weed of masturbation is a weed that no one seems to want to talk about but is as dangerous as any other sexual weed. Masturbation is when you sexually satisfy yourself by rubbing, touching or caressing your genital areas for sexual pleasure; that is, you are having sex with yourself. This may lead you to believe that you are not committing an illegal sexual act because you are not involving anyone else in the act physically, but in actuality you are abusing yourself sexually, emotionally and spiritually.

"And if your right hand causes you to sin, cut it off and throw it away. It is better for you to lose one part of your body than for your whole body to go into hell." Matthew 5:30

Just as taking a knife and cutting your wrist is harmful to your body, masturbation damages your way of thinking emotionally, sexually and spiritually. Masturbation is an unhealthy sexual outlet. When you masturbate, you receive a feeling from it that brings sexual pleasure. In a man, it is climaxed in ejaculation. In a woman it is done through an orgasm. When God institutionalized marriage, He designed it in a way where the man and woman would operate inter-dependently to meet each others' mental, physical, emotional, and sexual needs. In 1 Corinthians chapter 7, Paul the apostle gives advice to married couples and men and women who are single who desire to get married.

"Nevertheless, because of sexual immorality, let each man have his own wife, and let each woman have her own husband." 1 Corinthians 7:2

Some Christians wrote Paul letters asking if it was good to live a celibate life. Paul responds by saying, "Nevertheless..." What Paul is saying here is that although it is good to live a celibate life, there is a lot of sexual immorality in the present day culture. To counter the sexual immorality plaguing the culture, each man should have one wife and each woman should have one husband. This cancels out having multiple girlfriends or wives as a husband and if you are a wife, it cancels out having multiple boyfriends or husbands. The interesting thing is as a single or married person, when you have sex outside of the marital relationship, you become one with the other person. Becoming one with a person is a form of marriage. What you have in this scenario is an unauthorized, illegal marriage not recognized and stamped by God's covenant of marriage. There are many single and married people who have multiple unauthorized marriages. These unauthorized connections tend to cause dysfunction within God's covenant of marriage. And it should be noted that another man cannot be a wife and another woman cannot be a husband; that is, two men or two women cannot have a legitimate marriage recognized by God according to Paul.

"The wife does not have authority over her body, but the husband does. Likewise the husband does not have authority over his body, but the wife does." 1 Corinthians 7:4

The word *authority* means the right to control, command and determine. Before marriage, as a single Christian your sexual authority belongs to God. You do not have the authority or authorization to satisfy yourself sexually outside of marriage or through masturbation, illegal sexual encounters, or pornography because when you accepted Jesus Christ as your Lord and Savior you gave up the right to control, command, or determine how you engage your body sexually.

"There is more to sex than mere skin to skin. Sex is as much a spiritual mystery as it is a physical act. As written in Scripture, "The two become one." Since we want to become spiritually one with the Master, we must not pursue the kind of sex that avoids commitment and intimacy, leaving us more lonely than ever—the kind of sex where we can never "become one." There is a sense in which sexual sins are different from all others. In sexual sin we violate the sacredness of our own bodies, these bodies that were made for God-given and God-modeled love, for "becoming one" with another. Or didn't you realize that your body is a scared place, the place of the Holy Spirit? Don't you see that you can't live however you please, squandering what God paid such a high price for? The physical part of you is not some piece of property belonging to the spiritual part of you. God owns the whole works. So let people see God in and through your body."

1 Corinthians 6: 16-20 (MSG)

When you masturbate you are not glorifying God with your body and in your spirit. You are thinking about lustful thoughts and fantasizing about sexual encounters as you engage yourself in a sexually inappropriate way. Jesus spoke about inappropriate fantasizing in Matthew chapter five. Masturbation is an unhealthy sexually, emotionally and spiritually damaging habit.

What Paul is saying is that when a man and woman get married and become united as one, they lose the right to control, command, or determine when their spouse can receive sexual gratification from them. Remember, with masturbation you control, command,

and determine when you will give yourself sexual pleasure. You do not have to rely on God or your spouse and, as a result, this leads to underdeveloped self-control and discipline. This unhealthy habit also takes God's authority and your spouse's access to that authority over your body away, causing a selfish weed to be planted in your inner soul and in the garden of your marital relationship.

When you have a habit of self-stimulating yourself sexually before marriage and you bring that habit into the marriage, you short change your spouse and yourself from effectively sexually interdepending on each other. Your spouse is the only one who has the legitimate authority and authorization to satisfy you sexually. Before marriage, the habit of masturbation causes you to be in a self-seeking mindset when it comes to trusting your future marriage partner to meet your sexual needs interdependently because they will have access to your sexual authority. Masturbation creates a habit of personally satisfying yourself when God never designed your sexual organs to be handled in this fashion. In God's design of interdependent sex, your sexual organs were made for your spouse only, not your hands or manmade sex toys used as substitutes for the real thing. You and I were designed by God to be released sexually by our spouse, causing an interdependent sexual bond in marriage. Masturbation is a way to not have to interdepend on your spouse for sexual fulfillment.

A wedding ring which the bride and groom give to each other during a marriage ceremony is usually made of gold, platinum, or silver. When you exchange rings at the marriage ceremony, what you are saying and expressing is, "God, my sexual authority belongs to you, but I would like you to grant this one person access to my sexual rights through this union of marriage." In so many words, you make the statement to your spouse saying, "As you receive and accept this ring that I have chosen to give to you, I give my whole self mentally, emotionally, physically, and sexually to you." Your rings symbolize the approved unlimited access of your sexual rights that belong to God to now be accessible to your spouse through the union of marriage. God gives you the option to choose who this person will be. In the marriage covenant, you agree to the terms and conditions of God's marital covenant, operating and functioning within the marriage manual He provides in His Word. The rings serve as a visual reminder that your sexual authority, which belongs to God is now also accessible to your spouse. When you get married, your husband or wife receives special authorization from God to be the only person authorized to release you sexually; you and I do not have the authority to engage ourselves in a sexual way through masturbation or unauthorized sex. The ownership of your sexual authority is not transferred to your spouse after the marriage ceremony, only legal access to engage you sexually is approved by God. Once married you must still remain faithful to God first, then to your spouse in marriage.

Physical, emotional, sexual and mental intimacy in a marriage in accordance with love, respect, trust and forgiveness was designed to keep a man and woman united or glued together. Why? God knew that as a married couple you would have challenges, conflicts and disagreements.

When you experience conflict or have disagreements with each other, both parties are more motivated to resolve the issue quickly because sexually they know that their spouse is the only person who is authorized by God to connect with them sexually. Not only that, God knew we would need a way to cleave or stay glued to one another. Sexual fulfillment is one of His strategies for making this possible. When you do get married, you bring with you the habits you possessed prior to marriage, whether good or bad. There is no magical wand that will change your habits during the wedding ceremony. Many men and women have entered into a marriage relationship with the masturbation habit. So when disagreements or conflict arise, there is a tendency for some to not resolve the skirmish so that they may sexually connect with one another and stay glued to each other. Instead, they default into the habit of masturbation or some other form of illegal sexual habit, which eventually causes sexual dysfunction within the marriage relationship.

So before you get married, you must be disciplined in how you manage your body as it pertains to masturbation so that when or if you do get married, instead of only now relying on God, you have another person who you rely on secondary to God.

What should you do if you get the urge to masturbate? My advice is to pray and ask God for strength and deliverance from this sexual vice. I also suggest you re-read this section on masturbation over and over until the desire goes away. You need reasons to stop and if you find enough reasons to stop you will change. Picture yourself overcoming the habit of masturbation. Begin repeating this passage found in Matthew 4:4. "It is written that man does not live by bread alone, but on every word that comes from the mouth of God." Visualize yourself not masturbating and imagine what your life would be like without you having to masturbate or it having control over you. Imagine yourself having and applying the self-control and discipline to say no to yourself. The idea is to begin seeing yourself being victorious in your mind, which will eventually be reflected in your actions.

Choose someone qualified to be your accountability partner and to pray with you. Everyday this person should ask you how your night and day was and if you masturbated in the past 24 hours. You being open and honest with them will help you break this unhealthy habit. The reason this is possible is because you are more inclined to change a behavior or habit when you have to answer to someone other than yourself.

When you choose not to rely on God or your spouse to meet your sexual needs, you will ultimately be more vulnerable and tempted to explore other illegitimate options for sexual fulfillment. One of these options is pornography, which I will discuss next. Your sexual authority belongs to God and he gives your marriage partner access to that authority through the union of marriage.

The Weed of Pornography

If the weed of masturbation had a cousin, it would be the weed of pornography.

"But I say, anyone who even looks at a woman with lust in his heart has already committed adultery with her in his heart. Or if your eye—even your good eye—causes you to lust, gouge it out and throw it away. It is better for you to lose one part of your body than for your whole body to be thrown into hell." Matthew 5:28, 29

The definitions of pornography are sexually explicit videos, pictures, writings, or other material whose primary purpose is to cause sexual arousal. Pornography excites sexual arousal in a way that is unhealthy, degrading, and lustful. It creates this fantasy in your mind that is unrealistic. Pornography paints false pictures of what women and men are. Your perception of what intimate lovemaking is becomes skewed and reduced to a barbaric, selfish, lustful experience.

How does pornography affect your desires and perception of sexuality? Pornography constitutes about twenty five percent of all search engine requests, and is the fourth most common reason people give for going on the Internet. The not so shocking truth is that pornography has profound consequences for the brain and acts in many ways like a drug. With prolonged exposure, your sexual tolerance is increased and many often find themselves addicted. If you are in a dating or marital relationship, there is a tendency to become bored and withdraw from your mate because they cannot provide you the sexual high you are looking for. You also may feel that you have to go out and manufacture this feeling another way. So the excitement of an affair or illegal sexual encounters outside of the marriage relationship is not far from your thoughts. Though pornography is not a physical substance, it leads to the same general loss of control, the compulsiveness to seek out the activity despite negative consequences and withdrawal when it goes away. Much like that of gambling or running for example. The issue is that continued exposure can cause long term or even life long neuro-plastic change in the brain. Dopamine is released as a reward whenever we accomplish something whether it be eating to sustain life or sexual activity to produce future life. And this dopamine consolidates neural connections in order to drive us to perform the same activity in the future. In other words, it alters the brain cells to motivate certain actions. It rewires your brain. The National Institute of Health measures drug addictiveness by testing rats. The rat is trained to press a button in order to get a drug, and the harder it works to acquire that drug indicates how addictive the substance is. It turns out that the more addictive a drug is the more dopamine we see released. While there is, unfortunately, no rat porn that can be given to male rats, we do know that dopamine is also released during sexual excitement which pornography plays right into.

The more time you spend watching it, the more dopamine gets released which reinforces the behavior and makes you not only desire it in the future but require it. And as you begin to imagine these images away from the computer or while having sex, they become reinforced. Furthermore, each orgasm releases even more dopamine, which consolidates the connections made during the session. It's a feedback loop that becomes harder to escape and just like a drug your tolerance for visual stimulation has now compounded, making it more difficult to be turned on by reality.

Pornography addiction can often lead to finding your mate less attractive; the good news is that it doesn't have to be permanent. Usually, when people understand the mechanism and realize that it's affecting their relationships, they can stop. The brain is often described as a use it or lose it system because the neural connections you stimulate grow stronger and desire to be activated while the ones you ignore become weakened. Much like your muscles, which if sitting still all day itch for activity but after prolonged non-use they become complacent. Luckily, because of our "use it or lose it" brain, the same neuro-plastic system that proliferates these habits can also be used to acquire healthier ones.

Continued consumption of pornography leads to structural rewiring of the brain causing the following.

1. Numbed pleasure response.
2. Hyper-reactivity to porn.
3. Willpower erosion as the frontal cortex changes.

Pornography takes that which is sacred between a husband and wife in the union of marriage and creates this fantasy of lust, selfishness, and mistrust. Pornography affects your self-respect, making it hard to respect others. It numbs your conscience as it captivates your curiosity. During this process, it feeds the heart and emotions, making you feel as though you cannot live without it. It creates unrealistic expectations, which cause you to compare what you see in the pornographic images and videos with what you experience in reality. So when or if your husband or wife does not measure up to what you saw in a particular video or magazine, you can start to feel as though you are missing out on something in your sexual experiences with your spouse. You can begin to feel frustrated because the other person does not engage you in the way you think he or she should and is holding back from you sexually. It also skews your ability to be sexually aroused. Now it is more difficult to get and keep an erection as a man because your sexual tolerance level has been affected due to the rewiring of your brain.

Erectile Dysfunction

"Due to the pornography available on the Internet, we are finding out that this type of sex dysfunction is a real entity," said David B. Samadi, MD, chairman of the urology department and chief of robotic surgery at Lenox Hill Hospital in New York City. "It is a problem in the brain, not the penis."

Porn can lead to unrealistic expectations that increase a person's tolerance for sex. Samadi likened the phenomenon to what occurs when someone consistently drinks more and more alcohol. Eventually, that person has a harder time feeling inebriated. The same happens with porn and sexual performance.

As a man, when you are naturally aroused sexually, a signal is sent from the brain to the penis that starts the process of the penis becoming and staying erect. As porn begins to rewire the brain, this signal becomes weaker and weaker which causes erectile dysfunction in most men who view porn regularly.

Most boys start watching pornography by age 10.

-Simon Lajeunesse, PhD

Internet porn is not sex. Porn leads to arousal addiction.

Internet Porn is Killing Men's Sexual Performance. A survey by the Italian Society of Andrology and Sexual Medicine, February, 2011

"It starts with lower reactions to regular porn sites which often times lead to exploring hard core porn sites. There is a general drop in libido, and in the end it becomes extremely difficult to have and maintain an erection." –Dr. Carlo Foresta, head of the Italian Society of Andrology and Sexual Medicine

Porn-Induced Erectile Dysfunction

Recovery Times

Once a man stops watching pornography, it typically takes a younger man 4-5 months for his brain to be rewired back to its default healthy sexual state and 2 months for older men.

When you view and/or masturbate to pornography what you are doing is injecting your sexual being with sex cocaine. You get this unbelievable high that takes you to ecstasy. When the high goes away, you begin to desire it again. Your mate cannot compete with this sex cocaine. If you are no longer interested in and no longer desire your spouse sexually and you have a difficult time being aroused by them, it could be because you have affected your natural sexual appetite through the rewiring of your brain.

Engaging in pornography and masturbation is self-abuse.

In my first marriage I allowed illegal sexual encounters, pornography, and masturbation to rob me of the sexual intimacy in my marriage. I placed unrealistic expectations on my wife and pressured her to do things that I saw in pornography. I was so addicted to porn; I would sometimes refuse to or not want to have sex with her because I was not interested in being intimate with her. All I wanted to do was watch porn and masturbate to it. My behavior played a major role in destroying our sexual intimacy and her self-esteem. It created a sexual dysfunction in our relationship. This sexual dysfunction in our marriage was being reinforced by pornography and me masturbating to it. My wife did not even know what she was fighting against. I acted cowardly because I was not man enough to tell her what I was doing and how I was abusing myself. I kept it a secret from everyone. Pornography and masturbation competed against my wife for my mind and heart, and I chose them over her. I was completely consumed and deceived that she had the problem and not me. At times, it was very challenging for me to achieve an erection and sustain one long enough for mutual sexual fulfillment. I could not appreciate what I had before me. The selfish acts of adultery, masturbation, and pornography led me to want more and more and more. I was addicted to a fantasy only to realize that it was not reality, and my flesh would never be satisfied. I became completely desensitized and less patient and kind to her. The very thing that a relationship is built on—love, respect, sexual fulfillment, and romance—was not being demonstrated by me in a healthy consistent manner. Please understand that it is hard to be respectful, loving, have healthy love making, and romance when you watch and feed yourself material that does not mirror respect, love, romance and healthy love making. By sharing my story, my honest desire is that if you are a man or woman who feeds your heart and mind pornography or masturbates to it that you would stop abusing yourself and seek the necessary help. You may claim that you watch pornography to learn how to please your spouse or that you and your spouse watch it together to spice up your relationship. This is not a wise thing to do. The weed of pornography will destroy a marriage if not taken out of the marriage garden.

"I made a covenant with my eyes not to look with lust at a young woman." Job 31:1

Job was a noble man. As I read this verse, I decided to make a covenant with my eyes too. I'm going to have the same attitude that Job had! Not only had he avoided committing adultery, but he was not guilty of lusting after women with his eyes or in his heart. Job recognized that this sin was different from the other sins and was determined to not let it trip him up. A wife competes daily with pornography and scantily dressed women on the Internet, television, in magazines and movies in this sex-crazed world. How refreshing would it be to her to know her husband had the mindset of Job? How refreshing would it be to know that he loves God so much that he won't make her uncomfortable with his wandering eyes but remain committed to her through his faithfulness to God? I believe it allows women to feel more secure in their relationships when their husbands take on this type of attitude of eye control. Our bodies are a combination of dust and spirit. How we conduct ourselves in regard to sexual purity affects our spirit. When we commit a sex sin, it hurts God because it shows that we prefer to follow our own desires instead of the desires of God and being led by the Holy Spirit. It deeply affects our personalities, which respond with depression and anguish when we harm ourselves physically and spiritually. During this period of our lives our personal devotion, worship, service and praise to God are often affected drastically.

What do you do if and when you get the urge to watch pornography? I would say that you should pray and read this section on pornography over and over until the desire goes away. Take out a sheet of paper and list all the reasons why pornography is damaging and abusive to you and your well-being. List the reasons why you want to stop and review this list daily. What has this toxic habit cost you in the past? Was it worth it? Picturing yourself overcoming pornography in your mind will eventually lead you to developing the self-discipline to regain control of your life. Here is a great affirmation to repeat found in Matthew 4:4. ***"It is written man does not live on bread alone, but on every word that comes from the mouth of God."***

Choose someone to be your accountability partner who will pray with you and hold you accountable. Everyday this person should ask you how your night and day was and if you watched pornography in the past 24 hours, encouraging and standing with you as you battle this unhealthy habit.

"Confess your sins to each other and pray for each other so that you may be healed. The earnest prayer of a righteous person has great power and wonderful results." James 5:16

As you are open and honest with those who hold you accountable they (note positive peer pressure) can help you replace this habit with a new healthier habit. This is because you are more inclined to change a behavior when you have to answer to someone other than yourself. A renewed feeling leads to a renewed attitude. A renewed attitude leads to renewed actions. Renewed actions lead to renewed habits.

The Weed of Sexual Denial

There are two exceptions where Paul states that you can deny your spouse sexual access to your body. In 1 Corinthians 7:3,5 Paul talks about these exceptions.

"The husband should not deprive his wife of sexual intimacy, which is her right as a married woman, nor should the wife deprive her husband which is his right as a married man."

1 Corinthians 7:3

"Do not deprive one another except with consent for a time that you may give yourselves to fasting and prayer; and come together again so that Satan does not tempt you because of your lack of self-control." 1 Corinthians 7:5

Paul addressed married couples about sexual denial; strongly suggesting that the only time they should deny their spouse sexually is if they both agree to not engage each other sexually for a set period of time for fasting or prayer. This is because you hold in your hands the access key to your spouse's sexual authority. They also hold the access key in their hands to your sexual authority. As a married couple each person is authorized by God to engage their spouse sexually. When you say no to your spouse for selfish, manipulative reasons and deny their rights to sexually engage you, you open up the door for Satan to tempt the other person to use masturbation, pornography, or an emotional or physical affair to satisfy their sexual needs. So this is one area in which you must not play marital games by being immature and selfish.

You may be thinking the following question, "Do I really have to rely solely on my spouse for sexual fulfillment?" "What if they are not physically able to have sex?" "What if I'm denied my sexual right to have sex with my spouse?" What then? Although you have the right to have unlimited sex with your spouse in marriage, choosing to address sexual denial in a loving, respectful, and tactful way is where you start. If your right is being denied for whatever reason, know that you do not own the sexual rights of your spouse; you only have access to them. God exclusively owns the sexual rights to you and your spouse. If the above is present in the marital relationship know that an agreement has been broken and must be rectified. You may be saying, "I never agreed to these terms." Actually, you did when you said "I do" and got married. Does this term ring a bell, **"FOR BETTER OR FOR WORSE?"** Many times when "worse times" come along, we want to pack up shop. Or, we feel it is an excuse to not be responsible in our actions. If you are the person being denied, you must not pursue illegal activity in the form of sexual selfish acts that causes you to sin against God who owns your sexual authority. Why? Because in God's eyes you are trespassing on His private property that you do not have legitimate ownership of.

"For God bought you with a high price. So you must honor God with your body." 1 Corinthians 6:20

It is during these difficult times of adversity and marital conflict that we must operate with integrity, faithfulness, discipline, courage and consideration while seeking to achieve win-win scenarios. If you are the person denying your spouse because of selfishness or immaturity, understand that God sees Himself in the person who is being denied. This is because of the access He has granted them to you and because of the agreed marital covenant you have established with your spouse. To deny your spouse their God given right to sexual fulfillment is to deny and reject God.

Why? We as humans were created in His image. As a married couple, God has granted sexual access of your body to your spouse. To deny God is to reject God, which is the ultimate sin. With this sin you experience the ultimate consequence: separation or divorce.

We need food and water to survive. We as humans can live up to 40 days without food but only 3 days without water. To a man, **respect** is like water and love is like food. He will not last long without her respect. To a woman, **love** is like water and respect is like food. She will not last long without his love.

Are you thirsty in your marriage? Many married men and women wish their spouse would offer them a refreshing drink of love, respect, sexual fulfillment and romance. There are a lot of spiritually, emotionally and sexually thirsty, dehydrated men and women in their marriage relationships, now looking for "water" to drink from someone else. Because someone is married to you, you become the only water source that person can drink from to quench his or her thirst for sexual fulfillment. But too often many water fountains have a sign attached to them that says, "Out of Order." Men and women have needs that must be met to keep themselves in balance. Balance is the key to life and happiness. As you commit yourself to a relationship, in this case the marriage relationship, it is important to know that God designed people to relate interdependently with the person they are married to in order to meet certain needs. Once we communicate effectively and clearly define what those needs are, it is up to the other person to do his or her best to meet those needs consistently. Men fundamentally need to feel respected, and women fundamentally need to feel loved. This is why in the Bible (Ephesians 5:33) men are commanded to love and women are commanded to respect. If a married man decides to no longer unconditionally love his wife for whatever reason or if she decides for whatever reason to stop unconditionally respecting her husband, what they by default have decided is to become an accomplice to a potential crime of infidelity, whether it is mental, emotional or physical.

According to the Bible, does a husband or wife have the right to deny his or her spouse sexual intimacy? The answer would be yes, but only for a mutually agreed amount of time for fasting and prayer. If you are denying your spouse any type of sexual satisfaction, the key here is that you both must agree that it is for prayer or fasting. One person in the relationship cannot force the other person to give in because they simply do not want to participate in the sexual experience. It must be a mutual agreement for a set time for praying and fasting.

Please note that when God grants access to the sexual authority of your body to your spouse when you get married, that person should not abuse that access. It is not access without limitations; each spouse must function under divine authority to have legitimate sexual access in a marriage. There will be situations when it may not be appropriate to engage in sexual relations. In these times, because of the love and respect that you have for each other, you may decide not to seek sexual fulfillment from your spouse. For example, if your spouse has the flu and is not feeling well, expecting sex from that person does not show love and respect, even though you have the legitimate marital right to do so. If you are physically forcing your spouse to have sex with you against their consent you are not operating with love and respect, courage or consideration. Submission in sex means to voluntarily go along with; it is a person's choice. Are you making the right choice? Are you a person who denies your spouse sexual or emotional fulfillment because you lack the maturity or are selfish, manipulative, unloving and disrespectful? Well, you may be considered an accomplice to the potential crime of infidelity.

Eternal Triangles

A sexual or romantic relationship among three people that involves jealousy or other emotional conflicts.

"Why do some married men become interested in other women, more than their wives? I think it is not an exaggeration to say that "eternal triangles" have their beginning when men discover the lack of interest by their wives, in their occupation. It is a part of a man's nature to seek close association with those who show a keen interest in his work. A man's ego needs food in the form of personal encouragement, admiration, and affirmation, and no one is in as favorable a relationship to support him as his wife."
–Andrew Carnegie

Unfaithfulness in marriage seems to be common in both men and women. It is usually initiated by having an emotional affair with a person of the opposite sex. Having an emotional affair often leads to having a physical affair. An emotional affair is not to be confused with getting godly advice from a credible person. A person giving godly advice should not be looking to capitalize on your vulnerability because of your emotional state and should encourage you to seek counseling as a couple. Be wise when selecting someone to discuss your relational or marital challenges. There are times where counseling and mediation are necessary for getting the relationship back on track. If you and your spouse decide to take this path together, it is wise to make sure that the person is highly qualified and credible to provide relational care. Not all advice is beneficial. Getting poor advice from an unqualified source will do more damage to the relationship than good. If there is an issue or concern in your relationship, deciding to work it out with your partner is the best way to approach mediation. As you become comfortable sharing information with certain people, you can emotionally and physically be drawn into that person you are sharing your feelings with. This can lead to an unfavorable outcome if the person you are sharing with does not possess character and integrity. When you give someone access to intimate information who is not a credible person, your innermost thoughts, feelings and decisions can be manipulated and you run the risk of committing an emotional or physical affair.

Accomplice to Adultery

The definition of an accomplice is an associate in wrongdoing, especially one who aids or abets another in a criminal act as a principle or an accessory person. When a person decides to commit adultery they are responsible for their choice. We are responsible for our own actions. As a partner or spouse to someone who has had an affair, you also have a choice to be or not to be apart of the logic or reasons for which your partner had an affair. Your mindset should be that if your husband or wife wants to have an affair, that you choose not to be an accomplice to his or her choice. If your spouse has been unfaithful to you, did you contribute to their unfaithfulness? As a woman are you respectful? As a man do you love her unconditionally?

When a man chooses to stop loving his wife consistently or all together because of past hurt, pride, resentment, jealously, unforgiveness, or unfaithfulness but has made a decision to remain in the relationship and hold her hostage to her past, he has decided to become an accomplice to the potential act of infidelity. When the need of feeling loved is not met, it can lead a woman to begin searching for someone who will love her. It is not about her deserving your unconditional love and forgiveness; it is about you obeying God to love and forgive despite what she does or does not do. It is about loving her apart from her performance because God loves you as an imperfect person.

When a woman decides that she will not respect and forgive her husband either consistently or not at all because of past hurt, pride, resentment, jealousy, unforgiveness, or unfaithfulness but has decided to remain in the relationship with him, she too has made a decision - whether she knows it or not - to become an accessory to a potential crime of infidelity. Her unconditional respect and forgiveness that she should freely give is nonexistent, and it can lead a man to begin searching for someone who will respect him. It is not about him deserving your unconditional respect and forgiveness; it is about you obeying God to respect and forgive despite what he does or does not do. It is about respecting him apart from his performance because God loves and respects you as an imperfect person.

All relationships and marriages have challenges. It can be devastating to find out that someone you love and trusted has been unfaithful to you. If this has happened to you, it was not your fault. That person decided to commit adultery on his or her own free will. However, it is possible that you may have contributed to the affair by way of neglect. Neglect to listen and forgive, neglect to spend quality time, neglect to love or respect to name a few.

Do not make it easy for someone to be unfaithful. When it is all said and done let the record reflect that you played no part in their decision to be unfaithful.

Research shows that men tend to cheat largely for sexual reasons, while women cheat for emotional reasons. The majority of the reasons cheating men gave for their infidelity were directly or indirectly related to sex.

On the other hand, research shows that women who were cheating had different motivating factors. The primary motivating factors for women who cheat are unmet emotional needs or dissatisfaction with their marriage. I believe the lack of unconditional love is the primary antecedent that eventually leads a woman to be unfaithful to her husband.

I believe the lack of unconditional respect is the primary antecedent that eventually leads a man to be unfaithful to his wife.

Below are the 10 most common reasons cheating husbands and cheating wives use to justify their extramarital affairs. The following aren't the only reasons cheating men and cheating women were unfaithful to their mates. There are many other reasons as well.

Top 10 Reasons Why Men Cheat

1. More sex (the desire for a more active sex life)
2. Sexual variety
3. Opportunistic sex
4. To satisfy sexual curiosity
5. To reaffirm his sexuality
6. A feeling of entitlement
7. The "thrill of the chase"
8. The desire to feel respected, important or needed
9. Peer pressure
10. Sexual addiction

Top 10 Reasons Why Women Cheat

1. Lack of emotional intimacy (a desire for a close emotional bond)
2. Dissatisfaction with her man
3. Marital or relationship unhappiness
4. A desire for male attention (lack of quality time spent with her man)
5. To re-experience feelings of romance
6. To reaffirm her desirability (to feel wanted and validated as a woman)
7. A desire to feel "special"
8. Boredom
9. Loneliness
10. Sexual excitement

Avoiding An Affair

" It is written, man does not live on bread alone, but on every word that comes from the mouth of God." Matthew 4:4

Jesus was tempted by Satan to turn stones into bread because he had not eaten for 40 days. Bread can be classified as many different things. It can mean sex, money, power, fame, physical or emotional needs and desires. Are you trying to satisfy God-given desires at the wrong time and in an inappropriate way? Many of our desires are normal and good. God only wants us to satisfy them in the right way and at the right time. With the help of the Holy Spirit we can overcome sexual impurity.

As a final thought I just want to encourage you to be faithful to God and your spouse in marriage. Here are some strategies to do this.

1. Guard your mind. Every sin starts with a thought. That thought turns into an attitude. That attitude turns into a feeling. The feeling turns into an action, and repeated actions turn into habits and addictions. Avoid books, Internet sites, movies, music, people, places or things that will stimulate unhealthy thoughts. Feed your heart and mind the spiritual food necessary to nourish the soul.
2. Keep away from settings, places, and people who tempt you to be sexually impure. If you are in a dating relationship, set up boundaries in your relationship to keep from being impure and crossing the line.
3. Do not only think about the current moment. Today's thrill may lead to tomorrows ruin.

Physically, how does inappropriate sexual behavior affect the marital relationship?

1. It destroys family life.
2. It erodes a person's ability to effectively love and respect by replacing those virtues with lust and selfishness.
3. It degrades human beings and turns them into objects.
4. It can lead to disease and result in unplanned children.
5. They are against God's moral standards and you may lose the ability to fulfill commitments such as being faithful to God and your spouse. You can lose the ability to feel sexual desire for that person. It may also cause distrust and prevent you from being entirely open with your spouse.

Chapter 27

The Emotional Weeds of Immorality

Emotional weeds represent unjust conduct or thinking and are just as important to address as the weeds of sexual immorality. Emotional weeds fall into 3 categories. They are how you think, how you express emotion, and how you behave or make choices. If you were to take inventory of your garden, would you find fruitful thinking, emotions, and choices or would you find emotional weeds? Emotional weeds must be eradicated from the marital garden, so that healthy emotional fruit can be in abundance.

Energy Drainers

Get all the toxic people out of your life. It takes a lot of mental, emotional and spiritual energy to reach your goals. You can run faster with twenty people who want to run with you than with one around your neck. There are two types of relationships: toxic relationships and nourishing relationships. Nourishing relationships are the relationships that inspire you and motivate you to become the best person you can possibly be. They bring out the best in you. Toxic relationships are relationships where people always criticize you. All they do is find fault and highlight negative things about you, exploiting your weaknesses and reminding you of the mistakes you have made in the past. These types of people are bad for your health. Have you ever wondered why you have not yet reached your full potential? It could be that you are in a toxic relationship, and the mental, emotional and spiritual energy you need to be successful is being drained from you daily. Energy drainers in your life will kill your ambition. If one apple can spoil the whole bunch, one energy drainer can spoil your whole life. Thousands of people's lives have been ruined because someone was not good for them. You cannot change toxic people; they must want to change. Look at the people you most associate with and ask yourself these questions:

1. What kind of person am I becoming because of our association?
2. Are these people helping me to grow mentally, emotionally and spiritually?
3. Am I becoming a better person because of our friendship?
4. Do they bring out the best in me or the worst in me?
5. Do they inspire me?
6. Do they encourage me to develop my greatness?
7. Do they add value to my life?

Birds of a feather flock together. If you hang out with negative people or losers, you will become a negative person and a loser as well. But if you hang out with successful, positive people, then you will more than likely be positive and successful. It takes a lot of energy to achieve your personal goals so stay away from energy drainers.

The Weed of Hate

The weed of hate is more difficult to address in the marriage garden because many times they are deep-rooted. Hate, once implanted in the mind, tends to manifest itself as a long-term attitude rather than a temporary emotional state. Hate is associated with discord and dissension and will eventually dissipate a healthy marriage. Hate suffocates love. To hate is to dislike intensely or passionately, feel extreme aversion for or extreme hostility toward, or detesting someone or something. When you have hate for someone, you have a strong desire for something bad to happen to that person. Hate, when present in a marriage relationship, stirs up vigorous or bitter conflict, competition, rivalry, and discord. As a result of this, it has a negative effect, creating a hostile or unfriendly environment. Unresolved hate often leads to revenge, physical assault, damage to property, bullying, harassment, verbal abuse, or insults. Extreme hate for someone can create a state of mind where you want to destroy anything positive associated with the person you hate. Many are willing to risk their well-being and are willing to go to the extreme of losing their life and freedom to get even. The hate weed is a weed of division. The more you hate someone, the less you can unconditionally love him or her. Remember, love binds a husband and his wife together, and the opposite of love is hate. If your spouse has done something to you to cause you to feel extreme hate towards him/her, then you must make a proactive mature choice to forgive and love your spouse.

The Weed of Discord

The weed of discord represents disagreements or lack of concord or harmony between two people. In a marriage, there will be times when you will disagree with your spouse. Because the two of you are different, you will have disagreements. But the weed of discord is more than just disagreeing. It is the pride of not only disagreeing but also refusing to work and achieve harmony in the disagreement. Suppose you and I desire to purchase groceries together. I desire to purchase groceries at Whole Foods Market and you desire to purchase groceries at Wal-Mart. Thus we have a disagreement on where to purchase our groceries. Instead of coming up with a win-win alternative to solve the disagreement, I shut down because I feel we should go to Whole Foods Market. If I have discord in me or operate out of discord, I'm not even willing to hear why you believe Wal-Mart is a better choice to purchase our groceries. Harmony means to come together and operate in unity. The weed of discord in a marriage garden will kill the fruit of love. The fruit of love produces unity and harmony. For harmony to manifest itself, I must be willing to understand your point of view or reasoning before my point of view or reasoning is understood. I may not agree with you but I desire harmony between us, so I cooperate with you to find a solution that we both can benefit from. Where there is no harmony, there is no togetherness. Where there is no togetherness, there is separation. Divorce mentally, emotionally, or physically is being separated.

The Weed of Selfish Demands

Who desires to live with a dictator? Who desires to live with a person who has the mentality of "Do what I say because you have no voice in this relationship." The word selfish means to think only of yourself. The word demand means to strongly call for or command something of someone. Self-demands are strong request or commands to someone to do or be something, only thinking of yourself as you receive the benefit. The weed of self-demands has the characteristic of being controlling and manipulative. This type of person seeks to control and manipulate people, their time, resources, abilities, and feelings. They do not care who they hurt in the process as long as they get what they need and want. A dictator is a person who is inclined to rule another person arbitrarily while being overbearing and tyrannical. If a person makes a request for something they want or need, and the request is turned down, our selfish instinct often times encourage us to take more forceful steps to get what we want or need without being considerate. In order to sustain a healthy marriage, self-demands cannot drive your behaviors.

The Weed of Dissension

The weed of dissension is a weed of division. The characteristics of dissension are constant quarreling, arguing, fussing, and fighting. Not many people want to come home to chaos where constant quarreling and arguing are the norm. Day in and day out, night in and night out, you argue and fight. Most of the time, the arguments are not even about major things, and many times small things are blown out of proportion. It could be that you put too much sugar in the lemonade, and that turns into an argument. Maybe you left the top off the toothpaste, and that turns into a disagreement. Sometimes the things that married couples argue about are not even the real issues.

When a married man and woman communicate in this fashion, they are not functioning as husband and wife, and there is no harmony or peace. When you disagree with someone about a person, situation, or problem, there almost always is a third solution—a better way where both parties can move to a mutual agreement. The problem lies in the fact that most of the time we do not want to cooperate with the person because of fear, pride, or selfishness. This weed of dissension causes many men and women to confide in someone else when conflict arises. They believe that they cannot confide in their spouse because they are not understood, appreciated, or affirmed. The weed of dissension attracts infidelity and unfaithfulness to the marriage garden. There is no doubt that you will have to resolve conflict in your relationship. There is a right way and wrong way to do it. Using profanity, being rude, name calling, and screaming is no way to resolve the issues or concerns that you have. Just ignoring them or avoiding them will not resolve conflict either. You must be willing to work out whatever conflict presents itself in the relationship with consideration and courage.

The Weed of Uncontrolled Anger

The weed of uncontrolled anger is probably one of the most deadly and destructive weeds that can sprout up in the marital garden.

"One minute of anger weakens the immune system for 4 to 5 hours. One minute of laughter boost your immune system for over 24 hours. –Les Brown

Are you angry with someone? If you have not forgiven that person and are still holding on to anger you are literally killing yourself. Forgive and live! It is estimated that between 80% to 90% of all engaged or married couples who attend marriage counseling are said to be struggling and battling with uncontrolled anger.

Anger is a completely normal, healthy human emotion given to us by God. But when it gets out of control and turns destructive, it leads to serious problems. It causes problems at work and affects personal relationships and the overall quality of your life. Anger is the emotion of instant displeasure on account of something morally wrong or bad that presents itself to you. The emotional state of anger varies in intensity from mild irritation to intense fury and rage, according to Charles Spielberger, PhD, and a psychologist who specializes in the study of anger. It can be brought on from external factors or internal factors. The instinctive, natural way to express anger is to respond aggressively. Anger is a natural, adaptive response to threats; it inspires powerful, often aggressive feelings and behaviors, which allow us to fight or take flight. A certain amount of anger, therefore, is necessary to our survival, but it must be controlled. The Bible, our laws, social norms, and common sense place limits on how far our anger can take us.

The Bible doesn't tell us that we shouldn't feel angry, but it points out that it is important to handle our anger properly. People use a variety of both conscious and unconscious processes to deal with their angry feelings.

The three main approaches are expressing, suppressing, and calming. If vented thoughtlessly, anger can hurt others and destroy relationships. If bottled up inside, it can cause us to become bitter and destroy us from within. Paul, here in Ephesians is advising us to deal with our anger immediately. For some people, they have chosen to allow months or even years to go by before addressing their anger and the anger they have towards others. We must deal with anger in a way that builds relationships rather than destroys them. If you harbor the weed of uncontrolled anger in your marriage, you give Satan the green light and opportunity to divide and conquer the marital relationship. Are you angry with someone right now? Don't focus on what they did to you, but on what you can do to resolve your differences. As a man when I get married, I am called to love my wife unconditionally, even though, at the same time, I may not love how she is treating me or what she has done to me. I am not to attack her out of anger with murderous actions and unloving words. I am to address my concerns in love. I am to focus on the issue or problem—not the person. As a woman, you are called to respect your husband unconditionally, even though, at the same time, you may not respect how he is treating you or what he has done to you. As his wife, you are not to attack him out of anger with murderous actions and disrespectful words. It is wise to address the issue or concerns you have with a respectful tone and demeanor. A wise wife will focus on the issue or problem and not on him as a person. As stated previously don't let the day end before you begin the process of mending and addressing the challenges that you currently have with each other.

If this weed is not eradicated from the marriage garden, destruction, chaos, and divorce will remain once the dust settles.

The Weed of Murder

Related to the weed of anger is the weed of murder. In fact, when the weed of anger is present in the marital garden, it is almost certain that the weed of murder is not far away, because they tend to thrive in the same environment. The 6th commandment of the 10 commandments in the Bible is "Thou shall not murder." You may think you can skip this section on murder because it does not pertain to you. You've never killed anyone—this is what you may be thinking at this point. This commandment addresses the sanctity of human life. Human life has value; therefore, God is saying to not kill or murder human life. There cannot be any unauthorized execution, killing, or slaying of another individual. You cannot by your own determination take someone's life; it is not your decision to make. The word murder means the killing of another human being under conditions specifically covered in the law. Why does the 6th commandment exist? Because you and I are unique. We are created in the image of God. No one on the planet has your exact fingerprint.

We as humans beings have been given something animals and plants do not have. We have a soul and spirit. We are different and we are unique. We are created in the image of God. What about abortion? Is that unauthorized murder? Many men and women feel they have the right to choose. Some believe in pro-choice, while others believe in pro-life? I believe in pro-God. What does God have to say about pro-life or pro-choice? When the sperm of a man and the egg of a woman meet, the image of God is stamped on the fertilized egg. It now has infinite value because the image of God is within it. Something new has been created that will never be created again. God is upset because the infinite value He places on a life is treated as an inconvenience, or worthless in value. This is what I believe upsets our Creator. God is the creator and author of all creation. So if you abort what God has created and stamped His image on, you are in disagreement with God about life.

God has blessed men and women and given them the ability to create life as a gift in a marriage relationship. He has instructed us to do it this way so that our lives would have order and stability. Many times God's perfect plan for life is perverted by mankind's selfish ways. Many people have unauthorized sex because they are not married to the person they are having sex with and create a unborn baby together. Then, because of inconvenience or immaturity, many decide to abort what they chose to create. Is abortion right or wrong? No situation is the same and there are exceptions but I believe that God's stance is pro-life.

Are you thinking, "This does not apply to me? I am ready to skip to the next chapter. I haven't murdered anyone, and I am not thinking about murdering anyone?" You view yourself as a peace-loving person, and this information does not pertain to you. Well, let us take a look at Matthew 5:21 and 22 to see if you are in fact a murderer. Here in Matthew you have Jesus speaking. He says, **"You're familiar with the command to the ancients, 'Do not murder.' I'm telling you that anyone who is so much as angry with a brother or sister is guilty of murder. Carelessly call a brother 'idiot!' and you just might find yourself hauled into court. Thoughtlessly yell 'stupid!' at a sister and you are on the brink of hellfire. The simple moral fact is that words kill."**

The definition of murder goes deeper than physically taking someone's life. Jesus is saying that murder includes instances when you use your mouth to bring destruction and death to another person because you are angry or frustrated with them. Here you have committed spiritual murder. Jesus is saying that you are murdering their character, self-confidence, self-image, self-esteem or you seek to injure their soul with murderous words. If you have a habit of calling people distasteful names, you are attacking the image of God in that person. When you spew venom that tears down another person because you are mad, in God's court you have committed a form of murder. Many married men and women assassinate their spouse and children as they speak harsh words toward them. They use their lips as a weapon to cut deep into the soul of another human being. At the end of the massacre, what is left is a deeply wounded heart, mind, and soul. Many people are in ICU on life support because of repeated verbal assaults and abuse on their well-being. Notice I stated married men and women because when they speak with poisonous words to their spouse, they are not operating as a husband or wife. The author James in the Bible speaks about controlling what we say and the harmful effects of improper speech.

"A word out of your mouth may seem of no account, but it can accomplish nearly anything—or destroy it!

It only takes a spark, remember, to set off a forest fire. A careless or wrongly placed word out of your mouth can do that. By our speech we can ruin the world, turn harmony to chaos, throw mud on a reputation, send the whole world up in smoke and go up in smoke with it, smoke right from the pit of hell. This is scary: You can tame a tiger, but you can't tame a tongue—it's never been done. The tongue runs wild, a wanton killer. With our tongues we bless God our Father; with the same tongues we curse the very men and women he made in his image. Curses and blessings out of the same mouth!

My friends, this can't go on. A spring doesn't gush fresh water one day and brackish the next, does it? Apple trees don't bear strawberries, do they? Raspberry bushes don't bear apples, do they? You're not going to dip into a polluted mud hole and get a cup of clear, cool water, are you?'-James 3:5-12

Verbal Abuse is still ABUSE! It may start as only verbal abuse but more than likely it will lead to physical abuse.

If someone is abusing you verbally or physically, it is time to leave the relationship PERIOD-POINT-BLANK! Do not date, marry or stay married to anyone who verbally abuses you.

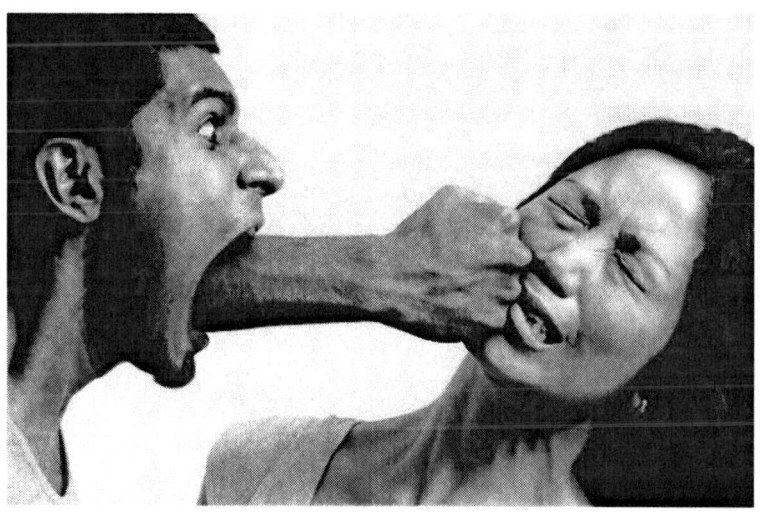

What you say or do not say is important. Proper speech is saying the right words at the right time while also controlling the desire to speak negatively. The harsh words we say to people can do great damage to their self-esteem. In a marriage when you allow your anger to become a weapon through uncontrolled, harsh, abrasive words you inevitability will disrupt harmony and intimacy. A few words spoken in anger can destroy a marriage that took years to build. We can apologize later, but the scars and damage remains. Even if we may not achieve perfect control of our tongues, we can still make a conscious effort to control the damage that our hurtful words cause. It is far better to make an effort to put out fires than to start them with our abusive speech.

As Christians, the Holy Spirit gives us increasing power to control what we say when we are offended. Before you speak, ask yourself the following questions.

1. Is what I want to say true?
2. Is what I want to say necessary?
3. Is what I want to say kind and uplifting?

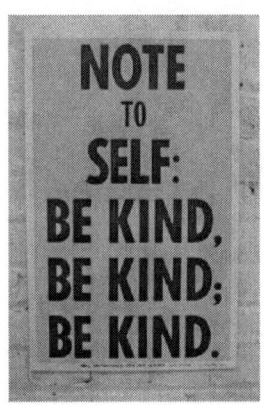

Based on what James is stating we have all committed murder at some point in our lives. What the person did may have seemed stupid, but you did not attack what they did, you attacked them as a person. It is one thing to say with love what you did or how you acted was wrong or unwise, but when you viciously attack someone personally you are not acting and demonstrating love.

Unresolved anger is the prelude to murder. One of the dominating emotions today causing all kinds of psychotic and psychological problems is unresolved anger. You may be angry with your parents because either one or both abandoned you, abused you or allowed someone else to abuse you. Maybe you saw your parents abuse each other. You may be angry with your spouse because he/she did not love you the way you desired to be loved or respected you the way you desired to be respected. Your anger is apparent because when you speak to people your words cut deep like a surgeon's scalpel. Hurt people hurt people. Many people in marriages are angry and have been since they were children; it is legitimate pain that they experienced as a child. Many adults still live with the scars of being physically abused or molested by family members or friends of the family when they were children. Many were told that they were worthless, were not given love and were not affirmed, appreciated, or understood by their parents. Many children who are now adults experienced death or divorce and were blamed for it, and they are still secretly carrying the resentment and anger today. This anger that they hold onto has gripped their soul and ripped them apart emotionally. This anger inside consumes, controls and imprisons them. When people get angry, you can tell if it is really deep-seated anger if they hurt the people they love. They are not just angry with the people close to them; they become angry with anyone in their space. Because of this, some mothers abuse, neglect, and punish their children because they are angry with the children's father.

As they tear down and destroy others with their malicious words, they inevitably destroy and tear down themselves. So how does one cope with the vice of murder? The same way you cope with the vice of anger. You forgive the person who hurt you. If you choose not to forgive you will be an angry, bitter person and that is not a healthy way to live. Forgiveness is for you so that you can move on in your life and start the healing process.

If you're an adult who experienced sexual abuse as a child, know that you are not alone. In the U.S., 44% of sexual assault victims are under the age of 18, and 93% know the perpetrator. Many perpetrators of sexual abuse are in a position of trust or are responsible for the child's care, such as a family member, teacher, clergy member, or coach.

No matter what, the abuse was not your fault. It's never too late to start healing from this experience.

What Are The Effects of Child Sexual Abuse For Adults?

If you experienced sexual abuse as a child, you may encounter a range of short and long-term effects that many survivors face. Adult survivors of child sexual abuse may have some of the following concerns that are specific to their experience:

1. Guilt, shame, and blame. You might feel guilty about not having been able to stop the abuse, or even blame yourself if you experienced physical pleasure. It is important for you to understand that it was the person who hurt you who should be held accountable—not you.

2. Self-esteem. You may struggle with low self-esteem, which can be a result of the negative messages you received from your abuser(s), and from having your personal safety violated or ignored. Low self-esteem can affect many different areas of your life such as your relationships, your career, and even your health.

3. Intimacy and relationships. It's possible that your first experiences with sex came as a result of sexual abuse. As an adult, intimacy might be a struggle at times. Some survivors experience flashbacks or painful memories while engaging in sexual activity, even though it is consensual and on their own terms. Survivors may also struggle to set boundaries that help them feel safe in relationships.

Why Do I Still Feel This Way?

As an adult survivor, you have been living with these memories for a long time. Some survivors keep the abuse a secret for many years. They may have tried to tell an adult and were met with resistance or felt there was no one they could trust. For these reasons and many others, the effects of sexual abuse can occur many years after the abuse has ended. Remember that there is no set timeline for dealing with and recovering from this experience. Please visit *rainn.org* for more information on how you can start the process of healing.

It is worth noting that there are emotional weeds that were not discussed in this chapter but you must still be on the look out for them and remove them from the marital garden. They are:

1. The weed of drunkenness.
2. The weed of illegal substances.
3. The weed of lying.
4. The weed of wild living.
5. The weed of arrogance.
6. The weed of homosexuality.
7. The weed of greed.

The husband and wife are to cultivate and protect their marital garden from these emotional weeds so that the marriage can produce fruit. There is one fruit that is produced when a marriage is free from harmful destructive weeds. It is the fruit of the spirit. The fruit of the spirit has nine characteristics that describe it. They are:

1. Love
2. Joy
3. Peace
4. Patience
5. Kindness
6. Goodness
7. Faithfulness
8. Gentleness
9. Self-Control

To experience and have a fruitful marriage a married couple must protect it from harmful and destructive weeds.

Chapter 28

What is a Wife?

What is a Christian wife? She is a woman who is married to a man. She is a woman who operates underneath and is answerable to Christ first then to her husband. Before she submits to her husband, she submits to the Lordship of Jesus Christ, obeying His instructions on how she will relate to her husband and to others. The definition of a wife is a married woman who helps compliment her husband as she catapults him to greatness. For a married woman to become an effective wife, she must adopt and implement the principle of respect and submission just as her husband must adopt and implement the principle of love and submission.

"He that finds a wife finds a good thing and obtains favor from the Lord." Proverbs 18:22

A noble wife captivates and stimulates her husband's mind, heart and soul while seducing him with her inner and outer beauty.

"The Lord God said, 'It is not good for the man to be alone. I will make a helper suitable for him." Genesis 2:18

The word "suitable" means appropriate to a purpose. Women, before you say "I do" to the man you desire to marry, you should ask yourself a question. Are you suitable to help him for a purpose? What is the "shared purpose" of the relationship? Many women have married men they were not suited to help. Your mission statement and his mission statement may not be the same, but they should complement each other. Here is another question a woman should ask herself. Do I know what my partner's purpose in life is? If he has not identified his life purpose or some goal or plan to serve and contribute to the greater good of humanity what does he need your help with? What will you receive out of marriage that you wouldn't receive by remaining single? Why are you getting married or why did you get married? Was it because of love? I believe that two people who want to get married should do so because together, married, they are better off than they would be as single people. But there must be a central purpose they share that cannot be accomplished as individuals, which makes marriage ideal. If you are just living with a person, and you want to get married because you have been together an extended period of time, you may be thinking the next step is marriage. But if you have no legitimate purpose that you both desire to accomplish together then you may want to rethink marriage. As a wife you are called to help your husband lead and manage the relationship effectively and efficiently. A marriage has systems, which I stated earlier, that a husband needs help with, making sure they operate efficiently. The word "help" in Hebrew means one who shares in the responsibility with whom you corroborate to fulfill a purpose. As men, we do not have all the information, perspective or intellect. The woman brings to the relationship her gifts, ideas, values, and emotions, so there will be a collaborative effort in doing what God would have us do as a couple. So the role of a wife is to complete what the husband is lacking. She is to be a person close to him, who understands him, to give a perspective to him he would not otherwise have.

Make Him or Break Him

You have probably heard the phrase that a man's wife can make him or break him. Well, this is a true statement, and I'll tell you why. The "making" and "breaking" is the result of the wife's understanding, or lack of understanding of the emotions of love, respect, sexual intimacy, and romance. Man's greatest motivating force is his desire to please a woman. Men who accumulate large fortunes, and attain to great heights of power and fame, do so mainly to satisfy their desire to please women. Take women out of their lives, and great wealth would be useless to most men. It is this inherent desire of a man to please a woman, which gives a woman the power to make or break a man. Most men will not admit this because of their ego. When a man and woman get married they create a marriage alliance connecting the minds of the two. The alliance between a man and woman in marriage creates a relationship that reaches deeply into the spiritual nature of both parties. Fortunate is the man who is married to a woman who devotes her life to strengthening her husband's mind power by blending it with her own, in a spirit of sympathetic understanding and harmony. That type of wife will never "break" any man, but she will most likely help him to rise to greater heights of achievement than he would have known without her help. A great psychologist once said that no two minds ever come into contact without there being, of that association, a third and intangible mind, or greater power than either of the two minds. Whether this third mind becomes a help or hindrance to one or both of the two contracting minds depends entirely upon the mental attitude of each person. No man is happy or complete without the modifying influence of the right woman in his life. The man who does not recognize this important truth deprives himself of the power, which has done more to help men achieve success than all other forces combined. –Andrew Carnegie

A Wife's Main Ministry

Private victories preceded public victories. Winning in your marriage allows you to win in the world. As a wife, your "main" ministry is the home then the world. Your first priority is the sole purpose of assisting your husband so that he fulfills what God has called him to accomplish with the gifts, values, talents, and abilities God has bestowed you with. When you get married as his wife, you merge your God ordained purpose into your husband's God ordained purpose. Your husband will not be able to accomplish what God is asking him to accomplish with maximum effectiveness, without your help, wisdom and guidance. The attributes of encouragement, respect, love, support, cooperation, companionship, wise counsel, healthy interaction, sexual intimacy, and healthy communication will manifest themselves in a harvest of unbelievable prosperity. As his wife you must be dependable, loyal, have ability and value, maintain a positive mental attitude, be willing to go the extra mile, and have applied faith.

Career Women vs. Wives

Should an ambitious woman undertake to divide her attention between marriage and a personal career? Napoleon Hill asked Andrew Carnegie this question as he was interviewing him about the principles of personal achievement. This was Andrew Carnegie's answer to this question in his own words.

" No, under no circumstances. Career women seldom make successful wives. Conversely, successful wives seldom make efficient career women. It should be one or the other. I have known of many marriages resulting in failure because of this very situation, where the wife endeavored to divide her attention between home and career. It may happen, and it sometimes does, that a married woman is forced to take a career because of the illness or disability of her husband, or his death, but the division of attention between home and career should never be a matter of choice." –Andrew Carnegie

Our careers demand so much from us and take a lot of our time and attention away from the home and our family lifestyle. It seems to be the norm for an employer to expect and require their employees to take huge amounts of unfinished work and projects home to meet important and sometimes unrealistic deadlines. Mr. Carnegie said, "Successful wives *seldom* make efficient career women, he did not say they never do."

Beware of Beautiful Ugly Women

I was watching a movie that came on television one weekend called "Shallow Hal." This is a brief synopsis of the movie: Following the advice of his dying father, Hal decides he will only date women who are physically beautiful. At work, Hal's co-workers accuse him of being shallow and caring about nothing but physical appearance. Hal wants to see women for their inner beauty, but his appreciation of physical beauty gets in the way. While going to work one day, by an unexpected twist of fate, Hal meets the famous American life coach Tony Robbins while stuck in an elevator. After having a brief conversation with Hal and understanding his situation, Tony hypnotizes Hal into seeing people's inner beauty—not their external selves. Hal, shortly thereafter, meets Rosemary, a grossly obese 300-pound woman, and as a result of being hypnotized, he is blind to her physical appearance. He only sees her inner beauty.

These are not the women I want to address. The women I want to address are women who do not seek to develop their inner beauty. They are the beautiful ugly women of the world. Yes, these women turn heads with their pretty eyes, luscious lips, sexy smiles, and gorgeous bodies, but on the inside they look ugly and act nasty. I believe that every woman is physically attractive to someone. So what I perceive to be beautiful physically, another man may find unattractive physically. We all know women who have been blessed with natural physical beauty. This is not a bad thing, but a blessing from God. What is disappointing is to overshadow that natural beauty with a nasty, mean, cold, disrespectful, conceited, inner ugliness. The personality and spirituality of the beautiful ugly woman has the residue of filth and sludge. Yes, she is physically beautiful, but she is ugly and unattractive on the inside. Solomon wrote about these beautiful ugly women in Proverbs 11:22:

"A woman who is beautiful but lacks discretion is like a gold ring in a pig's snout."

Are you that woman he is describing? Do you know someone like that? This woman is physically beautiful like gold, but her inner self resembles a waste management plant. Discretion, much like consideration, is your ability to decide responsibly in situations and circumstances. In other words, it's your response-ability or your ability to respond. This type of woman that Solomon is describing reacts inappropriately to situations or circumstances with immaturity and careless behavior. Her rationale for this type of behavior is " I am physically beautiful, and I can get away with treating people like crap and using them." Many physically attractive, beautiful ugly women act without discretion or consideration for others' thoughts and feelings. Confidence is not the same as being conceited, which is having an excessively favorable vain, proud, egotistical opinion of one's appearance. A married woman who is beautiful physically, but who murders her husband with her words, talks down to him to her friends and family, and dishonors him in the children's presence is not beautiful by God's definition. If the inner soul of a woman is ugly, no amount of makeup or beauty enhancement items can hide the inner ugliness.

Beautiful Ugly Women to Avoid

1. The Gold Digger- is a woman who cultivates a personal relationship in order to attain money. She likes you because of your wallet and not your walk with God. She loves your car instead of being attracted to your character.

2. The Shallow Woman- She may like you because you are her type physically. You are the right height, have the right build, hair, and eye color. Her interest in you is based solely on physical attraction.

3. The Status Hungry Woman- She just loves your status or the position you hold. If you have seen the movie *Just Wright* with Queen Latifah, you know exactly what I'm talking about. Her liking you has nothing to do with the God in you and nothing to do with your character, your godly walk, or your ambitions to help others. She is not impressed that you are a good-natured person. If you lose your status, you will lose her.

4. The Rebound Woman- You are her rebound. She spends time with you and hangs out with you because she is in between relationships, and you are available. She is the type of woman who cannot stand to be alone, and you satisfy her emotional need of loneliness. She uses you to attempt to fill voids only God can fill. So you become her "commercial" until she finds the TV show she really wants to watch. When another man comes along, she changes the channel.

5. The Cinderella Woman- She is just looking to fulfill a fantasy, and you are the main actor. She just wants to have a wedding. She is not concerned about being a godly wife and mother. She is in love with the fantasy of a wedding—not a marriage.

6. The Undeveloped Woman- She loves the *idea* of a godly man but is not ready for a godly man. A godly man is the cake and not the icing. Her cake is all the carnal things she desires in a man with a little spirituality sprinkled in. She has not taken the steps to develop her spiritual life but wants a spiritual man. Many women say, "Where are all of the godly men? Why can't I find a godly man?" Then you come along and now you are too godly or too spiritual because you pray over your food, read your Bible every day, and are spiritually plugged into God. Make sure she is not a penny looking for a silver dollar.

7. The Psycho Woman- She *loves* you before she *knows* you. This woman is borderline obsessed. It has only been three days and she is already talking about what the children's names will be. She should know you first before she falls in *love* with you.

8. The Babysitter Woman- She only likes you because you are good with her kids. There is nothing wrong with a woman who has children, who is a godly mother, and desires to be a godly wife. However, the woman I'm talking about is looking for "daddy daycare." Any man will do as long as he has a job and can babysit her kids.

Men, the point of this list is to help you familiarize yourselves with beautiful ugly women who have deviant motives. As men we must watch out and be selective so that we are not taken advantage of by these deceivers. These women are not concerned with giving and serving, which is the true definition of love. They are concerned with what they can get and how they can use you and the resources you have acquired.

I believe many men share my personal belief about women from the perspective that a beautiful woman who I am physically attracted to can get my attention. But a physically beautiful woman who is beautiful on the inside will keep my attention. She is a beautifully beautiful woman. In Proverbs the Bible describes a wife of noble character in Proverbs 31:10-30.

This woman described in Proverbs paints a picture of genuine inner beauty of a woman who loves God, her husband, and her family.

Proverbs 31:10-30 (NLT)

10: **"*Who can find a virtuous and capable wife? She is worth more than precious rubies.*"** With there being close to seven billion people on the planet Solomon is saying that a virtuous and capable wife is rare. What he means by rare is exceptional, extraordinary, and few and far between. She is held in great respect. This woman is extremely sophisticated and possesses special inner beauty.

11: **"*Her husband can trust her, and she will greatly enrich his life.*"** She is a woman deserving of trust or confidence. She is dependable, reliable, honest, and faithful. To enrich means to supply with abundance of anything desirable. She enriches her husband's mind with knowledge and wisdom. She adds greater value or significance to her husband as she relates to him. In other words, she upgrades him.

12: **"*She will not hinder him but help him all her life.*"** She is not an obstacle or impediment to the things that God has called him to accomplish as her husband. She cooperates with him and does not work against him. Her speech is kind. Her words are helpful. She is an encourager and his biggest supporter. She affirms, appreciates, and seeks to understand her husband.

13: **"*She looks for wool and flax and works with her hands in delight.*"** She works joyfully in her occupation without a negative and complaining attitude.

14: *"She is like the merchant ships, bringing her food from afar."* She is not satisfied unless it is the best quality of goods or food. She chooses only the best. She does not mind traveling a great distance to get the best deal.

15: *"She gets up before dawn to prepare breakfast for her household and plan the day's work for her servant girls."* She is not averse or disinclined to serve. She follows a set or system of rules and regulations to achieve goals and objectives. She is disciplined in focusing on the important and urgent tasks of the day.

16: *"She goes out to inspect a field and buys it. From her earnings she plants a vineyard."* She is a business-oriented woman ready to undertake projects of importance or difficulty or untried schemes. She is not afraid to take risks. She is energetic in carrying out any undertaking that shows a great potential of making a later profit. She is prudent with money and assesses a situation before she makes a financial investment.

17: *"She is energetic and strong, a hard worker."* She possesses or exhibits energy, especially in abundance. She is a go-getter.

18: *"She watches for bargains; her lights burn late into the night."* She does not spend money carelessly. She shops at thrift shops and retail outlet stores looking for the best bargains. She is a good steward over money and can make it stretch.

19: *"Her hands are busy spinning thread, her fingers twisting fiber."* She is consistent in her efforts to accomplish something. When she has a goal that she has set out to achieve, she is attentive and persistent in achieving it.

20: *"She extends a helping hand to the poor and opens her arms to the needy."* She exhibits a feeling of deep empathy, sympathy, and sorrow for another who is stricken by misfortune, accompanied by a strong desire to alleviate the suffering. She volunteers to help the less fortunate.

21: *"She has no fear of winter for her household because all of them have warm clothes."* She is proactive in her foresight of things and situations. She plans ahead carefully in her methods for the future.

22: *"She quilts her own bedspreads. She dresses like royalty in gowns of finest cloth."* She is tastefully fine or luxurious in how she dresses, her style, and what she designs for herself and others. She is gracefully refined and dignified in her preferences and habits.

23: *"Her husband is well known, for he sits in the council meeting with the other civic leaders."* She has the capacity or power of persons or things to be a compelling force on or produce effects on the actions, behavior, and opinions of others. Her husband is one who is of considerable importance or influence because of her.

24: *"She makes belted linen garments and sashes to sell to the merchants."* She is industrious, exhibiting great effort at what she does because she desires to be successful in her craft.

25: *"She is clothed with strength and dignity, and she laughs with no fear of the future."* She is a woman who is composed, dignified, and self-assured. Her character empowers her to act rather than be acted upon. It frees her from dependence on circumstances and other people. She is responsible, choosing to place her values over her feelings when responses, choices, and decisions are made.

26: *"When she speaks, her words are wise, and kindness is the rule when she gives instructions."* She is cognizant of her words when she speaks. She is knowledgeable and informed, discerning, and judging properly as to what is true or right. She is a person who educates and promotes kindness when instructing or directing.

27: *"She carefully watches all that goes on in her household and does not have to bear the consequences of laziness."* She is well informed of the pulse of the home. She aids her husband in the leadership and management of the home to bring about or succeed in accomplishing, sometimes despite difficulty or hardship.

28-29: *"Her children stand and bless her. Her husband praises her saying, 'There are many virtuous and capable women in the world, but you surpass them all'"* She is worthy of praise. She is to be commended, affirmed, appreciated, loved, respected, and understood for who she is and what she does. Her husband understands that she is far beyond calculable or appraisable value. In his eyes she is of inestimable worth. This husband is saying that who she is and the value she brings the marriage, as a wife is priceless!

30; *"Charm is deceitful and beauty is vain, but a woman who fears the Lord, she shall be greatly praised."* The power of pleasing or attracting through personality or beauty is misleading. Physical beauty, while it is important to some, is without real significance, value, or importance because it fades away. But a woman with a beautiful spirit and a heart for God in her ways carries more value than charm and physical beauty.

31: ***"Reward her for all she has done. Let her deeds publicly declare her praise,"*** She is to be shown honesty, fairness, and integrity. She is to be given love and high respect, for her worth and merit. She should be placed in high public self-esteem. In other words, this is a woman you brag on. You put your love for her on a billboard for everyone to see. As her husband you show your gratitude for the privilege of being associated with her and the favor you receive from such a respected person.

Some people have held the belief that the ideal woman is strictly domestic. Here we see a woman who is an excellent wife and mother who is invaluable, but she is also a manufacturer, importer, leader, manager, realtor, farmer, seamstress, financial consultant, and business owner. Interestingly, her strength and dignity do not come from her amazing achievements but from her respect for God. We live in a society where physical appearance is weighed heavily to express beauty. Surprisingly enough, her physical appearance is never mentioned. Her attractiveness comes entirely from her character.

So any man who does not utilize his woman for her mind, her skills, her intellect, her training, and her gifts is not acting wisely. Many men often argue logically but a woman normally tells you how she feels, so when what she feels does not line up with your logic, many times her feelings are dismissed. God has placed in a woman's emotional base or mind more nerve endings that pick up on perceptions and intuition, which logic does not pick up on or address. God gives the husband the final say of a matter in the marriage, but what God does not give the husband the right to do is make the decision without collaboration with his wife.

Men, here are 10 qualities that you should look for in a potential wife:

1. She shares your beliefs- When it comes to finding your wife, I've heard "equally yoked." It has nothing to do with weightlifting for those of you guys who like muscle women. Your potential wife should share common beliefs with you. If you don't share core beliefs….good luck.

2. She makes you a better man- If everyday is hell with her, that should be a red flag. Your potential wife should bring value to you and the relationship. You can get a good idea from your friends and family. Do they say you act differently in a bad way when you are around her? Not a good sign. She should bring out the best in you, not bring out heartache and frayed nerves.

3. She's trustworthy- In fact, she should inspire trustworthiness within you. If you don't trust her, you're probably making her as bitter as you're making yourself. Not worth it. If you can't trust her, maybe you're not ready to date her or maybe you need to work on confidence issues within yourself. If there's good reason not to trust her, don't even go there. Just like any cheater, it's bound to happen again.

4. She has ambition- She should have strength in character and carry herself with confidence. As a man, you should be the leader in the relationship, but for any dictators who feel justified here; we're talking servant leadership. You probably don't want the consummate follower either. She should have plans too. In fact, she should be a hard worker just like you. That doesn't mean having a job is a requirement. One of my friends is a stay-at-home wife with three kids, and she works harder than any of my friends with careers.

5. She's selfless- She should care about others. Look at the way she treats her family and her friends. If she's not close with her family, and doesn't have any good friends, that's not a good sign. If you start dating her, much less marry her, you will discover why soon enough. Some questions to ask yourself: Does she care about causes? Does she go out and volunteer? Does she give change to the needy or buy them a meal? These are important characteristics to consider.

6. She's attractive- In your eyes, she should be a "10." When my wife walks in the room, I'm awestruck by her every time. She's beautiful from the inside out. However, I've dated "hot" girls who ended up being downright ugly by the time we broke up. Personality plays into attractiveness big-time. Just remember, "charm is deceptive and beauty is fleeting." She should be beautiful down to her soul because that kind of beauty lasts forever.

7. She's smart- You're going to be spending a lot of time with her, so she should be able to hold a good conversation. She should be wise, smart, and give you good advice. Her woman's intuition should be strong.

8. She respects you unconditionally- If she's trying to change you to be another person, it's time to move on. Your future wife should respect you just as you are, regardless of anything you've done in your past. There will be minor adjustments along the way, but if she nags you about your core characteristics, it won't get any better in marriage.

9. She's responsible- Does she remember appointments and meetings? Does she make time for you? Does she keep her word? Does she flake out all of the time? She should already do a good job of managing her own life. If she's got loads of debt and doesn't work, you're going to be taking all of that on. Ultimately, she will have some part in your financial well-being, and guess what? Finances remain one of the leading causes of divorce.

10. She gets along with your family and friends- If she doesn't even try to connect with your family and/or friends, let her go. She shouldn't be critical of the people who you love and have been loyal to you throughout your life. There might be cases where your mom doesn't like your future wife, and that may require your intervention; but in general, she should be a good fit with the people in your life. Marriage is a joining of two lives that existed prior to meeting the other person.

Chapter 29

Unconditional Respect

A husband is to receive unconditional respect from his wife. Without respect, he reacts without love. When a husband feels disrespected it is especially hard for him to love his wife.

In 1 Peter 3:1 and 2, Peter talks about unconditional respect. He tells wives that if their husbands are being disobedient to the Word of God, they may win their husbands over to the Lord by their chase and respectful behavior. Carnal Christian men who are disobedient to Christ or disobedient to the Word of God are who Peter is addressing. Peter is not asking wives to respect when they feel like it; he is commanding them to show respectful behavior unconditionally. This is not about whether the husband deserves respect but about the wife's willingness to treat her husband with respect and without conditions. When your husband sees and experiences Christ in you, it can convict him to reopen his spirit to Christ, which allows him to reopen himself to you.

A man typically does not want to open up to his wife when he feels she has contempt for who he is as a person or when she has strong feelings of disapproval and aversion toward him. A wife is to display a respectful expression and demeanor when her husband fails to be the man she wants him to be. She is to give her husband unconditional respect in tone and expression while confronting his unloving ways. He may deserve being despised, dishonored, or disgraced, but treating him as he deserves to be treated will not win him over any more than using harshness and anger to win over the heart of a woman. Most men and women believe respect is earned and love is unconditional. Men usually shut down when they have to unconditionally love a woman who makes him earn her respect.

He then becomes responsible for doing all the loving and respecting and, therefore, becomes overloaded. When a husband thinks he is being disrespected, he has a natural tendency to react in ways that seem unloving to his wife. This is the reason the command to love his wife was given to the husband. When a wife feels she is unloved, she has a natural tendency to react in ways that feel disrespectful to her husband. This is the reason the command to respect her husband was given to the wife.

Sometimes, what you say is not received as you intended another person to receive it, and what you think you heard is often times not what the other person meant at all. A man or woman can be right in what they are expressing, but the wrong tone, language, or demeanor can come across in a disrespectful or unloving way. Many times we see things based on our needs and perceptions. Long-term tension can be sparked by miscommunication. When a man is insensitive in his actions toward his wife, his insensitivity causes her to feel unloved. This feeling of not being loved causes many women to start to criticize, making the husband feel disrespected.

There is a famous song by Aretha Franklin titled *Respect*. All she is asking for is a little respect. But what most people do not know is that this song was written by a man named Otis Redding two years before Aretha ever sang it. Otis released it as a single on August 15, 1965 as his message to his wife. The primary meaning in Otis Redding's song is a cry from a man's deepest soul that says, "Respect is what he needs when he gets home and he's got to have it." But what is respect? According to *Webster's Dictionary*, respect means "to hold in high esteem, honor, and to show regard or consideration." Many men and women want their spouse to respect them but do not show the same level of respect. They feel as though it is a conditional thing based on how they feel. The Bible does not give men or women the option of loving or respecting each other when they feel like it. The Bible commands us to love and respect without ceasing. Here are some examples of what respect is. A wife must use respect as a tool to help keep the marital relationship intact. Here are some examples of different respect tools she must have in her toolbox.

>Respect is...listening without interrupting.

When you and your spouse have a conversation about something and your spouse has the floor to speak, do you allow your spouse to finish what he or she has to say without interrupting them? Do you seek first to understand them before you are understood? Do you listen with the intent to reply or learn? When they are talking do you cut them off to interject what you want to say? If so, you are being disrespectful.

>Respect is...taking your spouse's feelings into consideration.

When a decision has to be made about a particular event or issue, do you only think about yourself and how your decision will affect only you? Or do you take into consideration how your decision will affect your spouse and your family? If you only think about how your words, actions, attitude, and habits affect you, you are not taking your spouse's feelings into consideration and therefore you are being disrespectful.

Respect is...keeping an open mind.

The people most likely to gain knowledge are those who are willing to listen and keep an open mind. It is a sign of strength, not weakness, to pay attention to what others say. People who are eager to listen continue to learn and grow throughout their lives. If we refuse to become set in our ways, we can always expand the limits of our knowledge. When a new idea is introduced to you, are you open to hearing those new ideas and thoughts? Do you welcome and encourage your spouse to share their ideas and feelings with you so that a decision can be made that represents both parties involved? Do you honor your spouse's opinions and encourage him or her to share them with you? If you think your way is the only way and you have no regard for your spouse's opinions and feelings, then you have a closed mind. Has pride kept you from being open to new ideas? If you exhibit this type of behavior you are being disrespectful by not keeping an open mind.

Respect is...agreeing to disagree.

Sometimes you cannot come to an agreement on a decision or issue. No two people are alike so no two people can think exactly alike. There will be times when you have to agree to disagree. When you choose to agree to disagree you do not have to belittle one another's ideas, thoughts, or feelings. You still can respect each other's ideas, thoughts, and feelings even if they do not match your own. Ultimately, respect says we must come up with a win-win agreement, but if that is not possible then we will compromise or exercise a no deal agreement (agreeing to disagree).

Respect is...attempting to understand your spouse's viewpoint.

There were four friends exploring in an Amazon forest. One of the four friends decided that he wanted to climb a humongous mountain for fun. While he was climbing the mountain his other friends continued to explore the forest. One friend stopped and shouted, "Hey, I found a snake." The other friend shouted, "It is not a snake; it is a tree trunk." The last friend yelled and said, "It's not a snake or a tree trunk; it is a jump rope." The friend climbing the mountain heard the conversation and yelled down to his friends and said, "All of you are wrong; it is an elephant." All the friends thought that what they saw was the actual thing they were looking at. But the friend who had climbed the mountain was able to see the whole picture because of his position. You may not want to understand your spouse's viewpoint about a situation or issue but it is worth noting that just as you may see a jump rope, a tree trunk, or a snake, it could be that you are looking at an elephant.

Respect is...loving yourself.

When you understand the love God has for you and what He has done through His Son Jesus on the cross for our sins, it is much easier to pass that love along to others. God made you the way He wanted you to be. You are created in His image, and God said everything that He has made is good. When you respect and love yourself, it allows you to extend it in your relationship. In relationships of all kinds, mutual respect for the other person's thoughts, feelings, and actions allows you to develop the love aspect of the relationship.

Bobby L. Sneed Jr.

Respect is...being trustworthy and honest.

As you look to develop your relationship or marriage, having trust and honesty must be the foundation. If you cannot be honest with your thoughts, feelings, and actions, then the relationship has little or no chance of surviving. This is because when you interact as a couple, your personal actions directly and indirectly affect the other person. So the decisions you choose to make or not make must be trustworthy and honest, and by doing this you are showing respect to your spouse.

Respect is...giving each other space.

Becoming one in marriage is the fundamental process that a husband and wife should strive for. However, you need space in your "togetherness." What this simply means is that you should have time apart where you can each spend with God, friends, and family. Sometimes you just need a break from the one you are with. Going to work out or playing a sport allows you to have that personal time for growth, reflection, or devotion. Allowing each other the time and space necessary to do this is showing each other respect for each other's space.

Respect is...nonviolence.

When you respect someone, you are not violent toward him or her. You are not abusive with your words or actions. Violence in a relationship of any type is not love, and you are not showing respect for a person if you act out in violence. If you are physically, mentally, or emotionally abusive or being abused, understand that as the abuser you are not giving respect and as the person being abused you are not receiving respect. Respect is showing no violence toward others.

Marriage: It's In Your Hands

Respect is...effective communication.

When someone annoys or insults you it is natural to want to retaliate. But this solves nothing and encourages trouble. Instead, effectively communicate slowly and quietly, choosing your words carefully. Your positive response will achieve positive results. A gentle answer turns away anger and demonstrates respect in communication. Because no one person can read another person's mind, effective communication is a must in order to express love and respect in a relationship. The key to effective communication is to do it in love. There are times when concerns must be addressed, and you may feel uncomfortable discussing the issue at hand. When you communicate in love and not out of anger, you are more likely to be acknowledged by the person you are communicating with. Yelling, screaming, cursing, and name calling are all immature ways of communicating, and by doing so you show the other person you are not being respectful in communication. You can also communicate non-verbally. Although some people correctly understand what people intend to communicate through nonverbal cues, it is better to sit down or take a walk together and discuss what the concern or issue is. This shows that you are willing to be respectful in your communication with your spouse.

Respect is...building a person up instead of tearing him or her down.

There is a saying that you can catch more bees with honey than you can with vinegar. Similarly, you can greatly affect your spouse's feelings, mood, and self-esteem by how you treat him or her. Are you an encourager or do you always criticize and put your spouse down? There was a study done in which couples were interviewed about the positive reinforcement that took place within their relationships. Couples who spoke one positive comment to one negative comment had a 98% divorce rate after 3 years. However, couples that had a 5 to 1 ratio of positive to negative comments had a 90% chance of staying together. The tongue is a small part of the body; however, it can do massive damage if used inappropriately. You have not mastered respect or self-control if you do not control what you say. Unkind words cut and destroy a person. If you want to build someone up, begin with what you say. If you have the urge to be negative and tear down your spouse, stop and think before you act or speak. Respect builds a person up with kind words and actions. Husbands are called to love and as their love is demonstrated to their wives they will exhibit respect. Wives are called to respect and as their respect is demonstrated to their husbands they will exhibit love. When you love you are willing to respect. When you are respectful you are willing to love. Dr. Emerson Eggerichs in his book *Love & Respect* explains what respect means to a husband. The acronym he uses is

C-H-A-I-R-S. It is an acronym that stands for six major values that your husband holds. They are **C**onquest, **H**ierarchy, **A**uthority, **I**nsight, **R**elationship, and **S**exuality.

Conquest - Appreciate his desire to work and achieve.

Hierarchy - Appreciate his desire to protect and provide.

Authority - Appreciate his desire to serve and lead.

Insight - Appreciate his desire to analyze and counsel.

Relationship - Appreciate his desire for shoulder-to-shoulder friendship.

Sexuality - Appreciate his desire for sexual intimacy.

Understanding and applying C-H-A-I-R-S is the foundation to practicing unconditional respect in the marital relationship. Reading the book *Love & Respect* will give you further understanding and insight on how to respect your husband unconditionally.

Just because you feel unloved or disrespected does not mean your spouse is sending that message intentionally. Many times we focus on our own needs and ignore and look over the needs of the other person. When a wife is complaining, criticizing, or crying, it is quite possible that she is sending a message that she wants her husband's love. Whenever a man is being insensitive, speaking harshly, or not speaking at all, it is quite possible that he is sending a message that he wants his wife's respect.

Chapter 30

Building the Marriage Foundation

The rock foundation that a marriage must be built on is love and respect. Unconditionally practicing love and respect is the challenge many couples face. This is why first-time marriages end in divorce 50% of the time. Many marriage relationships have a poor foundation that ultimately fall with a mighty crash when they experience bad weather.

"Anyone who listens to my teaching and obeys me is wise, like a person who builds a house on solid rock. Though the rain comes in torrents and the floodwaters rise and the winds beat against that house, it won't collapse, because it is built on rock. But anyone who hears my teaching and ignores it is foolish, like a person who builds a house on sand. When the rains and floods come and the winds beat against that house, it will fall with a mighty crash." Matthew 7:24-27

When Jesus was teaching this sermon, he wanted us to practice obedience. To "build on a rock" means not only to be a hearer to the word of God but also a doer. God has given us instructions on how to build our marriages. Practicing obedience to what God has said about marriage becomes the solid foundation to weather the storms of life.

Love and respect are the most important ingredients in the foundation of a marriage. Attempting to build a marriage foundation with materials consisting of money, infatuation, selfishness, and lust is like having a $250 dollar foundation supporting a $100 million dollar hotel building. The reason many of us have the wrong view of marriage and the expectations that come with it is because we have gotten our information and data from a social secular source or have adopted Hollywood's viewpoint rather than a biblical viewpoint.

When we as men decide to pursue a woman (Proverbs 18:22) and get married, God gives us instructions and has expectations on how we are to treat and relate to our wives. When a wife takes the hand of her husband in marriage, God gives her instructions on how to relate to him. What we sometimes do is ignore what God has said for us to do and lean to our own understanding. This is exactly what Adam and Eve did in the garden. They chose to ignore what God said about the tree of knowledge of good and evil and ate from it. God said that Adam would surely die the day he ate from that forbidden tree. And that is exactly what happened. He was separated from God. Another word for separate is divorce. Here you see the first divorce recorded because Adam and Eve thought that their finite minds were wiser than the infinite mind of God. God says the same thing in Ephesians 5:33. If you choose not to obey what God has said, death will occur in your relationship. Why? God designed men with a primary need for respect and women with a primary need for love. This is not a suggestion but a command from God. What I'm about to say next you must hear in the spirit and be under its influence. Please allow me to reiterate this point. In the Bible the husband and wife relationship can be summed up in two words: *love* and *respect*. Husbands should love their wives, and wives should respect their husbands.

Men speak the language of respect. Women speak the language of love. No wonder God commanded a man to love. Men do not naturally love because that is not his native language. As men, we have to be taught how to love and develop and operate out of the principle of love. Women do not naturally respect because that is not their native language. No wonder God commanded a woman to respect. Women have to be taught how to be respectful and develop and operate out of the principle of respect. Men understand respect and speak the language of respect but are commanded to *love*, so the best way to respect a woman is to *love* her.

Women understand love and speak the language of love but are commanded to *respect*, so the best way to love a man is to *respect* him.

In Matthew 5:25 Jesus said, **"Every household divided against itself will not stand."** Who is mentoring you as an individual as you prepare for marriage? Who is providing instruction to you as a couple to stand and grow together? More than fifty percent of couples in their first marriage fail to become one, which ultimately leads to some form of divorce. This is because of one of the following: each person has not taken the time to become the right person in his or her private life, or each person does not know how or choose not to effectively interact with each other, effectively communicate with each other, and effectively cooperate with each other.

I pray that this book has served as a step-by-step guide to help you achieve a successful marriage. Remember, It is a true saying that whether your marriage flourishes or perishes is truly in your hands.

From The Author

Whether you received this book as a gift, borrowed it, or purchased it yourself, I am glad you read it and I pray that you were blessed by it.

If this book has blessed you and you know someone who would benefit from reading it please share it with them or bless them with a copy. My life-purpose is to help save and strengthen marriages, develop families and prevent divorce and I need your help to do this.

For more information about this marriage ministry, speaking engagements or if I can be of help to you or someone you know, please email me at

marriageitsinyourhands@gmail.com.

Thank you for your love and support. –Bobby L. Sneed Jr.

Sources/References

Introduction: It's In Your Hands

1. Brian K. Williams, Stacy C. Sawyer, Carl M. Wahlstrom. *Marriages, Families & Intimate Relationships*, 2005.

2. Darel Rutherford. *So, Why Aren't You Rich* (DAR Publishing Third Edition 1998), pp. 111-134.

3. Proverbs 23:7, New King James Version.

Chapter 7: Development

1. Stephen R. Covey. *The 7 Habits of Highly Effective People* (Free Press 2004), pp. 43-49, 51-52.

Chapter 9: The Principle of Agape Love

1. *Life Application Study Bible NIV Version* (Tyndale House Publishers 2005), pp. 103.

2. "Are We There Yet?" *Wikipedia.com*. Wikipedia, n.p Web August 2010.

3. "Holding grudge for someone shows emotional imbalance." *Charminghealth.com*, n.p 2009.

Chapter 11: The Principle of Self-Control

1. Stephen R. *Covey. The 7 Habits of Highly Effective People* (Free Press 2004), pp. 67-68, 70-72.

2. George Sylvester Viereck (October 26, 1929). "What life means to Einstein: an interview." *The Saturday Evening Post.*

Chapter 12: The Principle of Having a Vision

1. Steven R. *Covey, The 7 Habits of Highly Effective People* (Free Press 2004), 98, 100-101, 104-106, 108-111, 122-123, 138

Chapter 13: The Principle of Managing Yourself

1. Stephen R. *Covey. The 7 Habits of Highly Effective People* (Free Press 2004), pp. 149-151, 162-165.

Chapter 14: A Prelude to Marital Interdependence

1. Emerson Eggerichs. *Love & Respect* (Thomas Nelson 2004), pp. 15,16.

2. Darel Rutherford. *So, Why Aren't You Rich* (DAR Publishing Third Edition 1998), pp. 163-166, 171-184.

Chapter 15: The Principle of Interdependent Interaction

1. Stephen R. *Covey. The 7 Habits of Highly Effective People* (Free Press 2004), pp. 206-214, 223, 224, 232, 233.

Chapter 16: Marriage Systems

1. David Ferguson, Ferguson, Teresa, Terri Snead. *Intimate Encounters* (Relationship Press 2006), pp. 192-207.

Chapter 18: The Principle of Interdependent Communication

1. Stephen R. *Covey. The 7 Habits of Highly Effective People (Free Press 2004), pp. 237-241, 245.*

2. Stephen R. *Covey. The 7 Habits of Highly Effective People Personal Workbook (Free Press 2004), pp. 110.*

Chapter 19: The Principle of Interdependent Cooperation

1. Stephen R. *Covey. The 7 Habits of Highly Effective People Personal Workbook (Free Press 2004), pp. 122, 125.*

Chapter 20: The Principle of Self-Renewal

1. Stephen R. *Covey. The 7 Habits of Highly Effective People (Free Press 2004), pp. 288, 296-298.*

2. "Sleep Disorders Health Center" Webmd.com. n.d Web 2010.

Chapter 22

https://rainn.org/get-info/effects-of-sexual-assault/adult-survivors-of-childhood-sexual-abuse

Chapter 23: The Emotional Weeds of Immorality

1. "Hulk" Wikipedia.com. n.d Web 2010.

2. Tony Evans. "The Sixth Commandment MP3" tonyevans.org. n.d Web 2010.

3. *The Wife List: 10 Qualities*
http://goodguyswag.com/the-wife-list-10-qualities/

For continued development of your marital relationship, I recommended reading the following books:

The Bible by God

Love and Respect by Dr. Emerson Eggerichs

The Act of Marriage by Tim & Beverly LaHaye

No More Excuses by Dr. Tony Evans

Theology You Can Count On by Dr, Tony Evans

The 7 Habits of Highly Effective People by Steven R. Covey

So, Why Aren't You Rich by Darel Rutherford

Prayer Rain by Dr. Daniel Olukoya

Before You Say "I Do" workbook by H. Norman Wright & Wes Roberts

The Purpose Driven Life by Rick Warren.

Attached. By Amir Levine and Rachel S.F. Heller

The Power of Your Subconscious Mind by Joseph Murphy

CPSIA information can be obtained at www.ICGtesting.com
Printed in the USA
LVOW07s1212200216

475966LV00001B/71/P